Transforming
CONVERSION

Transforming CONVERSION

RETHINKING THE LANGUAGE *and* CONTOURS OF CHRISTIAN INITIATION

Gordon T. Smith

Baker Academic

a division of Baker Publishing Group
Grand Rapids, Michigan

© 2010 by Gordon T. Smith

Published by Baker Academic
a division of Baker Publishing Group
P.O. Box 6287, Grand Rapids, MI 49516-6287
www.bakeracademic.com

Printed in the United States of America

Library of Congress Cataloging-in-Publication Data
Smith, Gordon T., 1953–
    Transforming conversion : rethinking the language and contours of Christian initiation / Gordon T. Smith.
        p.   cm.
    Includes bibliographical references and index.
    ISBN 978-0-8010-3247-9 (pbk.)
    1. Conversion—Christianity. I. Title.
BV4916.3.S65 2010
248.2′401—dc22   2010005989

Except as otherwise indicated, Scripture quotations are from the New Revised Standard Version of the Bible, copyright © 1989, by the Division of Christian Education of the National Council of the Churches of Christ in the United States of America. Used by permission. All rights reserved. Other versions occasionally cited: KJV, from the King James Version; NIV, from the New International Version; TNIV, from Today's New International Version; and REB, from the Revised English Bible.

10   11   12   13   14   15   16   7   6   5   4   3   2   1

to joella

Contents

✛

Introduction

✢

Evangelicals are walking through a paradigm shift in their understanding of conversion. While revivalism has for more than a century shaped their language of conversion, a new way of speaking of salvation, redemption, and conversion is emerging—a change that has profound implications for our vision of the Christian life and the life and mission of the church.

Older revivalism assumed that conversion was punctiliar, that the focus of a converted life was religious activities, in anticipation of a life "in heaven" that would come after death, and that this "conversion" was essentially an interior, personal, and subjective transaction. Revivalists had little appreciation of the place of the sacraments or the intellect in the spiritual life. For the revivalist, the church has only one agenda: to obtain conversions; to be successful, congregations should have plenty of growth by conversions.

All this is changing. It is not that evangelicals are not attending to the matter of conversion; to the contrary, it continues to be a critical concern and passion. It is rather that the fundamental assumptions and categories of revivalism are being questioned as never before. Several factors have led to this change. Biblical scholars are calling for a more comprehensive theology of salvation, including both the corporate and cosmic dimensions of the work of God in the world. Evangelicals are also learning from voices that have given critical attention to the nature of religious experience, including philosophers and developmental theorists. Evangelicals are also taking account of the insights of theologians within other traditions—Orthodox, Roman Catholic, mainline Protestants—and these exchanges have had an invaluable impact on how evangelicals think about the experience of conversion.

Further, the face of evangelicalism is changing; the majority of evangelical Christians now live outside the West, and most of these are self-identified Pentecostals. A current discussion of the meaning of conversion must take account of this development: What does it mean, for example, to come to faith from a Muslim background? Further, how do we consider the meaning of conversion in light of the Pentecostal experience of the Spirit?

Another influence factor in this discussion is that church historians are forcing evangelicals to rethink their theological and spiritual heritage as Christians and especially as evangelicals. This calls us to recover the wisdom on conversion from the early church, the pre-Christendom church, and also to draw afresh on the wisdom of the evangelical heritage of the late eighteenth century, before the rise of revivalism in the nineteenth century. Yet most of all we pastors and we ordinary Christians are eager to make sense of our own experience and the ministry of congregations. We are eager to rethink the meaning of conversion and what this means for the life and witness of the church. The revivalist paradigm may have served us in the past; but there is an urgency in our recognition that we need a new way to think about how women and men come to faith in Christ and what this means for the congregations of which we are a part.

What follows, then, is an attempt to distill this extraordinary conversation on conversion from the past quarter century; and then to demonstrate what this might mean for how we do church. I will begin with an assessment of revivalism; we need to be clear on the language that has been so influential to date. Next I will consider the witness of the Letter to the Ephesians, the witness of the church's history, and a reappraisal of the goal or objective of conversion. In the second half of the book, I will delineate the contours of a Christian conversion.

Finally, I conclude with advice-giving chapters. First, I give counsel to individuals who seek to make sense of their own conversion experience through the spiritual practice of spiritual autobiography. Second, I counsel congregations that long to be spaces where the children of the church are coming to an adult faith in Christ and where inquirers and seekers are discovering the wonder of God's love through the witness of communities of faith.

1

The Language of Conversion

Revivalism and the Evangelical Experience

What is the biblical vision of conversion, and how is this reflected in the actual experience of those who come to faith in Christ Jesus? What implications does this have for our understanding of the church and the ministry of the church? What implications does this have for our understanding of the actual character of the Christian life as a whole? The challenge is clear: to think *theologically* about conversion, to ask What is its fundamental character?

How we think and speak of conversion matters deeply, for conversion is the genesis, the point of departure for the rest of our Christian life. Our conversion establishes the contours for our experience of God and of the salvation of God. The whole of our Christian experience is the working out of the full meaning and implication of our conversion. To live in truth is to act in the world in a manner consistent with or at least reflecting our conversion. Therefore, it only makes sense that we should give attention, intentionally and theologically, to what it means to come to faith. This requires that we establish a clearly outlined, theologically informed, and consistent understanding of conversion.[1]

We need an outline of the nature and character of conversion that has internal congruence but also congruence with our own experience. With this outline in mind, we should be able to understand and interpret our own experience, to strengthen and deepen that experience, and to assure ourselves that our experience leads to transformation. The apostle Paul frequently appeals

---

1. For those who identify with the evangelical Christian tradition, there is particular incentive to think about the experience of conversion, especially if D. W. Bebbington is right in his suggestion that conversion is one of the four defining features of the movement and his observation that conversion is the content of the gospel for evangelicals; see *Evangelicalism in Modern Britain: A History from the 1730s to the 1980s* (London: Unwin Hyman, 1989), 3, 5.

to the conversion experience of his readers as a basic and elemental point of departure for his teaching about the Christian life.

Thinking theologically about conversion requires language; language provides us with meaning and structure for our understanding. Yet this is precisely where we—I speak here as an evangelical Christian—have a problem. For many evangelicals, the language of conversion that permeates the public life, worship, and witness of the church does not reflect their own experience. They feel distant or alienated from their own experience because it does not fit the pattern of what they believe a conversion should look or feel like. This leads them to wonder whether their experience is legitimate. However, if our experience of conversion does not fit the language we use to describe it, then we are not speaking the truth about the way in which God works in the life of individuals or the congregation as a whole.

An additional complication flows from this: if our language about conversion does not portray how people *actually* become Christians, our approach to evangelism will not correspond to the ways in which the Spirit brings people to faith in Christ Jesus. Evangelism is vital to the life of the church and to our growth as Christian believers, and our approach to evangelism must be congruent with the way in which the Spirit of God draws women and men into the kingdom of the Lord Jesus Christ.

Many rightly observe that the language and theology of conversion that permeates our evangelical psyche is not so much that of the New Testament as it is the language and theology (and the premises) of *revivalism*. As a religious movement, revivalism is heir to both the seventeenth-century Puritans and the renewal movements of the eighteenth century. Yet revivalism largely emerged in the nineteenth century and was broadly institutionalized in major conservative denominations in North America and within many parachurch and mission agencies, which then expanded the movement within North America and globally. Contemporary Christianity is greatly indebted to this movement; it would be hard to conceive of the global presence of the Christian faith if it were not for the mission agencies whose vision for evangelism was fueled by this particular understanding of both the need for and the character of conversion. An extraordinary number of Christians today have come to faith through the witness of those who are heirs to this movement.

The revivalist heritage includes two invaluable affirmations. First, it stresses that conversion is necessary and possible. Revivalism affirms the reality of the human predicament and that the only hope for humankind is a radical inbreaking of divine grace: no self-help program will resolve the human predicament. Our only hope is conversion, and conversion is possible. Thus there is a deep hopefulness to this spiritual heritage: evil does not have the last word. Second, the revivalist heritage appropriately emphasizes the need for people to take personal responsibility for their lives and for their response to the claims of the gospel. When this emphasis is not located within a broader appreciation of divine sovereignty and initiative, the result can easily be a distorted understanding of human agency. Nevertheless, we can and must affirm this insistence on human responsibility.

Though this movement has given contemporary Christians much for which to be thankful, it has also left us with some baggage—in particular, a way of speaking about conversion and religious experience that is problematic in many respects. It is urgent that we identify this language and seek a thorough rethinking of the way in which we speak about the experience of conversion and about the Christian life as a whole. Revivalism's language of conversion permeates evangelicalism in at least twelve ways.

1. Conversion and Salvation Confused

One of the noteworthy features of the language of revivalism is that the words *conversion* and *salvation* are used synonymously. To be converted is to be saved; to be saved is to be converted. This means, for example, that those within the movement are inclined to use the language of salvation almost entirely in the past tense (one is "saved"), and this reference to being saved is directly linked to some action that the person in question has taken. A person has prayed a prayer or has "accepted Christ into one's heart" and is now, as of that action, "saved." This emphasis on right words and intentions leads many to believe that, having done it right and simply, they are "good to go." They can be "assured" that they are children of God.

The problem with this is twofold. First, it represents an overly narrow conception of the salvation of God. No doubt some New Testament language does highlight the reality that through a conversion experience one has confidence that one is a child of God, but other aspects of salvation language in the New Testament are overlooked or downplayed. As a result, evangelicals have consistently struggled with Pauline language that speaks of "work[ing] out your own salvation with fear and trembling" (Phil. 2:12–13) or that speaks of salvation as a future experience. Yes, past-tense language is there (for example, Paul speaks in Titus 3:5 of the day in which God "saved us"), but this is only one aspect of the language of salvation in the New Testament.

There is a second and even greater problem here, though this one-dimensional view of salvation is problem enough! Within revivalism, not only is the word *salvation* used almost exclusively in the past tense, but it also is consistently linked with human activity: one is saved when one prays the so-called "sinner's prayer" or when one, to use other language typical of the tradition, "receives Christ into one's heart." When one does these things, one is declared to be "saved," so much so that one can ask another, "When were you saved?" The acceptable answer is to identify a time when the particular human action or decision was made.

Although the tradition rightly seeks to emphasize the importance of human agency ("What must we do to be saved?"; cf. Acts 16:30) and appropriately affirms that our actions matter, the evangelical heritage has not adequately sustained the vision of conversion as a human act in response to the gracious initiative of God. Conversion is certainly human activity, but God alone saves. This is why it is so important that the words *conversion* and *salvation* not be viewed as synonymous: salvation is the work of God; conversion is a human response to the divine initiative.

The revivalist tendency to combine these two ideas was driven, in part, by the desire to provide a basis for assurance: how is one to know that one is saved, accepted, forgiven, justified? While we understandably long to know, with confidence, that we are children of God, the route to this confidence is not by linking the salvation of God to a human choice, the action of choosing God. Conversion is about choosing, and human actions and responses matter, but assurance of salvation arises from the interplay of a number of factors, which we shall examine in detail later. For now, we simply note this problematic merging of two ideas that, though intimately linked, need to be kept distinct. The one, salvation, is the work of God; the other, conversion, is a human *response* to the saving initiative of God.

2. The Emphasis on Human Volition

Within revivalism, the language of conversion focuses on volition, an emphasis inherited, at least in part, from the Puritans. For the revivalist, the heart of the human predicament is the human will, which is in rebellion against God, and salvation comes when we surrender our rebellious will to the will of God. If the essence of sin is rebellion (a refusal to obey God), then the essence of life and holiness is a meek submission of the will (the ideal state being one of compliance with the will of God).

From this perspective, to become a Christian is thus to make a *decision*, which is specifically the surrender of the will. A corollary to this is that any subsequent problem in the Christian life can be attributed to an "unsurrendered will." For many Christians who grew up in this movement, the recurring question was "Is your all on the altar?" And they were repeatedly reminded that freedom and life come with submission. Revivalist preachers, then, really have only one question for the non-Christian, "Will you surrender your life to God?" and one for the Christian, "Will you rededicate your life to God?"

The movement needs to be commended for understanding that, as Bob Dylan (1979) put it, "You've gotta serve somebody" and that, as the apostle Paul makes clear in Romans 6, we are either slaves of sin or slaves of righteousness. They grasped that our only hope for transformation is to present ourselves to God (Rom. 12:1). However, a one-dimensional perspective on the

4

human person that too closely links our salvation and ultimate transformation with our will can easily cause those within the tradition to think that they are transformed by the surrender of the will rather than by the renewal of the mind (Rom. 12:2). Such a perspective discounts the significant place that the intellect and the affections have in human transformation.

When we view the human will as itself a problem, as the great threat to the Christian life, then the only hope for getting children to submit to God is to first teach them to submit to their parents and other authority figures. The revivalists apparently inherited this view from their Puritan fathers and mothers, who believed that the chief task in raising children was to break their will, because the will was viewed as the problem. Good children, then, were obedient children, meaning *compliant* children. In this environment, any proclivity toward independence or mischievousness or creativity, or any threat to parental authority, was quickly branded as rebellion, the greatest possible affront to God.

A popular contemporary book on child raising that reflects the revivalist heritage actually focuses on what is termed a "strong will" and speaks of the "strong-willed child" as an unfortunate problem and challenge. The implication surely is that if the child has a strong will, then it will be a little tougher to "break." All of this implies that what parents in the revivalist tradition want is nice, compliant children.

Ironically, we observe that one aspect of the genius of the great saints in the biblical narrative and in the history of the church was the power of their will. Their strength of character was matched by their strength of will and by their capacity to engage God with this strength of will. Surely what young people need as they head into the cauldron of peer pressure in high school is strength of will. The will does indeed need to be challenged and directed, but having a strong will is not, in itself, a problem, and the heart of parenting is surely not to "break" this will.

3. Conversion Is Punctiliar

The emphasis on volition leads us to what is perhaps most noteworthy in the revivalist perspective on conversion. The language of salvation and volition (or surrender) is all wrapped up in the assumption that conversion is *punctiliar*. You can date it. You can mark it. You can know when you were saved, because you know the exact moment when you prayed what is typically called "the sinner's prayer." Preachers can count conversions, if they have more than one "decision," and conversion is linked to this "decision." Conversion is punctiliar, and salvation is punctiliar. They are tied to the moment in which one made the decision, said the prayer, and thereby "accepted Jesus into one's heart."

5

Yet revivalism fails to appreciate the complexity of the human person and the complexity of religious experience. Despite the depth of the human predicament, despite the complex character of human emotions and pain, and despite the deep ambiguities of life, revivalism expects that a person can suddenly become a Christian. It also expects that this act can be recorded, measured, and counted. The assumed simplicity of conversion has often meant that one could identify how many people became Christians in this place at this time or over this period of time. Yet if religious experience is more ambiguous and complex, it means that this language of conversion does not enable us to speak accurately about what it means to become a Christian, what it looks like, what it feels like.

Without doubt, the greatest problem with the assumption that conversion is punctiliar is that it rarely ever is. Many people do not have a language with which to speak meaningfully about their own spiritual experience for the simple reason that they have not experienced conversion as a punctiliar event in their lives. Whether they are second-generation Christians (more on this below) or whether their journey to faith and of faith does not fit the mold, they do not know how to tell their story, how to give expression to their encounter with God's grace. J. I. Packer states it well:

> Conversion itself is a process. It can be spoken of as a single act of turning in the same way that consuming several dishes and drinks can be spoken of as a single act of dining, . . . and revivalism encourages us to think of a simple, all-embracing, momentary crisis as its standard form. But conversion . . . is best understood if viewed as a complex process that for adults ordinarily involves the following: thinking and re-thinking; doubting and overcoming doubts; soul-searching and self-admonition; struggle against feelings of guilt and shame; and concern as to what realistic following of Christ might mean.[2]

Most, if not all, conversions are actually a series of events—often a complex development over time, perhaps even several years. Yet for many Christian communities, there seems to be no way to speak meaningfully about believers' experiences of coming to faith. Further, the proclivity toward thinking of conversion as singular and punctiliar has been matched by an assumption that the power of divine grace is evident precisely in the drama of the moment. There is a corresponding failure to appreciate the wonder of the Spirit, who often works slowly and incrementally in the natural course and context of our lives, bringing about God's saving purposes.[3]

2. J. I. Packer, "The Means of Conversion," *Crux* 25, no. 4 (1989): 14–22.
3. My work gives me opportunity to travel extensively, and I often sit down with pastors and theologians to reflect on the experience of conversion. While writing this book, I was in conversation with a Pakistani theologian who commented that he knows many Christian converts from the Muslim faith who have two conversion narratives—one that is an honest reflection of their

In the late 1980s and early 1990s, a British study of conversion experiences came to the following remarkable conclusion: "The gradual process is the way in which the majority of people discover God and the average time taken is about four years: models of evangelism which can help people along the pathway are needed."[4] What we urgently need is a language of conversion that accounts for the process—often an extended process—by which a person comes to faith; only then can we develop an understanding of congregational life and evangelism that is congruent and consistent with the way that the Spirit is *actually* bringing women and men to faith in Christ.

4. Ambivalence about the Intellect, If Not Actual Anti-intellectualism

When we talk about "the scandal of the evangelical mind,"[5] we are not speaking of the Puritans, Jonathan Edwards, or John Wesley, and most certainly we are not referring to the Reformers. The evangelical theological and spiritual heritage is actually known for its deep commitment to the life of the mind, the vital place of good scholarship in Christian mission and witness, and the importance of teaching, study, and learning for the health and well-being of the church. But we now live in an era of evangelicalism when the devoted scholar is viewed almost as an oxymoron. On one side are those who do not appreciate that the best scholarship is informed by prayer, and on the other are those who do not recognize that prayer and worship must be informed by good scholarship and that study, learning, and libraries are vital to the health and vitality of the church.

We have a generation of Christians who do not appreciate what it means to love God with one's whole mind, who do not see that transformation comes through the renewal of the mind and that Christian mission is about taking "every thought captive to obey Christ" (2 Cor. 10:5). Contemporary worship now routinely features songs that foster a particular way of feeling good without attention to whether we are singing as intelligent people. The great hymns of the faith, which are substantial expressions that engage heart and mind, are now set aside for musical offerings that are trite and sentimental. As one pastor put it to me, our music is "happy clappy," but it has little substance. We need to acknowledge the huge part that the revivalist heritage has played in this.

experience and another that describes a singular, punctiliar event, which they tell to satisfy the expectations of foreign missionaries!

4. John Finney, *Finding Faith Today: How Does It Happen?* (Swindon: British and Foreign Bible Society, 1992), 25.

5. Cf. Mark A. Noll, *The Scandal of the Evangelical Mind* (Grand Rapids: Eerdmans, 1994).

We should also acknowledge that this downplaying of the life of the mind has fostered a corresponding elevation of the place of emotions and affections in religious experience. Whenever we seek to incite a particular emotional response without reference to understanding and good doctrine, we are being manipulative, using emotion to achieve a particular end—whether a good feeling in the worship service or the making of a religious decision. Routinely, the heirs of revivalism have made no apology about using music to create a particular emotional landscape that in turn is viewed as the context in which significant religious choices can be made.

Evangelism must engage understanding, with a vigorous intellectual honesty. It needs to establish an intellectual beachhead from which a person, in becoming a Christian, can eventually come to a comprehensive reorientation of their thinking toward a Christian worldview. We need to turn from our propensity to think that evangelists are not scholars (or that scholars cannot be evangelists, for that matter). We need to turn from the inclination to be minimalists when it comes to what a person needs to know in order to come to faith. Without apology, we need to introduce inquirers to the magnificent spread of the biblical narrative—creation, fall, and redemption—and even, on a basic level, to the ancient creeds that anchor our understanding of who it is that we proclaim when we say the name "Jesus."

This runs counter to a revivalist heritage that speaks of becoming a Christian as "accepting/receiving Jesus into your heart" and has led a generation of Christians to answer the question "You ask me how I know He lives?" with a thunderous "He lives within my heart!" I am not for a moment questioning the vital place of the heart or of Christian affections in authentic religious experience, and I am not suggesting that our faith rests on certain facts that amount to, as a popular 1970s book put it, "evidence that demands a verdict." I am not calling for a cerebralism that fails to appreciate the significance of the arts and beauty in evangelism. However, evangelism that does not engage the mind in critical understanding of the truth is not truly Christian evangelism.

We need to rethink our language so that when we describe what it means to become a Christian, we do so in a way that clearly assumes and effectively describes a process or event in which there is a fundamental change of mind, a reorientation of one's thinking, and a clarity of understanding by which a person comes to see and appreciate the wonder that truth sets us free. Ignorance is hell, not bliss, and truth has a power, simplicity, and glory that is compelling.

When we proclaim the gospel to those whose background and upbringing are secular humanist or post-Christian, who know little if anything about the Bible and its message or anything of the grand narrative of the people of Israel or the person of Jesus, then this grasping of the truth of the gospel will not and cannot come easily or quickly. We need to accept that it will often be a multistep process before a whole new way of thinking is approached and ultimately engaged. This new vision of life's meaning will take time to establish.

5. Conversion Is an Individual Transaction with God

The emphasis on volition has also meant stressing conversion as a largely personal and individual experience. We are indebted to the Puritans for their powerful and legitimate insistence that we all need to come to terms with our own spiritual destiny. The Puritans went even further, insisting that we all need to have our own conversion narrative; we need to be able to describe how we have come to faith. Yet there was a key difference from revivalism: the Puritans insisted that the church would mediate this experience, that one did not transact this whole matter entirely on one's own.

Not so for the revivalists. They believed that you could become a Christian at a soccer stadium, on your own, in isolation from the faith community. It was a personal, interior, individual transaction. Even if someone prayed with you, it was *your* experience. It did not need to be linked to the church, and you did not need to become a member of the church to be a Christian. It was between you and God. Indeed, the revivalist insistence was that one could be "saved" without any reference to the church. For some, it was even a matter for celebration that this necessarily did not include the church. Robert E. Webber puts it well in his critique of modern evangelism: "Unwittingly, a wedge was driven between Christ and the church. In the worst-case scenario of modern evangelism, a person can be a Christian without an active life in the church. This approach to evangelism contributed to the privatization of faith, to a personal, me-oriented gospel that undercut the role of the church."[6]

The revivalist perspective failed to see how the church necessarily mediates the experience of conversion. And then, as a natural counterpart to this, by insisting that conversion is simple and individual, this perspective also downplayed that conversion leads to affiliation with a community of learners who experience transformation in community. If the genesis of the spiritual life is largely an individual transaction, then it follows that the rest of the spiritual life is transacted on one's own, in one's own space, on one's own terms. If one can be "saved" without reference to the community, then one can presumably live the rest of one's Christian life without reference to community. And while one might still attend church and be active in a Christian community, the individualism of one's conversion fosters a sense that the church is nothing more than the sum of its parts, a collection of members, of individuals. Such a Christian lacks a covenant relationship with the community of faith, lacks a sense of vital dependence or, better, mutual dependence upon the community, lacks a sense

6. Robert E. Webber, *Ancient-Future Faith: Re-thinking Evangelicalism for a Postmodern World* (Grand Rapids: Baker Books, 1999), 143.

of oneself maturing in the faith "as each part" does its work (Eph. 4:16). And the church is seen as a dispenser of religious experiences and opportunities that I can take or leave; hence, I can leave and affiliate with another congregation if I conclude that the other church will better "meet my needs."

We must recover a deep appreciation of the communal character of all religious experience, beginning with conversion. When we begin with conversion as communal experience, then it will naturally follow that the Christian life is indeed an experience of God while we are in the company and fellowship of others. We love God even as we live in love with others; we meet God only insofar as we are at peace with others.

6. Ambivalence about the Sacraments, If Not Actual Anti-sacramentalism

Revivalism is marked by an emphasis on inner and subjective experience, with a particular focus on volition, on a personal decision that one makes "to receive Jesus into one's heart." This results in an ambivalence about the mind and the intellectual dimensions of religious experience and an individualistic mindset about what it means to be in community, to be the church, and to have our experience of God mediated by the church. There is also an ambivalence about the *sacramental* actions of the church. In some cases, this goes beyond ambivalence to a discounting of the value and significance of these actions.

For many, baptism has become optional; indeed, it is not uncommon for the heirs of revivalism to conclude that baptism is not necessary. If conversion is viewed as a personal, individual, and subjective transaction between oneself and God—an *interior* act—then it only follows that the external, embodied, and communal action of baptism becomes, at most, secondary and incidental to the experience of conversion.

Baptism becomes separated from conversion, not incidentally but intentionally! Revivalism insists that Christians must not view baptism as having any redemptive value. In baptismal services, it is affirmed that the event has no particular value in itself but functions merely as a sign pointing toward the real conversion experience, which happens before baptism. Although some see no need for baptism, others accept the need for baptism but see it merely as a witness to their conversion. They may agree that they need to obey the clear mandate of Scripture, but they continue to insist that it is an individual transaction, something that can be done with a friend at the seaside or in a pool but not necessarily something to be mediated by the community of faith, the church.

However, the New Testament intimately links baptism and conversion. We are called to make disciples, and this call includes "baptizing them in the name of the Father and of the Son and of the Holy Spirit" (Matt. 28:19). On the day of Pentecost, when the first apostles were asked what one should do in response to the preached Word, the answer was simple: "Repent, and be baptized . . . so that your sins may be forgiven" (Acts 2:38). Routinely one finds that the New Testament links the inner experience of repentance with the external and communal act of baptism.

One of the challenges of our day will be to restore the close biblical affinity between baptism and conversion. Many will resist this out of a fear of "baptismal regeneration," the belief that the act of baptism itself is inherently redemptive, and they will counter that only God saves and thus that baptism cannot save. I concede this, but the New Testament will not allow us to tear conversion and baptism apart. We must find a way of speaking about baptism and conversion that affirms unequivocally that God is the savior but also that sacramental actions have a vital place in Christian experience. We need a better understanding of conversion, one affirming that as embodied souls our inner faith needs to be sacramentalized. And our language needs to reflect this by speaking of baptism as integral to, rather than subsequent to, conversion. By recovering the vital place of baptism in conversion, we will also recover the central and critical place of the Lord's Supper in the ongoing life of the Christian.

7. Conversion Is Easy and Painless and Certainly Not Costly

For the revivalist generally, conversion is simple and easy: all you need to do is "accept Jesus into your heart." It is easy and relatively pain free. Even though the words of the Gospels might urge an inquirer to count the cost, the emphasis in revivalism is that salvation is a gift, freely given, and consequently it comes easily.

Though salvation is certainly a gift, the language of the New Testament has a different ring to it. We read of Jesus telling a young man that he needs to sell everything, give his money to the poor, and then come and follow him. We read of the first disciples leaving everything to follow Jesus. We read of the foolish person who did not count the cost before venturing into a building project. The revivalist propensity toward making it easy and simple, uncomplicated and not costly, is part of a vision of evangelism and conversion that is oriented toward the afterlife: doing what is needed in order to have salvation in the next life, or as it is often put, doing what is needed in order to "go to heaven" after one dies.

Quite apart from a questionable cosmology and a view of heaven that does not incorporate the biblical vision of a deep continuity between this earth and the new heavens and the new earth, what is alarming is the failure to appreciate how conversion is as much about this life as the next. It is as much about becoming who we are called to be now, women and men who through an experience of God's saving grace are enabled to be now, in this life, thoroughly and redemptively engaged with our world.

This has resulted in a change in the way the term *disciple* is now used. The language of the New Testament assumes that the word disciple is a noun: through conversion, a person becomes a disciple, a follower of Christ. But in language inherited from revivalism, a person is first converted and then is "discipled": the word is used as a verb.[7] This minimalistic view no longer sees conversion as the foundation on which the rest of the Christian life will be built. It fails to see that the depth and breadth of our conversion is the basis on which the whole of our subsequent Christian life is lived. Surely we do not want such a weak foundation.

We urgently need a language of conversion that is deeply oriented toward transformation, maturity, and radical discipleship and that portrays conversion as a good beginning and solid foundation for what is yet to come. There is a deep continuity between evangelism and discipleship. They are not two distinct acts of the church; evangelism is integral to the call of the Scriptures to make disciples.

8. Evangelism Is a Technique

The revivalist heritage has left many contemporary Christians with the belief that conversions are the fruit of the right practices or techniques. By learning these techniques, one can become a "soul winner"; with the right methods, one could learn how to "lead people to Christ." Some Christians have been taught simple formulas in a one-size-fits-all approach to evangelism: ask the right questions, lead people through a series of simple statements, guide them through a timely prayer, and one can state with confidence that these persons have become Christian believers. Reducing the procedure to a formula, the father of revivalism, Charles Finney, put it this way: it is all a matter of getting the approach right so that what follows is a "result of the right use of the constituted means—as much so as any other effect produced by the application of means."[8]

Part of the wonder of the gospel is the reality that women and men can speak meaningfully about this good news to others and do so in a manner that provides an authentic witness to the reign of Christ (the kingdom). We *can* testify to the person of Christ as Lord of creation and as the hope for humanity, and we can speak personally of our own experience of God's grace

---

7. In Matt. 28, the word *disciple* is used as a transitive verb, "make disciples" as one word, but it is best translated as a noun; "disciple" is not so much something we do as something we are. We make disciples.

8. Charles Finney, *Revival Lectures*, rev. ed. (Oberlin, OH: E. J. Goodrich, 1868), 12.

in Christ. God consistently uses the witness of Christians to enable others to know the gospel, and to know it in such a way that they can respond and become fellow believers. But the revivalists' emphasis on technique, method, and formula has diminished our appreciation of the conversion experience as the fruit of the Spirit's work in a person's life. Our human participation in the process must honor the rhythms of the Spirit's work. Evangelism involves discerning the work of the Spirit, learning to be attentive to how the Spirit is at work in this person at this time and in this place.

Further, it is never a matter of "winning souls." There is only one who brings people to Christ: it is the Spirit, the Third Person of the Trinity. As demonstrated again and again by even cursory overviews of conversion narratives, some plant, others water, and still others harvest; yet only God "gives the growth" (1 Cor. 3:7). Indeed, I would go so far as to say that in the hundreds of conversation narratives I have read, there is no example where only one person played a defining and determining role. Rather, multiple people played diverse roles in the process, and sometimes those who played a particularly crucial role did so unintentionally! No one person can conceivably be spoken of as the "soul-winner." Conversion is purely and solely the work of the Spirit through multiple agents and avenues.

9. God Has No Grandchildren

From its Puritan roots, revivalism inherited the deep conviction that "God has no grandchildren." This perspective rightly recognizes that becoming an adult means taking adult responsibility for one's life and that one does not inherit faith but must choose for oneself to be a follower of Christ. No one, including our parents, can do this for us. But something important has been missed in this insistence. Those of the revivalist heritage often fail to appreciate the distinctive experience of second-generation Christians, those who have been raised within a faith community. Insistence on the individual act of choosing God is often expressed in a way that discounts that children are part of a covenant community of grace. The spiritual identity of the children of believing Christians is not the same as that of those whose parents are not Christian believers.

Some affirm the unique identity of believers' children through infant baptism. Those who do not accept infant baptism must find a way to recognize and affirm that the spiritual experience of the children of believers will be different from that of those who are not raised in a Christian home. The language of revivalism has left us with a vacuum here because of its focus on conversion as punctiliar: a person either is or is not a Christian, in or out. We do not know how to speak meaningfully about those who are *coming* to faith. We lack a way to speak about the spiritual identity of children, especially in their

13

teen years, as they move through adolescence and are in the process (often over an extended period of time) of seeking to understand their own identity (differentiation) and to make sense of their parents' faith.

We need a language that enables us to speak meaningfully about our children's *distinctive* journey to faith in Christ, both in their younger years and as they become adolescents or young adults. This rethinking is needed regardless of whether our particular religious tradition baptizes infants or waits until they make their own faith confession.

10. No Meaningful Connection between Conversion, Baptism, and the Gift of the Spirit

Long before revivalism appeared on the scene, the church had already established a precedent of separating "conversion," or the beginning of the Christian life, from the conscious appropriation of the gift of the Spirit. The Roman Church, for example, distinguished baptism (typically infant baptism) from confirmation (and thus chrismation, or the gift of the Spirit), which typically came later, in one's teens. Revivalism reinforced this split. Within Reformed and Baptist circles, some maintained that there is no explicit reference to the gift of the Spirit at baptism since it can simply be taken for granted that a baptized person receives the gift of the Spirit. Those within Holiness and Pentecostal circles assumed that baptism (and thus conversion) was an experience of Christ but not necessarily of the Spirit. The Spirit's work came later in what was commonly spoken of as a second experience of grace. The first was an experience of Christ, the second an experience of the Spirit.

Revivalism failed to provide the church with a vibrant understanding of the work of the Spirit in conversion, expressed if not actually experienced in baptism and then dynamically present in the life of the new convert. As we shall see, however, New Testament teaching and example insists on a close and intimate connection between conversion, baptism, and the gift of the Spirit.

Also, Christians who are heirs of revivalism do not typically have a helpful and doctrinally consistent way of speaking of the Spirit as a person (rather than as merely a force or "power") in whom we are baptized and by whom we are filled. This kind of language makes many uncomfortable because it suggests that the gift of the Spirit can be manipulated or controlled by the church or by sacramental actions. Others, who are happy speaking about the gift of the Spirit, typically separate it from the experience of Christ and the cross reflected in the New Testament doctrine of baptism. Against these two extremes, we must affirm a close connection between conversion and the gift of the Spirit and find a language that consistently maintains what might be called the "independence" of God. God is not obligated by our actions; there is not a one-to-one connection between the work of God and the work

14

of the church. Our language needs to reflect the language of Scripture and demonstrate—concretely and meaningfully—that in coming to Christ one receives the gift of the Spirit and that water baptism points to the baptism or filling of the Spirit, which is integral to conversion and baptism.

11. The Church's Mission: Obtaining Conversions

One of the gravest weaknesses of revivalism is the lack of a strong and dynamic ecclesiology, which is evident in language and practice. For the revivalist, the church is reduced to nothing more that the collection of individuals who have decided to become Christians, and their common identity is reduced to a common purpose: to get other people to join the club.

The revivalist heritage has led many congregations to gauge their identity and accomplishments by how many conversions have happened in the church in the last year, as if it were the sole indicator of congregational health. This makes congregational life one-dimensional: everything is geared toward getting people to become Christians. Worship is oriented toward trying to persuade people to come to faith, and even such ministries as TESL (teaching English as a second language) are justified as a means to this particular end rather than as a service to those who need to learn the language of their new homeland.

The best corrective for this kind of thinking is for the church to be, unapologetically, the church: to be a community of persons who grow in love for Christ and for one another; who are maturing together in faith, hope, and love; who are engaged together in mission in the world as a community that serves as a sign pointing to Christ's reign, seeking to make a difference for good through word and deed; and who are inviting others who need to be challenged with the call of Christ to join them and participate in this vision and work. In this way, we will not reduce or undercut our identity as the people of God by an exclusive focus on evangelism. Rather, as I will argue toward the end of this book, we will be a church that is passionate about Christ in our worship and passionate for the kingdom of God in our service. When integrated into this multidimensional picture, evangelism is simply our inviting women and men to join us as we worship Christ and serve the ascended Christ in the world.

The revivalist understanding of conversion assumes that religious experience can be measured, counted, and reported. Churches and ministries are then judged by whether or not they elicit conversions. Such congregations evaluate a program or worship service by one criterion: "Were there converts? If not, how can this program or activity be justified?" And at the end of the year, they want to know, "How many conversions did this church have?" They ask their missionaries after one year on the job, "Were there conversions?" If not, then support for the missionary may be put in question, or the missionary

15

is at least expected to rethink the chosen approaches to ministry in order to achieve better results, that is, more conversions.

But if the experience of coming to faith is not so clearly demarcated (i.e., is not punctiliar) and if everything that the church does is ultimately evangelism (i.e., we foster conversions not so much by being explicitly evangelistic but by simply being the church), then we need to learn how to be comfortable with ambiguity. Some, indeed many, people are on their way; they are seekers or inquirers. It may not be clear for quite some time whether they are "in" or "out." In the meantime, we live with ambiguity, comfortably so, knowing that a whole range of religious experiences cannot be counted or measured or controlled. Effective preaching may or may not lead to an immediate response. Often, even with good preaching, there is no immediate evidence of transformation. It takes time. The work of the Spirit happens below the surface, hidden from human eyes, and we need a language of conversion that takes account of this. Transformation happens most fully and completely when the church seeks to be the church, allowing the Spirit to do the Spirit's work in the Spirit's time.

12. A Focus on the Afterlife with Minimal Reference to This World

In his high-priestly prayer in John 17, Jesus explicitly asks the Father not to remove his followers from the world but to "sanctify them" in "the world" (esp. vv. 17–19). This depiction of Christian discipleship has often been aptly spoken of as being "in, but not of, the world." While Christian identity is rooted in and founded on Christ, our lives as Christians are lived out in the world. Yet the revivalist language emphasizes "getting saved" so that one can "go to heaven." As a result, conversion is oriented toward the afterlife, toward one's postdeath existence rather than toward transformation for life and work now, in the present world, in anticipation of what is coming.

The biblical notion of conversion, as we shall see, is about both this life and the life of the kingdom that is yet to come. It is about "eternity," certainly, but also about our present existence, and we must recover the truth that conversion transforms women and men for life *in* the world: in the marketplace, in the arts, in every sphere and sector of society. The revivalist notion of conversion frequently leaves Christians assuming that the only activity that counts is religious activity, church work, especially religious activity that fosters more conversions, producing more people who leave the world and wait for the consummation of the kingdom.

Seeking a New Language of Conversion

When these twelve indicators of the language and influence of revivalism are put on the table, it is clear that what is urgently needed is a new way of speaking about conversion, about how people come to faith. This will have a huge impact on how we speak about the church, about what it means to be a community of faith, and it will have a substantial impact on how we speak and think about evangelism. We urgently need a language of conversion that is more congruent with the New Testament and the actual experience of those who are becoming Christians.

We need to be able to speak with simplicity and frankness about how a person can come to faith in Christ, but we also need to be able to live with the complexity of it all, with the ambiguity of religious experience, with the fact that many are "on the way" and that their coming to faith may take months or even years. The church needs to be a place where this transitional status is okay, a safe place for those who have no previous Christian identity or orientation as well as for those who have been raised in the church and who are, through the grace of God, coming to an adult affirmation of their faith.

We must recognize that the language of revivalism is deeply embedded in the psyche of North American evangelicals and that it will take persistence and intentionality to begin speaking differently, to embrace a new language of conversion. This new language of conversion will reflect several dynamic tensions:

1. It will integrate heart and mind, following the wisdom of such giants as John Wesley and Jonathan Edwards, who rightly speak of religious affections as the heart of Christian experience but also maintain that these affections are guided by intellect and understanding. It will refuse to pit heart and mind against each other.
2. It will integrate body and soul, refusing to polarize them and refusing to accept a piety or spirituality that is purely interior, subjective, and expressive. It will without apology assert that if conversion is not embodied, it is not truly Christian. It will affirm the priority of the interior but also the vital place of baptism in conversion, without succumbing to baptismal regeneration, affirming subjectivity and interiority along with embodiment and sacramentality.
3. It will affirm the individual in community, that conversion is not merely an individual transaction but an experience that makes evident that we do not know God in isolation from the community of faith.
4. It will affirm human agency as vitally involved in our choices, our willingness to believe, our act of the will to believe, accept, and follow. Yet it will view this human agency within the context of divine initiative and insist that salvation is the work of God, that this work is the mysterious outworking of the Spirit's ministry, and that conversion is a response to the saving initiative of God rather than God's "saving" coming in response to human initiative.

5. It will sustain the dynamic tension between arrival and beginning. Through conversion we come home, we find ourselves and we find God, and we know the salvation of God (we are saved), but this "arrival" is a point of departure for the rest of the Christian life. Conversion is both arrival and departure simultaneously, and our new language of conversion must not only assure us that we are the children of God but also remind us that the journey has just begun, as we work out our salvation with fear and trembling, looking forward to the day of our salvation.

6. It will reflect the New Testament's assumption that in Christ we are baptized in and by the Spirit and that the very goal and purpose of baptism is that we would know this grace. It will affirm the need to speak of this and even formalize it in our rites and acts of Christian initiation, while also affirming the sovereignty and priority of God.

7. It will help us make sense of the experience of our children and thus the children of church, fostering a helpful understanding and tension: the children of believers must affirm the faith for themselves but they are also raised in, and formed in, the faith and therefore do not need to be "evangelized."

8. It will enable us to turn from disengagement to engagement with the world, to being *in* but not *of* the world. It will correct the language of revivalism, which assumes that the experience of conversion is about the afterlife and about abandoning this world and hoping for a world to come. Instead, it will empower us to embrace our vocation to be in the world as agents of peace and justice while asserting the profound discontinuity between "the world" and God's kingdom.[9]

How will we obtain and sustain such a dynamic language of conversion that embraces so many tensions and seeming contradictions—heart vs. mind, body vs. soul, individual vs. community, arrival vs. departure, human agency vs. divine initiative, *in* but not *of* the world—without losing either side of the balance?

First, it will come through a careful and thorough reading of the New Testament text, in which, as much as we are able, we allow the text to speak for itself, striving to read without imposing our revivalist heritage or other theological mindset. We cannot read with pure objectivity, but we can learn to read the Bible plainly and to let the language and thought forms of the New Testament increasingly shape the way in which we speak of conversion and the whole of the spiritual life. In the chapters that follow, I will give particular

---

9. I believe that many so-called seeker-sensitive approaches to congregational life have sought to correct revivalism by affirming links and connections to the world (holding worship services in movie theaters, for example) but in so doing have failed to demonstrate adequately the discontinuities between the world and the inbreaking of the reign of Christ.

focus to the Letter to the Ephesians and the book of Acts. Ephesians provides the theological contours for conversion; Acts describes the experience.

Second, we will need to recover our theological and spiritual heritage, appreciating the wisdom that comes from the tradition. For evangelicals, this will mean giving particular attention to the wisdom and insights arising from the sixteenth-century Protestant Reformation and the Great Awakenings of the eighteenth century. This will soften some of the false polarizations that have come through the language of revivalism. When we reflect on our own heritage, it is vital that we do so in dialogue with Christians from other traditions—Roman Catholic, Eastern Orthodox, and others—so that they can challenge our language, our categories, and our assumptions. We can be evangelical without being sectarian. We must read the Bible as those who are attentive to our past, our heritage, but who are also in conversation with Christians of other traditions.

Third, the language of conversion is necessarily informed by experience— the experience of the church and particularly the experience of those who come to faith in Christ. In other words, we attend to conversion narratives and recognize that these are a witness to the way in which the Spirit brings people into a transforming encounter with Christ. We will be looking at the experience of the early church, as described in the book of Acts; but we will also look at conversion narratives from subsequent chapters in the history of the church. These narratives illumine the biblical text for us and broaden our appreciation of the nature of conversion. In this way, our theology of conversion will be informed by the biblical text, the church's tradition, and the experience of those who come to faith, recognizing in this experience a witness to the work of the Spirit.

2

Conversion and the Redemptive Purposes of God

If we are going to speak a more helpful and dynamic language of conversion, it will only be as our language is thoroughly informed by the theological vision and language of the New Testament. One way to approach this is to ask two questions of the Bible: First, what on earth is *God* doing? Second, what was the character or nature of the *response* to this work of God? The first speaks of salvation, the second of conversion. Both sides of the equation are essential as we seek to make sense of the conversion experience.

All of this presumes that we are making a distinction between "salvation" and "conversion." Salvation is the work of God. God alone saves: the only hope for humanity is that God has acted in the cross and resurrection of Christ and the outpouring of the Spirit and is now acting, now at work, through the saving actions of the ascended Christ and the continuous work of the Spirit.

Conversion, in contrast, is the human response to the work of God. Thus when we speak of conversion, we speak of both divine action—salvation—and human response to the saving work of God. We reject any idea that we save ourselves or even that there is a one-to-one correlation between our actions and the salvation of God. But conversely we also reject any theological orientation that discounts human agency and says, in effect, "It is all God."

We seek to recover the dynamic, biblical vision of a God who acts (in saving gracious action) and who then invites a response and takes this response seriously. We seek a theology that affirms divine sovereignty and initiative, and the priority and indispensability of God's grace. But then, without hesitation, we also seek a theology that recognizes the significance of human agency: our actions matter, and they matter to God. We do not need to polarize the will of God and human volition. They are distinct, and the will of God clearly has priority. And yet this never either overrides or discounts human choices.

Thus conversion is a personal response to the saving work of God in Christ Jesus. It is a response to what God is doing in the world through Christ and by the Spirit. Hence, we can only speak meaningfully of conversion if we do so in the light of what God is doing. We need to locate our theological reflections on conversion (our response to God's initiative) within the broader context of a biblical theology of salvation (Christian soteriology) so that our theology of conversion is consistent with what God is doing in the world.

The first question, again, is What on earth is God doing? For this question, I am going to take the Letter to the Ephesians as a primary reference. Later in this study, I will consider the message of the book of Acts for a response to the second question, What then shall we do?

What on Earth Is God Doing?

Using Ephesians as a primary reference, consider the following:

1. The character of the human predicament
2. The gracious response of God, in Christ
3. The cosmic scope of the salvation of God
4. The purposes of God in salvation: to form for himself a people
5. The necessary call to spiritual maturity/transformation (in Christ)

These five points pivot on the second and third: the redemptive purposes of God are centered in Christ, and they are cosmic in scope. Further, it is vital that we also recognize that there is an undercurrent running throughout this whole description of the redemptive purposes of God: the human response is faith.

The Depth of the Human Predicament

We only appreciate the biblical understanding of conversion if we take the human predicament seriously (see Eph. 2:1–3; 4:17–24). When a theological perspective is weak on the need for conversion, it is invariably so because there is not a corresponding appreciation of the problem. We cannot appreciate the gospel, the fundamental message of Holy Scripture, unless we locate the gospel against its backdrop: we humans have a serious problem. And unless we see this and feel the full force of this predicament, we will not appreciate why the gospel is precisely that: gospel.

The Bible makes this very clear; our conception of the gospel and of Christ and of Christ's work rests on this appreciation. If Christ came to provide a solution to a problem, a resolution, then it follows that we surely need to admit the problem, and we need to have an understanding of the nature of the problem. Though it might be easy enough to say there is a problem, it is equally important that we are clear about the *nature* of the problem. Sometimes even when we feel fine, the doctor will tell us that we are sick and perhaps seriously so. It is the doctor's work to tell us as much. At other times, we know we are sick and perhaps know that it must be serious, and what we long for is a good diagnosis: tell me not only that I am sick, if I am sick, but also precisely what the nature of the disease is.

This is surely the genius or part of the genius of the Scriptures: the Bible provides humanity with a declaration that we are sick, and it provides us with a divine diagnosis. From this, we have an appreciation of the divine response. We allow the Scriptures to provide us with a description of the depth and nature of the human predicament; only then can we have a sure point of departure as we seek to understand the work of God in Christ Jesus and the character of our response to God's saving work. In the Letter to the Ephesians, Paul does two things: he provides both theological analysis and graphic description. The one establishes theological precision; the other strikes us with an affective awareness of the depth of our problem.

He does not open the letter with the human predicament; rather, he opens with a description of God's work in Christ. But it soon is apparent that the human predicament is the backdrop for everything he wants to say about God's work in Christ: understanding the nature of the human problem makes all the difference. We will not see how desperately we need Christ unless we see what humanity is like apart from Christ. Paul does not first address the human predicament but rather first gives the solution to this predicament. He thus reminds us that we do not reflect on sin in despair or hopelessness but only through the lens of the cross. Any other vantage point would overwhelm us and lead us to despair; rather, we see the problem, but we see as those who know that however deep the problem, the cross points to the sufficiency of the divine response. We read Ephesians 2:1–3 as already anticipating the great line of verse 4: "But God . . . in mercy . . ."!

With this perspective, then, notice what we have in Ephesians 2:1–3, 12 and then also in 4:17–19. It is not a pretty picture. One has the feeling that one is sitting in the doctor's office, receiving the worst kind of news possible, and the words that Paul uses to describe our predicament are severe, poignant, and pointed in their analysis.

Death

Paul begins by describing the problem as death (2:1); death is opposed to life; death is opposed to all that is truly human. This is an important place to begin: that we appreciate the deadly character of sin. It is significant that Paul highlights this. In Genesis 3, one of the most staggering and stunning lines recorded in Scripture occurs when the serpent says to Eve, "You will not die"

(v. 4). Eve has just advised the serpent that God has declared this eating from this particular tree to be a matter of life and death, and the serpent brazenly suggests that this is not the case. Ever since then, this remains the heart of the matter: does humanity believe that sin is a matter of life and death and that, apart from God, we do not have life?

Oppression

Paul then goes further. Having affirmed that we are in death, he highlights our problem as one of bondage and oppression. Ephesians 2:2 links the human problem directly with the forces of darkness, the spirit of disobedience. This is sobering: our problem is linked with the cosmic forces of the universe. This is not just a human problem; it speaks rather of a whole infrastructure of sin, bondage, and oppression that is *much* bigger than the human condition.

It is important to stress this because we do not appreciate the human predicament unless and until we see that there is no hope for self-salvation; we have a problem, and we are incapable of fixing the problem. We must stress that our hope is not a self-help program. We are too far gone; we are in bondage and oppression, bound by forces of darkness that are bigger than we are and more powerful than anything humanity has in store. Our only hope is divine intervention; our only hope is conversion.

Alienation

The depth of the human problem is aptly captured by a significant image: alienation from God and from one another. Paul highlights this in 2:12 by noting that in sin and death, we are alienated from the people of God, without hope and without God! More to the point, then, is 4:18: we are alienated from God himself. This is but another way of emphasizing that sin is death, for God is life and truth and goodness, and we are in dire straits if we are alienated from God, separated from the Creator and the source of life.

Futile Thinking

Paul takes the mind very seriously, so it is no surprise that his description of the human predicament includes an explicit reference to the intellect. He speaks of the futility of the human mind apart from God (4:17) and of being darkened in our minds when alienated from God (v. 18), which then speaks of the reality that humanity is living not in truth but in ignorance (v. 18).

Moral Fragmentation

For Paul, it is important to highlight this side of the human problem. In 2:3 he stresses that in death and sin we follow the passions of the flesh. This is his way of highlighting the reality of moral dislocation: humanity turned in on itself, skewed and disoriented, enslaved to its own disordered desires. In 4:18 this moral fragmentation is expressed as the *outcome* of misguided thinking: the darkened understanding leads to greed, impurity, licentiousness (v. 19). Verse 22 seems to almost turn this sequence around: our thinking is distorted by our moral dislocation; it is deluded by lusts. This is likely Paul's way of highlighting that in lust and passion we think we are seeking life, but in actual fact we find that we are pursuing death.

Condemnation and Judgment

Apart from God, Paul stresses in 2:3, we are "children of wrath." This is but another way of stressing that we are guilty and thus personally responsible for our predicament. We are victims, to be sure; we are born into a world under the judgment of God. But Paul stresses that we are not only victims; we are also responsible. We are part of a cosmic dilemma and predicament, but we are also responsible for our situation and are morally culpable, judged for who we are and what we have done.

Over the centuries theologians have tried to capture all of this in a word. Calvinism is well known for its introduction of the word *depravity* into our theological lexicon, and this word captures it well: depravity is a desperate situation or moral confusion and ineptitude. Others have suggested that it is helpful to think of this situation as like a terrible sickness or infection. This is helpful to a point, though we must insist that it is a *thorough* infection: it runs through the whole course of our being and poisons the whole. This is no passing flu; the problem is not a low-grade fever; rather, we have a cancer that cuts to the bone and infects the whole of who we are.

As mentioned, we only see and appreciate the gospel if we come to some sense of the problem, an informed recognition that our only hope is found in *outside* intervention—specifically *divine* intervention. Unless God acts on our behalf, we are a pitiful lot, for in and of ourselves, we are incapable of a resolution; there is no self-salvation.

Darrell Johnson, a friend and colleague, has rightly stressed that true preaching is not so much good advice as it is good news. What we need, most of all, is good news. We need the gospel. Why? Because, in the end, good advice will get us nowhere! We need God to break into our world and make all things new; we need the divine healer to intersect our sick, broken, and infected lives to make all things well. In Christ and in Christ alone is there hope, because there is no hope in ourselves; in Christ we find healing and hope, moral integrity and reconciliation; in Christ we find forgiveness and life. What this means is that we do not have a good theology of conversion until and unless we have clarity about the human predicament: the depth and complexity of sin and thus the need for a radical solution, one that only God can provide.

How do we respond to all of this? The operative word in the Letter to the Ephesians is *faith*. In 1:15, Paul celebrates the faith of his readers; in 2:8, he emphasizes that we are saved by grace, through faith; and in 3:11–12, he speaks of believers' access to God through *faith* in Christ. Any truly biblical understanding of conversion will, essentially, be an exposition of the meaning of faith and the character of the experience of faith. The Bible stresses, emphasizes, and insists that the only hope for humanity is found through faith in Christ Jesus. Faith is crucial. It is not an incidental dimension of our response to Christ. True faith will be focused on Christ, to be sure (and we will consider this further below), but what is also noteworthy is that faith arises precisely out of an appreciation of the desperate situation in which humanity finds itself.

To live by faith is to live while conscious of our predicament but also to live deeply conscious that life, hope, and healing are found in God. This is a vital dimension of faith; this is radical dependence on the source of life and forgiveness. There is certainly more to faith than this posture of heart, but we must begin here if we are to cultivate a biblical and genuinely Christian faith in our hearts. We truly live when we live in awareness of our radical need for God. Self-sufficiency is the mark of death. And so we pray that God would keep us from this kind of spiritual contentment with ourselves, from the blindness that so easily infects our world, from where we fail to see how desperately we need God and how God in Christ so deeply and thoroughly addresses the human condition.

Implications for the Christian Perspective on Conversion

Apart from the critical place of faith in conversion, we can affirm that, at the very least, the theological vision of Ephesians leads us to three observations. First, conversion is absolutely necessary because the only hope for humanity is divine intervention. God must act; God must take the initiative. Conversion is an act of response, an acceptance of God's initiative. Though it is a human act, it is specifically an act of desperation. No self-help program will solve this problem.

Second, conversion is an act of faith: what is emphasized throughout the New Testament, as well as in Ephesians, is that we cannot save or "justify" ourselves: faith is the act of abandonment of the self to God and to what God has done in Christ.[1]

Third, conversion needs to be both radical and comprehensive. The problem is pervasive and complex. Because sin is pervasive, conversion will be radical,

---

1. As will be evident in the chapters to come, this emphasis on faith in no way discounts the place of or the need for what are typically called "good works." Here too, Ephesians and the whole of the New Testament are clear: we are saved for that for which we were created: "good works" (Eph. 2:10).

reaching to the core of our beings. Because the problem is complex, conversion will need to be comprehensive, affecting the whole of our beings.

I stress that conversion itself is but a beginning. It will not, as a single or even complex experience, lead to a complete resolution of the human predicament. We are not suddenly made whole and completely healed persons. However, we are "a new creation" (2 Cor. 5:17 NIV) in the sense that a beachhead has been established. The old identity is gone; we have entered into a new identity that is grounded on faith ("The just shall live by faith," Rom. 1:17 KJV) and that supports the transformation that will follow.

The Gracious Response of God in Christ

As mentioned above, the Letter to the Ephesians actually begins here, with its central message: in response to the human predicament, God has acted. And what is so breathtaking and compelling is how this gracious response of God is so particular, so focused on the person of Christ. Consider Ephesians 1:3–14; 2:4–10.

We have a problem, and Paul provides the answer. And the answer, the good news, is that God has acted in and through Jesus Christ. All that God has done and is doing for the church and for the cosmos is through Jesus Christ. It is our great need that the truth, glory, and wonder of the gospel invade and penetrate into every aspect of our lives—so much so that our lives are, quite literally, animated by the gospel, by the reality that God has acted and continues to act in Christ Jesus. This is what it means to live in truth: not merely to believe certain things to be true but also to allow the truth to inform, reform, and transform who we are. And this happens only when the gospel shapes and informs the particulars of our lives.

When we meditate on Paul's Epistles—all of them, but this is particularly evident with the Letter to the Ephesians—we are meditating on correspondence between Paul and his original hearers. He is writing to a particular people at a particular time, with a definitive vision: he wants the gospel to penetrate the particularity of their lives. When we pray with the Gospels, we are seeking the same grace: that the gospel would penetrate *our* particularity. For this to happen, it will require a twofold exercise: (1) that we have a good comprehension of the gospel and (2) that we would honestly face the particulars of our lives.

Ephesians is especially accessible in this regard: the first half of the book is a cogent summary of the gospel; the second half of the book addresses the particulars. The danger, always, is that we would consider the particulars before we have a good read of the gospel. An appreciation of the gospel, in its most fundamental form, requires that we come to terms with three realities, which together constitute the theological framework that makes up the gospel:

- The human predicament is death, alienation, oppression, condemnation.
- God acts in and through Jesus Christ.
- This is an act of mercy.

With regard to the second reality, the extraordinary wonder of the gospel is that God has not been passive or oblivious to the human dilemma. God has acted. God chooses to engage the broken world, to respond to that world in a way that would bring healing. And consider this: God's response is explicitly christocentric.

What is pointedly clear from the words of Paul in the opening chapter of the Epistle to the Ephesians is that God's answer to our problem is focused on the Lord Jesus Christ. He could hardly emphasize this more in these verses. Notice the emphasis and, in particular, the use of the phrase "in Christ" to capture, cogently, the fundamental character of the work of God:

- God is identified as the Father of the Lord Jesus Christ, who blesses us "in Christ" (v. 3).
- We were chosen in Christ (v. 4).
- We are destined ("designed," one might say) for adoption "through Jesus Christ" (v. 5).
- "In him" (that is, in Christ) we have redemption through his blood (the shed blood of Christ Jesus; v. 7).

Paul stresses this in the context of a description of the grand plan of God's redemptive work, a plan that is, in the words of verse 9, "set forth in Christ." Thus, says verse 11, we have our inheritance "in Christ." What is so masterfully outlined for us, then, is that the purposes of God are pointedly christocentric: God's work of redemption finds expression, purpose, and means in and through Jesus Christ. All things are fulfilled in Christ; all of God's gracious work is mediated through Jesus.

In other words, in this important perspective, Christian faith is decidedly trinitarian: in our confession of faith we commonly use the Apostles' Creed to highlight this conviction. We believe in the Triune God, who is eternally Father, Son, and Spirit. But while our faith is trinitarian, it is also christocentric. Without apology, we can focus our energies, our vision, our passion, and our love on the Lord Jesus Christ. And our worship is a yearning from the core of our beings to see Jesus, know Jesus, and follow Jesus, who is the Christ, the Son of the living God. And rightly so, for the gracious purposes of God are fulfilled in him.

Observe the correlation between the human predicament and Christ:

28

death	Christ brings life; we are made alive in Christ.
oppression and bondage	Christ brings freedom.
alienation	In Christ there is reconciliation.
futility in our thinking	Through Christ our minds are renewed.
moral fragmentation	In Christ there is healing.
wrath and judgment	In Christ there is forgiveness.

Thus when we speak of faith, it is specifically faith *in Christ*.

An appreciation of the gospel includes this correlation between the human predicament and the divine response in Christ. But further, the Bible makes it abundantly clear that God's response is gracious. It is an act of mercy. When we speak of the gospel, we do so against the backdrop of the human predicament: death, alienation, condemnation, and oppression. In response, we also highlight the work of God in and through Jesus Christ. Yet we do not fully appreciate the wonder of the gospel unless and until we affirm and embrace the wonder that this is a *gracious* work that God does through Jesus Christ. Thus we read in Ephesians 2:4–8 that God, who is rich in mercy (v. 4), has loved us and made us alive together with Christ (v. 5a). It is by grace that we are saved (v. 5b), as a powerful demonstration of God's "kindness toward us in Christ Jesus" (v. 7). By grace we have been saved through faith (v. 8).

There is no authentic or true appreciation of the gospel that does not at the center sustain this fundamental principle: the gospel is good news precisely because we are hopeless apart from Christ. But more, it is also good news because God so freely and willingly *loves* us! And he loves us enough to send his Son as Savior to enable us, through Christ's shed blood (Eph. 1:7), to know saving grace. Salvation comes through God's grace: nothing but grace. It is not earned or merited; there is nothing we can do to persuade God to do this for us and to us. It is all gift and nothing but gift. It is an act of mercy, thanks be to God (Eph. 2:4). God is rich in mercy!

The structure of the Letter to the Ephesians is important here: we begin with the summary of the gospel, which becomes the basis for a reflection on the particulars of our lives. If we are eager and receptive to the gospel, then it necessarily means that the gospel penetrates the particulars of our lives: to our work and our relationships, to our approach to finances, to our sexuality, to our leisure as much as to our times of productivity. It penetrates the way we live as the people of God both in the world and as a community of faith. The gospel has the capacity to animate and empower, to enliven and transform, but only if we have a good grasp of what it is that we mean by *the gospel*. It really is quite simple: we have a problem, and it is a severe predicament. We do not really believe the gospel unless we embrace this reality. We have a dramatic solution: God acts in and through Jesus Christ, his Son. Central to this is the energy that drives God's response: his goodness, kindness, and generosity. God

29

is rich in mercy; it is all of grace. Mercy precedes transformation: Romans 5:8 says that God loved us while we were yet sinners.

Our Response

How then do we respond? The Bible makes it clear that we are, as we read in Ephesians 2:8, "saved through faith." What does it mean to live by faith, to respond in faith to the work of God and thus experience his saving grace? An appropriate answer to this is quite simple; it is not the whole answer, but it is a good beginning.

First, it is to believe in Jesus Christ. As Paul puts it in Ephesians 1:13, he commends the Ephesians because they heard the truth, the gospel of salvation, and believed in Jesus, and it is this faith in the Lord Jesus Christ that is celebrated in Ephesians 1:15. Faith here has a distinctly intellectual character: it is a reflection of one's understanding, of one's mental convictions. It comes in response to truth.

The Christian faith takes the mind seriously, and thus Paul stresses that the Ephesians' own experience of God's salvation came in response to hearing the word of truth and believing the truth. In addition, faith also has a distinctly affective dimension. We are certainly saved through faith (in the words of 2:8), but this is not merely a matter of clarity in our understanding. In 3:17 Paul stresses that Christ dwells in our hearts through faith when we are rooted and grounded in love. This highlights the reality that faith includes a radical trust in the love and providential goodness of God. To have faith in Christ necessarily means that we believe in him but also that we trust him, knowing and living in the reality that we are loved, a knowing that Paul says in 3:19 surpasses knowledge and enables us to live in the fullness of God.

Faith has an intellectual and an affective dimension, then. Actually, it also has a volitional element: Paul stresses that faith leads to good works (2:10), for example. But for the moment it is nevertheless appropriate to focus on these two and to realize that faith is not merely a matter of an initial response to Christ, something we do when we *become* Christians. To be a Christian is to live by faith, and thus faith is the most fundamental element of our Christian identity. To be a Christian is to have faith, to grow in faith, to learn what it is to mature in the experience of genuine Christian faith.

Implications for a Christian Understanding of Conversion

First, as a fundamental working principle, conversion is a response to the saving initiative of God. We can hardly overstate this point.

Second, it is focused on Christ Jesus: to become a Christian is to believe in Christ Jesus, to trust in Jesus, to become a disciple of Christ, a follower of Christ. And when one is baptized, it is a baptism into Christ, to be united with Christ in his death and resurrection (Rom. 6).

Third, it is an act of faith—or indeed, multiple acts of faith, multiple ways in which faith finds expression and is bred into our bones and becomes the very fabric of our way of being and living.

And fourth, the act of conversion is never meritorious; it earns us nothing. We are responding to the mercy of God: "Just as I am, without one plea, / but that your blood was shed for me" (Charlotte Elliott, 1835).

The Cosmic Purposes of God

The Letter to the Ephesians highlights a distinct tension that must be sustained if we are to have an adequate understanding of authentic religious experience and thus of conversion. It is the tension between the world—the "cosmos," meaning the earth and all of God's creation—and the inbreaking of the Christ's reign, or what we typically speak of as the kingdom of God.

First, we must highlight that the depth of the human predicament is cosmic and that, in turn, the redemptive work of God through Christ is, as would be expected, cosmic. The whole cosmos has been plunged into darkness through human sin, fragmenting a world that was "one" in Christ. Restoration comes through Christ, who, as the head of a new humanity, reconciles all things to himself. And so, while the salvation of God is centered on Christ, its impact is immense—so immense, indeed, that it incorporates all that God has made.

The scope of the purposes of God in Christ incorporates the whole of God's creation; Paul puts it this way in Ephesians: "With all wisdom and insight he has made known to us the mystery of his will, according to his good pleasure that he set forth in Christ, as a plan for the fullness of time, to gather up all things in him, things in heaven and things on earth" (Eph. 1:8–10).

This is accomplished through Christ, specifically in the ascension: "God put this power to work in Christ when he raised him from the dead and seated him at his right hand in the heavenly places, far above all rule and authority and power and dominion, and above every name that is named, not only in this age but also in the age to come. . . . And he has put all things under his feet" (1:20–22).

What we anticipate, then, is the day when all things will come under the authority of Christ. This benevolent authority is redemptive, therapeutic; all things are restored and reconciled to Christ by Christ—through the cross and then, on the basis of the cross, through his reign (see also Eph. 2:16; 2 Cor. 5:19–20). Thus the prayer of the church is simple: "Thy will be done in earth, as it is in heaven" (Matt. 6:10 KJV). And thus also, the apostle Paul speaks of the groaning of creation: as though in childbirth, it anticipates the day when the children of God will be revealed (Rom. 8:18–25).

The destiny of the human race is intimately linked with the destiny of the whole creation. We cannot speak of the salvation of humankind without at

31

the same time speaking of the heavens and the earth. The God of creation and the God of salvation is one and the same God. Salvation cannot be spoken of merely as the saving of individual "souls" that are whisked away to a heaven that is far from this earth—essentially an escape from a world that is going to hell. Such a way of speaking of God's salvation flies in the face of the clear scriptural witness to the cosmic purposes of God.

Appreciating this certainly requires that we anchor our faith and our understanding in a biblical doctrine of creation, and this means that we begin with Genesis 1 and affirm that the creation is other than God but that it reflects the will or purposes of God, having been brought into being through the Word of God. Genesis 1 resounds with the repeated phrase "and God said . . ." as the precursor to whatever it is that God creates. Further, Genesis 1 affirms the fundamental goodness of creation, as the text resounds with yet another repeated phrase, "and God saw that it was good." Indeed, the climax of the text comes with the declaration that it is *very* good (Gen. 1:31)! This particular highlighting of the goodness of creation comes specifically with the creation of humanity and the call to the human creatures to care for and steward what has been made. And here we have the first hint of the close interplay between the human vocation and destiny and that of the whole cosmos.

This doctrine of creation, in turn, lies behind the continual references to the creation in the Psalms and in the Prophets, notably in Isaiah; indeed, one could easily conclude that the prophecy of Isaiah cannot speak of the salvation of God except through the lens of a twofold reality: that God has created all things (we do not appreciate the capacity of God to redeem until and unless we have some sense of God as the Creator), and further, that the redemption of God is typically viewed through the reconciliation of the created order to itself and as such to humanity ("the wolf shall live with the lamb"; "the nursing child shall play over the hole of the asp"; Isa. 11:6, 8).

The Letter to the Ephesians gives meaning and thus clarity to what it means to be a Christian: it is much more than merely understanding what it means to be "in Christ," though it certainly begins there and includes this; rather, there is a distinctly cosmic orientation to this identity: the believer is located within God's creation.[2] Yes, the church is a central theme of the Letter to the Ephesians; we will come to this matter and to what the church means for a Christian conversion, but before this, we must affirm that all discussion about the church is located within God's grand scheme to reconcile all things to himself in Christ (Eph. 1:9–10; cf. 2 Cor. 5:19).

The Letter to the Ephesians declares that this redemption comes in and through Christ, through the crucified, risen, and ascended Lord. And in the meantime, the church can sing, "This is my Father's world" (Maltbie Bab-

---

2. I am indebted for this reading of Ephesians to Peter T. O'Brien, *The Letter to the Ephesians*, Pillar New Testament Commentary (Grand Rapids: Eerdmans, 1999).

cock, 1901)! However, what is equally clear is that though this is "my Father's world," a false prince rules on the earth (Eph. 2:2; cf. 2 Cor. 4:4). The deep fragmentation caused by sin means not only that there are pockets of sin and evil here and there but also that the world is governed by what Paul calls "rulers and authorities," hostile forces that war against the inbreaking of the reign of Christ (Eph. 3:10; 6:12).

Because the power of sin is so present in our own lives, even within the church, we cannot be naive about the deep disconnect that exists between the reign of Christ and the "world." A conversion is an experience of deep continuity *and* discontinuity. Although through conversion we are certainly not called to abandon the world or escape from it—Jesus insists on this in his prayer of John 17 (see v. 15)—we nevertheless recognize that there is a profound discontinuity between the values and mores of the world and those of the reign of Christ. The whole process and experience of conversion is one of moving out from under this foreign authority and moving under the reign of Christ, the cosmic Lord and head of a new humanity (cf. Col. 1:13–14). The Christian will, then, always live within this tension: the interplay of this age and the age to come. As Andrew T. Lincoln puts it in his commentary on Ephesians: "Those who have been seated with Christ in the heavens are at the same time those who must walk in the world (cf. Eph. 2:10; 4:1, 17; 5:2, 8, 15) and stand in the midst of the continuing battle with the powers (cf. 6:11–16)."[3]

Implications for a Christian Understanding of Conversion

We only fully appreciate the biblical doctrine of salvation as we begin to grasp the interplay, in this biblical vision, between the cosmos, the church, and the individual. The revivalist vision of salvation tends to begin with the individual. The focus is on the person who might "accept" Christ and then be saved. Then, hopefully, they will join the church. The world, or the cosmos, is almost an afterthought if it is remembered at all: so much revivalist thinking is escapist. The individual is considered first, then the church, and then the cosmos.

The biblical vision is the reverse. It *begins* with the cosmic purposes of God and then highlights the church (as we shall see below) as the critical means by which the gospel permeates the cosmos and only then comes to the individual—with the assumption that the individual only witnesses to the inbreaking of Christ's reign in the cosmos as a full participant in the life and witness of the church.

The point here is that this vision begins with the cosmic purposes of God. We are only faithful in our preaching if through our preaching and teaching we sustain this cosmic vision of what God is doing. Conversion is thus an

3. Andrew T. Lincoln, *Ephesians*, Word Biblical Commentary 42 (Dallas: Word Books, 1990), 109.

encounter with and an active response to the risen and ascended Christ; it is an experience in which and by which we recognize the cosmic authority of Christ and the radical implications of Christ's authority for the false kingdoms of this world. So in the end, conversion is not merely about finding personal fulfillment, and to speak of it as "accepting Jesus into my heart," however meaningful that might be on one level, hardly captures the grand vision of the New Testament, wherein conversion is a radical assignment with the cosmic purposes of God.

On the one hand, this will mean that we embrace the fundamental human (and thus Christian) vocation to steward the created order, to live in peace and justice within the creation, so that the cross of Christ intersects each sphere and dimension of human life and work. It is possible that through conversion a person might be called to leave an occupation; but it is just as possible that their conversion would transform their vision of life and work and that in coming to Christ they are emboldened and empowered to embrace the call of God to business, the arts, education, and other worthwhile occupations.

An authentic Christian conversion fosters our capacity to discern the call of God to be in the world. However, a Christian conversion just as surely enables the believer to see and feel, to understand affectively, that their identity is not anchored in a world that is alienated from Christ. Or to use the language of the Letter to the Colossians: "Seek the things that are above, where Christ is, seated at the right hand of God. Set your minds on things that are above, not on things that are on earth, for you have died, and your life is hidden with Christ in God" (3:1–3). In other words, there is a profound and radical discontinuity such that though we are in the world, we are not "of" the world. Our identity is other. The whole process of conversion necessarily needs to highlight and cultivate this *discontinuity* or, quite simply, it is not a Christian conversion.

Continuity and discontinuity—it is so very difficult to sustain and maintain this tension. Evangelical seeker-sensitive worship services, some of which are actually held in theaters, obviously assume that *continuity* is the order of the day. Yet Eastern Orthodox theology and liturgy unapologetically profile the distinct otherness of life in Christ—the deep *discontinuity*. So the question naturally arises: What is the best way to manage this tension so that a person is truly converted to Christ and transformed for life and work in the world; so that we are in but not of the world (to use the imagery of John 17); so that, in the language of Romans 12:2, we are not "conformed to this world" but "transformed by the renewing of [our] minds"? Is this likely to happen in a theater? Or is it more likely to happen within a Byzantine Orthodox church— such as the one just outside Toronto that is a perfect mirror of what an Eastern church would look like in Moscow, with no accommodation to local styles or culture? The litmus test between these alternatives, and all options in between these two poles, is whether our worship fosters a real-time encounter with the

34

risen and ascended Christ and whether in this worship and coming from this worship, we are transformed for life and work in the world.

The Purposes of God as a Means to an End: The Formation of a People

To appreciate the purposes of God as delineated in the Letter to the Ephesians, several points must be made. We need to see the depth of the human predicament matched by the christocentric character of God's response. Then also, we need to appreciate the cosmic agenda: God is reconciling all things to himself in Christ. But how? What is the means by which Christ will fulfill this agenda? And the answer inevitably, in Ephesians, brings us to the church. Any reading of the Letter to the Ephesians highlights that, in this regard, God's agenda is twofold: (1) God is forming for himself a people, which is the body of Christ, and (2) God's intention is that this people becomes mature, specifically, that they would be mature in Christ.

If we consider the question What on earth is God doing? it inevitably means that we appreciate the ecclesial, or churchly, character of the divine purposes. This is probably nowhere more apparent in the New Testament than it is in the Epistle to the Ephesians (consider 2:11–3:6 and the first half of Eph. 4). This is Paul's mature vision for God's redemptive work: this big picture (the cosmic perspective) of the full scope of his theology when it comes to the mission of God and, in particular, the vision for a people who would be the people of God.

We must affirm that the purposes of God are not limited by or to the church. God is establishing a liberating reign, to which the church is a sign. However, there is no avoiding the churchly character of the purposes of God—as a witness to the reign of Christ, and also because both the experience of conversion and the fruit of conversion are churchly. The first message of Ephesians is that God is reconciling all things to himself; the second message is that God is forming for himself a people. If we want to know God's grace, God's salvation, it will necessarily mean that his purposes for us as individuals will by definition be part of what he is doing as he forms for himself a people. If this is the case, to be a Christian means being part of the people that is being formed by God through Christ Jesus. The church then becomes a living sign, an abiding witness, that indeed the powers of darkness have been defeated and that all things will one day be reconciled in Christ.

In Ephesians, Paul approaches this topic of the purposes of God by highlighting an issue that was present to his Ephesian readers: the need for clarity about the identity of Jews and Gentiles (non-Jews) and the purposes of God for both. The backdrop to this was the Old Testament clearly establishing that God has a covenant with the Jewish people, a covenant with them such that they are the "people of God." By this perspective, non-Jews, or Gentiles, are "out" and not "in." As Paul notes, under this covenant, it would make sense to conclude that, as he puts it in 2:12, they were aliens to Israel, strangers to the covenant. They had no hope.

But then he insists that now the two have become one. There is no dividing wall between them (2:14). A new covenant has been established, and in this new covenant there is no Gentile or Jew (Gal. 3:28). Thus God has, through Christ, made for himself "one new humanity" (Eph. 2:15), one body (v. 16), one household (v. 19), one temple of the Holy Spirit (vv. 21–22). Then in 4:4 he comes back to this insistence that there is one body. Does this mean that God has abandoned the Jews? Of course not. Paul makes clear in Romans 9–11 that the purposes of God within the new covenant take account of the Jewish people. God's mission in the world will and must include the Jewish people. But it is not because there is a special covenant with them or for them. It is because there is one people of God, and they are necessarily a part of it. Nothing could be clearer in this respect than the words of Paul in Ephesians 2–3. Theological systems that conclude otherwise are clearly out of alignment with the message of the New Testament.[4]

Part of what makes the Letter to the Ephesians so compelling in this regard are the images that Paul uses to capture different aspects or perspectives of what it means to be the people of God. He uses them naturally and easily, and he weaves them into his discussion in a way clearly showing that they are integral to his theology of the church. Along with "the people of God," which is essentially an image that portrays the community of faith in unique relationship with the Father, we have three others that arise in these verses:

2:16	In speaking of the reconciliation between two people into one people, Paul speaks of "one body," an image he picks up again in 3:6 and 4:4; the church is the body of Christ.
2:19	Paul speaks of a "household of God," using a variation of a theme that comes up elsewhere in Paul, that the church is the family of God.
2:20–22	The church is viewed as a building, established on the foundation, and this building is portrayed as a temple, which is the dwelling place of God. The church is the temple of the Holy Spirit.

With these images as a backdrop, Paul proceeds in chapter 3 to highlight and celebrate the wonder that God's work in the world is through the church.

4. Here it is important also to note that the reconciliation of Gentile to Jew is not that of a proselyte who has been fully joined to Israel; rather, the intent of the Letter to the Ephesians is to highlight how God has formed a new entity that transcends what was formerly spoken of as Israel, a new entity that is no longer ethnic specific and that incorporates both Jew and Gentile. This is the new humanity of which Christ is the living head. Both Jews and Gentiles were alienated from God, both are now reconciled to God in Christ, and in Christ they form a new community, which is the body of Christ.

It is clear that the mission of God is intimately linked with the life of the church.

Beginning with verse 7, Paul speaks of his own calling and ministry but then stresses that his own calling is but an extension of, and integral to, the calling of the church. Thus, in verse 10, it is through the church that "the manifold wisdom of God" is made known (KJV). Paul's personal ministry of proclamation is rooted in this greater reality: the church is the medium by which the gospel is known in the world.

Therefore what we clearly see is that the theological vision of Ephesians celebrates something consistent with the entire witness of the Old Testament, that God is forming a people for himself. These people are those who are "elect" in Christ. The first choosing is the election of Christ, and then God calls forth a people who are elect in Christ Jesus. And these people are on a mission, collectively, as a people who together witness to the inbreaking of the reign of Christ.

Implications for a Christian Understanding of Conversion

First, God's salvation is always portrayed in corporate terms, never to the exclusion of the individual, but always with the assumption that the individual is an integral member of the community of faith. Thus we cannot in the end conceive of or portray a biblical doctrine of conversion except with a distinctly ecclesial character. Religious experience, in other words, is never purely individual, personal, and interior. It will (and must) be individual, personal, and interior, but it will never be *solely* individual and interior. Further, it will not be individual and personal and interior *unless* it is grounded in the common experience of the people of God, unless it has a corporate dimension. True Christian experience is anchored to the common faith of the church, and it is the common faith that gives authenticity to our personal and individual faith. It is the church's ancient and historic experience that gives meaning to our personal experience.

Few things challenge the revivalist vision of salvation as much as this. For revivalism, salvation and thus conversion are individual transactions between the person and God; the individual experience of salvation comes before the experience of the church and of community. The biblical vision places the priority, both theologically and existentially, with the church. The church, not the individual, is the center of the divine purposes of God. This means that the church is not merely the sum of its members, the collection of individually saved people; rather, the church is an organic, dynamic, and living entity in its own right, of which the individuals are vital and active members, to be sure, but not as an afterthought to the experience of God's salvation.

Second, this means that a person is not a Christian unless they have a distinct sense of their identity as a participant in the people of God. By this I mean that we cannot conceive of our relationship with God except as it is intimately linked with our relationship with others. The one dimension of Christian experience (with God) is interdependent with the other dimension (with others, notably the community of faith). Coming to Christ means that we are incorporated into his body, which is the church. We cannot be in Christ unless we are grafted into his body. This is the basis for the mission of God: not merely the salvation of individuals here and there, but chiefly the formation of a people.

Third, all of this is a reminder that the mission of God finds expression through the church. Thus the means of conversion—Word and Spirit, which I will address below—will be mediated through and housed in the experience of the church. In other words, in some form or another the experience of conversion will be derivative of the church (Eph. 3:10). This is a theological affirmation, but it is also consistent with the experience of converts. This is the way people come to faith in Christ.

One of the most vital expressions of this identity in the church is baptism: there is "one baptism" (4:5), one essential mark of this identity as the people of God, the temple of the Spirit, and the family of God. Baptism becomes not only a sign of our union with Christ but also an indicator of our *common* identity in Christ.

Yet having affirmed, and necessarily so, that the church plays a key part in the redemptive purposes of Christ, this point must always be made with a distinctive caveat: the church is a means to an end; it is not the end. The church is called into being to witness to the inbreaking of Christ's reign. We affirm the church, yes. God chooses a people, certainly. But the whole point of Ephesians is that we are not ultimately converted to the church. We are converted to the risen and ascended Christ, by whom and in whom we live in the kingdom. Without this perspective, we are not truly the church, and conversion is not truly Christian; we are only joining a religious club that gives itself to certain Christian activities, perhaps, but it is not the church. By its very nature, the church is oriented not to its own maintenance but to the kingdom of God. We are not ultimately interested in church growth or church planting or the extension of the church, but to the kingdom. The real test of the church is not how large it is or how fast it is growing but whether its members are equipped to be kingdom agents in the world. And conversion is not about joining a religious club but rather about becoming part of a faith community that is impassioned in its call and mutual commitment to be a sign to God's kingdom.

The Purposes of God in the Character of the People of God: Maturity in Christ

When we ask What on earth is God doing? we recognize that God is reconciling all things to himself: to this end, in Christ he is forming a people for himself.

38

But it is not just any people; we also need to speak of their character, of what it is that God is intending for this people. God is forming for himself a people. This is clear. But it is also important and vital for us to stress that God has a very particular agenda for this people. They are the people of God, the body of Christ, the temple of the Spirit. What does God intend with all of this?

As already mentioned, God's intent is that through this people, his wisdom would be made known. Yet there is something equally fundamental to the purpose or agenda of God, something central to any Christian theology, evident in what Paul says in Ephesians 3:14–4:16, especially in 4:7–16 as well as 5:25–27. In the last part of Ephesians 3, Paul urges his readers to be rooted and grounded in love, strengthened by the Holy Spirit. Then in Ephesians 4 he speaks about gifts that are given to the church: apostles, prophets, pastors, given to equip the people of God. And all of this—the assurance of love, the promise of the Holy Spirit, the ministry of the Word through prophet, apostle, and pastor-teacher—all are given with a distinctive and intentional goal. God is forming for himself a people who are *mature* in Christ (4:13–16).

Here are some affirmations. First, maturity is the goal of our common identity in Christ. Basic to Paul's thought is the notion that the intent of God for each of us individually, but more to the point, for each of us as participants in the community of faith, is that we "grow up." Indeed, it may well be that this corporate expression of maturity is its first and most fundamental expression. But the main point here is that this spiritual maturity is basic and not incidental to the purposes of God. Ephesians 5 provides the big picture: "Christ loved the church and gave himself up for her" (v. 25), cleansing the church by the washing of water through the Word so that he might present the church as a pure bride (vv. 26–27). Frequently this latter reference is assumed to belong with the consummation of history; and yet it is clear from the rest of the Letter to the Ephesians, if not the whole New Testament, that this is meant to mark the *current* experience of the church.

Second, this is a maturity that takes its focus and character from Christ. This growth is not merely a personal self-fulfillment program, though Christian maturity is surely the fulfillment of our Christian identity. Neither is it merely a program of self-discovery or self-realization, though in Christ we surely find ourselves; rather, it is a maturity that is focused in and through Christ. To be mature is to be mature in Christ, to grow up in him and be grounded in his love, oriented toward his character: to be like Christ and be aligned in thought, word, and deed with his call on our lives. Ultimately, it is a union with Christ by which we can affirm that we abide in Christ even as Christ abides in us.

Third, we mature in Christ as we grow in love. Paul stresses that we grow up as we grow in love, yes, but it is a growth in love that is rooted in our knowledge of God's love for us. This experience of God's love, which finds expression in our love for each other, is the very stuff of our common life;

it is the basic ingredient that holds us together and enables us to be all that we are called to be. In Ephesians 3, Paul stresses the need to be rooted and grounded in the love of God. But then in Ephesians 4, the focus shifts to our love toward others:

- Showing humility, patience, and gentleness, we bear with one another in love (4:2).
- Speaking the truth in love, we grow up into him who is the head (4:15).
- The community of faith grows as it builds itself up in love (4:16).
- We are called to live in love as Christ has loved us (5:2).

Therefore, the spiritual maturity to which we are called is not something achieved or experienced in isolation from the people of God. And the mark of this common identity, the very soil in which this spiritual maturity is found, is mutual love.

Fourth, all of this assumes that our individual and personal growth is interdependent with that of the community of faith. We *need* one another. We all grow up into Christ, as Paul puts it, as each part contributes to the whole. It is essential to the identity and practices of this community for us to affirm that this happens and can happen only as we are filled with the Spirit (5:18); we are strengthened by the Spirit as we are grounded in the love of God (3:14–17). The common life of the church is effected by the gracious ministry of the Spirit.

Implications for a Christian Understanding of Conversion

Some critical affirmations can be made in terms of our understanding of conversion. First, conversion is but a beginning; it is the benchmark by which the Christian life is established with a particular objective, so that the individual and the community may experience what it means to be transformed in Christ. The intent of conversion certainly has otherworldly implications, but what Ephesians and so much of the New Testament speaks to is what happens in this life.

We become Christians so that we might experience the transforming grace of God. If this maturity in Christ does not develop, the whole purpose of conversion is aborted. Conversion is an initiation into a growing and maturing community, an interdependent network of individuals who in love serve one another and who together, in mutual dependence, grow up in faith, hope, and love. Thus conversion is only Christian if it explicitly means an experience by which a person is incorporated into precisely this kind of community, which will enable the very purpose of conversion to be fulfilled.

Conclusion

Eventually, in our thinking about conversion we need to consider the question: What then must we do to be saved? Though the Letter to the Ephesians does not provide the explicit response to the question (we will look elsewhere for this), it nevertheless provides five invaluable and crucial guiding principles that will shape our answer to the question.

First, our understanding of conversion must take account of the extent of the human predicament, its depth and complexity. It will come as no surprise to us that the conversion experience itself will probe deeply and, in turn, take account of the complexity of our lives. It will have an intellectual, affective, penitential, and volitional dimension. Further, it will be an experience that cuts to the core of our beings, involving body and soul, heart and mind, understanding and behavior. Significant in this regard is the fact that there is no reason for this to be a punctiliar experience, momentary or specific to one time and place. This does not make it less dramatic or miraculous. What we seek is an understanding of conversion that cuts through the whole of our identity. This may well take some time to occur; that is fine!

Second, it will be an experience of Christ Jesus. In the chapters that follow, I will make the case that it is not an encounter with ideas, principles, or laws, although it is clearly an experience of the intellect that will include a change of understanding. The bottom line is that conversion is an encounter with a person, the Lord Jesus Christ.

Third, we need to speak of conversion in a way that takes account of the cosmic work of Christ in and for the world. Indeed, as we have stressed, we begin here and then speak of the church, the next point, and then speak of the individual. Our understanding of conversion needs to be located in the light of the in-breaking of the reign of Christ.

Fourth, conversion will have a distinctively corporate character to it, from beginning to end. Conversion will certainly be personal: we can affirm the need for each person to choose whom they will serve. But this experience and this choosing never happens in isolation from the community of faith.

And fifth, we have a truly biblical understanding of conversion only when what we experience in conversion is a beginning of a life in which one ultimately experiences the sanctifying and transforming grace of God. It must lead to spiritual maturity. It is a good beginning.

We will get to the question What must we do to be saved? But these are five essential parameters for our response to that question.

A final word: There is something that holds all these together, something around which this whole discussion coheres. Christ is now at the right hand of God, in the heavenly realms. This becomes determinative of the identity of the church: Christ is *now* exalted. And it is our identification with the ascended Christ that puts us in opposition to the kingdoms of this world. Yes, the full expression of this is yet to come. But even now, in real time, Christians and the church are in dynamic and living communion with the ascended Christ (we are seated above; Eph. 2:5–6). All this is in anticipation of the consummation of history. To become a Christian is to be initiated into this new identity, this new and dramatically different way of being "in the world." We are in the world but not of the world.

3

Chapters in the History of an Idea

Part 1

Any consideration of the meaning of conversion would do well to give an account of the way in which Christians in previous generations of the church have sought both to understand and to explicate this dimension of their experience. What I hope to demonstrate is that the understanding of the church regarding conversion has been shaped, significantly so, by the experience of conversion. This overview will provide an interplay between the experience of conversion and critical reflection on the nature of conversion.

In this chapter and the next, I am going to consider a number of what might be called "chapters" in the history of the idea of conversion, reporting how the church has understood the experience of coming to faith in Christ. I am going to consider six such chapters, beginning with the idea of conversion that emerges from the descriptions within the book of Acts itself, and thus the experience of the apostolic church. From there, I will move to five subsequent eras, or chapters, in the history of the church.

The Book of Acts and the Early Conversion Experience

The book of Acts is not the only place where we have conversion narratives within sacred Scripture. In the Old Testament, the book of Isaiah in particular makes clear that the call of the prophets was not merely to the people of the covenant community; we also find a call to the nations to acknowledge that Yahweh and Yahweh alone is God and is thus the Creator. The response of Abram to the call of God is essentially a conversion, a definite and radical move to live by faith in God (Gen. 12). Rahab (Josh. 2:1–21) and Ruth are not part of the covenant community; yet, as outsiders, they choose to acknowledge that the God of Israel is and will be their God; the faith of Israel becomes their faith. In Ruth's narrative, what strikes the reader is the recurring mention of God's mercy and kindness; Ruth's response is one of choosing God—and God is specifically the God of this people, the covenant people of Israel. There are other examples. Noteworthy is the conversion of the people of Nineveh, who hear the word declared by the prophet Jonah, and in response, believe in God, repent, and choose the way of faith and obedience. Their response to the preaching of the Word is mentioned in the New Testament (Matt. 12:41; Luke 11:32) as an example of conversion, reflecting a deep commitment of the prophetic witness: the means of conversion is, precisely, the word of the prophet.

The Gospels also provide us with conversion narratives, the most notable being the experience of the disciples. Here too it is clear that they became disciples of Jesus in response to the preaching of Jesus. Jesus announces the kingdom, his reign, and invites disciples to join him in living in the kingdom. Throughout the Gospels we see that the call of Jesus was not merely universal and general but also particular: to the disciples as they struggled to bring the overload of fish to the shore (Luke 5), to the rich young governor (Luke 18), to Zacchaeus the tax collector (Luke 19), and to many more. Some respond, but not all. Those who did respond positively became disciples, and they entered into a life of dynamic communion with Christ and a life lived under the authority (or reign) of Christ, the abiding theme of the Gospels.

Yet our fullest understanding of the conversion experience needs to take account of Pentecost; in many respects, the call of Jesus anticipated this, as is evident from both the Gospel of John and the opening chapter of the book of Acts. We turn to the experience of those who came to faith on and following the day of Pentecost. In Acts we do not have complete conversion narratives, with the possible exception being 2:38–42. This narrative—Acts 2:38–42—is significant; indeed, the text sets the stage for the whole of the book of Acts. It may well be the most definite description of conversion found anywhere in Scripture. Thus it merits focused attention, and we will come to this in an upcoming chapter. But for now, I wish to profile the descriptions of individual conversions that we have in the Acts of the Apostles.

New Testament scholars often observe that there are six accounts of conversion in the book of Acts, apart from 2:38–42. There are many, many references to conversion experiences, but Acts presents six accounts that are noteworthy or prominent.

1. The story of the Ethiopian, in Acts 8:26–40, describes a God-fearing Gentile, a court official, heading home from Jerusalem to Ethiopia or, what is more likely, the region now known as the Sudan.[1] He is reading the Scriptures and raises a

---

1. Most commentators see "court official" as the likely meaning of "eunuch"; see, e.g., I. Howard Marshall, *The Acts of the Apostles: An Introduction and Commentary*, Tyndale New Testament Commentaries (Grand Rapids: Eerdmans, 1980), 162.

question about the meaning of Isaiah 53, wondering if the author is speaking of himself. We read that Philip then comes alongside in response to a prompting from the Spirit—the actual reference in the text is to "an angel of the Lord" (Acts 8:26). He is sent to help the Ethiopian interpret what is he is reading.

Philip speaks to him about Jesus as the fulfillment of the Isaiah text. As they travel together, it seems that as the Ethiopian comes to a fuller and more complete understanding of the gospel, he is open to the call of the apostles to repentance and baptism. When they come to water, perhaps a stream or an oasis in the desert, we read the compelling request "Look, here is water! What is to prevent me from being baptized?" So Philip, convinced of the Ethiopian's faith in Christ Jesus, baptizes him. Philip is taken away by the Spirit, and the Ethiopian continues on his journey, we read, "rejoicing" (8:39).

2. Without doubt the most famous conversion narrative of all is that of the apostle Paul, which is reported in three texts: Acts 9:1–19; 22:6–16; and 26:12–18. Paul is headed to Damascus on a mission to root out the emerging Christian movement; he is going under the authority of the high priest. En route, not far from Damascus, he is blinded by a light and hears a voice, clearly the voice of Jesus, asking him, "Why do you persecute me?" (9:4). It is a personal encounter with the risen Christ, depicted as light (an important motif in Paul's conversion, his movement from darkness to light, from blindness to sight), and Paul hears a voice as Jesus speaks directly to him.[2]

His companions lead him, blind, into the city. For three days he fasts, perhaps struck by the enormity of his experience and not knowing how to proceed. Again, much as Philip was led to the Ethiopian, Ananias is called by God to go to Paul. Ananias, despite his understandable reservations (he apparently knows something of Paul's mission), goes to Paul and places his hands on him. He advises Paul that he has been sent by the Lord Jesus so that Paul's sight will be restored and that he will be filled with the Holy Spirit. Paul receives him and is baptized, to have his "sins washed away" (22:16). Following the baptism, he eats, for he has gone without food for three days following his encounter and blindness on the road to Damascus (9:19).

Soon Paul is in the synagogues, insisting that Jesus is the Son of God; this puts him in trouble with the authorities. To help Paul escape a threat on his life, his fellow Christian disciples let him down from the city wall in a basket, enabling him to return to Jerusalem. There Barnabas is pivotal in seeing that Paul is incorporated into the city's Christian community.

Many students of this conversion narrative note that this may not be so much a description of a conversion as a calling: Paul's commission to take the

---

2. He is Paul, also known as Saul. It was a common practice for individuals to have two names, one used in the Jewish world (here Saul) and the other in the Gentile world (Paul). It is common to think that his conversion led to a name change, but Acts does not speak of this. Also, the Scriptures do not mention the mode of Paul's transportation from Jerusalem to Damascus. We do not know if he was on foot or if he was on a horse (as traditionally thought).

gospel to the Gentile world. The point is valid. The "calling" motif emerges early: the blinding light is accompanied by the voice of Jesus, anticipating that he has a unique calling, and he is to go into Damascus to learn what it is to which he is being called.[3] Perhaps the best way to think about the account is to appreciate that it is both conversion and call; yet even this may not be a full account of Paul's conversion if, indeed, this is first and foremost an account of the calling.

3. Peter's role gives particular significance to the conversion of Cornelius. In Acts 10, as is commonly recognized, we essentially have two conversions in the works. Cornelius comes to faith in Christ, is baptized, and receives the gift of the Spirit. But the text also profiles the "conversion" of Peter as he comes to appreciate, in those immortal words, "that God shows no partiality" (10:34). This leads to two follow-up observations: "The Holy Spirit had been poured out even on the Gentiles" (10:45), and "God has given even to the Gentiles the repentance that leads to life" (11:18).

What occasions these observations is the conversion of Cornelius, a Gentile. He is a devout man, a God-fearer—meaning that he is not a proselyte and has not undergone circumcision. Through a vision, he is called to be open to the visit of Peter. Peter in turn also has such a vision, responds, and heads out to visit Cornelius's house, where he recounts the Jesus event: his life, death, resurrection, and ascension, and his mandate to preach the gospel of forgiveness.

As Peter is speaking, the Spirit comes upon those present. It is hard not to be deeply moved by Peter's response: "Can anyone withhold the water for baptizing these people who have received the Holy Spirit just as we have?" (10:47). Indeed, it is the visible and tangible evidence that they have received the Spirit that leads Peter, a few days later, to defend his actions with Cornelius before the apostles and the Christian community by recounting that Jesus had promised a baptism in the Spirit and that these Gentiles had been baptized in the Spirit. He silences his critics with this definitive observation: "If then God gave them the same gift that he gave us when we believed in the Lord Jesus Christ, who was I that I could hinder God?" (11:17). His critics are not merely silenced; they also respond with doxology.

In Acts 2:38, Peter urges those who are present to "repent, and be baptized, . . . and you will receive the gift of the Holy Spirit." Cornelius receives the gift of the Spirit, and the response is that he and those with him should be baptized. Peter links baptism and the gift of the Spirit, even if the link is not causative or sequential.

---

3. For references to the apostle Paul's vocation, in the conversion narratives, note the line in 9:6: "You will be told what you are to do." See also 22:10: the call of Ananias to go to Paul is linked to the calling of Paul to go to the Gentiles. See especially Acts 26:16–18, 20, 23, where Paul defends himself before Agrippa. Here the "conversion" narrative is secondary to Paul's recounting his calling to the Gentiles, "to open their eyes so that they may turn from darkness to light" (Acts 26:18).

4 and 5. We come to Philippi and two noteworthy conversions. Acts 16:14–15 describes the conversion of Lydia. Paul and his associates come to Philippi, and on the Sabbath they speak with some women outside the city gates, by a river, at a place where people typically came to pray. Lydia, a businesswoman of some means and a devout worshiper of God, responds eagerly to what Paul has to say after the Lord "opened her heart" (v. 14). She and her household are baptized, and then we read that she "prevailed" upon Paul and his colleagues to stay, saying: "If you have judged me to be faithful to the Lord, come and stay at my home" (v. 15).

One thing leads to another, and Paul and his colleague Silas are flogged, thrown into prison, and held in an inner cell in stocks. Through the night the two men are in prayer and singing hymns[4] when an earthquake destroys the prison foundations, loosing the prisoners. The prison guard assumes that he will be charged with the escaped prisoners and hence intends to kill himself, but he is stopped by Paul's call, assuring him that the prisoners are all present and accounted for.

The guard comes running to the two and falls to his knees, asking, "Sirs, what must I do to be saved?" (16:30). And the answer is given: "Believe on the Lord Jesus, and you will be saved, you and your household" (v. 31). More is offered; the text says that they "spoke the word of the Lord" to the jailer and his household. Clearly the response of the jailer does not come out of a vacuum. Perhaps he heard Paul and Silas earlier in the day; perhaps he knew something of the emerging Christian movement. Either way, the message and demeanor of the two, along with what he has already learned, is all that the jailer needs. His response is nothing short of delightful: he tends their wounds, he and his family are baptized, and he offers Paul and Silas food to eat.

6. The sixth defining conversion narrative is found in Acts 18:1–8, in Corinth. We read that many Corinthians "became believers and were baptized" (v. 8), and what stands out is that this group includes the official of the synagogue: Crispus.

Paul, Silas, and Timothy have come to Corinth from Athens; now here in Corinth, their ministry focus is the synagogue, where the emphasis is on seeking to persuade Jews that Jesus was indeed the anticipated Messiah (v. 5). But Paul's message is rejected, violently so. This seems to settle things for Paul. He leaves the synagogue and resolves to focus his ministry on the Gentile community. He begins next door, immediately adjacent to the synagogue, in the house of Titius Justus, a God-fearing Gentile. And something amazing happens: Crispus the synagogue president, and his household, come to faith in Christ, and they do so in the house of this Gentile.

Each of these conversion accounts is surely unique, but noteworthy and interesting are the common themes of these conversion experiences. While

4. With tongue in cheek, I might point out that they are singing "hymns," not contemporary choruses—something to consider if one hopes for prison-breaking earthquakes!

none of these narratives is comprehensive (each is a window or a segment of an experience), they are nevertheless instructive, providing insight into the early church's understanding of conversion, particularly when we consider the common elements. Before considering these, a few things are worth noting.

It is apparent that these are not just samples from the experience of the early church. There is a literary intentionality, and the sequence is noteworthy: each narrative, though significant in its own right, is also part of a larger story. We observe three distinctive movements when the narratives are considered together as part of a whole:[5]

1. With the exception of Paul's conversion, there is a movement outward. In Acts 2 we have the conversion of Jews; in Acts 8 the conversion of Samaritans; then also in Acts 8 and into Acts 10 and the first part of Acts 16, we have the conversion of God-fearing Gentiles: the Ethiopian, Cornelius, and Lydia. With Lydia there is a movement outward in that her coming to faith occurs in Europe. Then, still in Acts 16, we have the conversion of the Philippian jailer, a pagan. Finally, in Acts 18 we have the conversion of a Diaspora Jew. This last might seem like a reversal unless it is viewed through the lens of the second movement, from synagogue to household.

2. The movement outward is complemented by another perspective: from synagogue to household. Although early Christian evangelism began in the synagogue, it was not long before the venue changed. For Cornelius, the pivotal moment is in his house; for Lydia, again, the orientation is her house, and we read that her household is converted; and for the Philippian jailer, the focal point is also the house and the household. In other words, the religious space in which people come to faith in Christ moves from synagogue to household. By the time we come to Corinth, the move is complete. Paul goes to the synagogue but is rejected, so he moves to the house of Titius Justus (18:7), which then becomes the center for Paul's ministry in the region. The significance of this last should not be missed: the official of the synagogue is converted not in the synagogue, but in the house of a Gentile![6]

3. There is another movement, a movement to a genuinely Gentile faith, and what makes this so intriguing is that it happens around meals. The new converts offer meals to those who have preached the word to them. In the case of Cornelius and Lydia, who are God-fearing Gentiles, the offering of food would likely be kosher—something that would surely be important to both Paul and Peter, but especially Peter. But the same cannot be said for the Philippian jailer, and this would have caught the attention of any first-century Jewish reader. Paul and Silas

---

5. For many of these insights, I am indebted to the work of David Lertis Matson, *Household Conversion Narratives in Acts: Pattern and Interpretation* (Sheffield: Sheffield Academic Press, 1996).

6. We should not confuse "household" with "family." Though a household may well have included parents and children, more often this designation suggests an extended family system and household servants.

eat in his house and thus demonstrate—this in Acts 16, following the council decision of Acts 15—that the Gentiles do not need to become law-observant Jews in order to become Christians. The Philippian jailer does not go to the synagogue to become a Christian, and equally dramatically, Paul goes to the house of a (converted) pagan and eats with him and his household! Then in Acts 18, in an extraordinary full-circle spin, Crispus, the (Jewish!) official of the synagogue, is converted not in the synagogue but in the house of a Gentile.

Andrew F. Walls makes the following cogent observation: the earliest church was thoroughly Jewish, certainly, but it is noteworthy that when it came to the early church's understanding of conversion, it was clear that to become a Christian, one did not need to become Jewish. Walls makes the distinction between a convert and a proselyte and insists that what is so significant in the book of Acts is that those who responded to the gospel were not proselytes—joining a religious movement or sect—they were converts, affiliated now not with a religious movement per se but with Christ Jesus himself. Thus Paul and the other early church leaders rejected any inclination to Judaize those who were coming to faith. Their new affinity was not to the religious identity of the evangelist; they were not proselytes. They were *converts*, whose identity, loyalty, and obedience were now owed exclusively to Jesus.[7]

So, with this broader perspective in view, we can consider common elements in these conversion narratives:

1. Divine initiative and activity. Luke is at pains for the reader to appreciate the working of divine grace demonstrating that only God could have brought this about (e.g., Peter to see Cornelius and Philip to meet the Ethiopian, and the blinding light that Paul experienced on the road to Damascus). The divine initiative includes preparation for what is yet to come: the preaching of the Word or the proclamation of Jesus, for example. But the main point is that what is effected in the life of the new believer can only be explained as a direct intervention of God. An "angel of the Lord," a messenger of some kind, calls Philip to meet the Ethiopian. In a dream, Peter is told to go and meet with Cornelius. Ananias has a vision telling him to go to a house on Straight Street. In providing these narratives, Luke clearly has a theological agenda: to demonstrate the priority of divine initiative and even the divine choreography of human religious experience. This does not mean that human volition and response are incidental or that human response does not matter; it is rather to stress the priority of divine initiative and grace.

2. There is an openness, an inquiry, a desire to know more, either explicit, as with the Philippian jailer's "What must I do to be saved?" or implicit, as with Lydia's heart being opened to the message of Scripture. Each saw their need for God.

7. Andrew F. Walls, "Converts or Proselytes? The Crisis over Conversion in the Early Church," *International Bulletin of Missionary Research* 28, no. 1 (2004): 2–6.

3. There is preaching or instruction about Jesus. In some cases this is explicitly linked to the Scriptures; in other cases it is implied. Either way, we notice the participation of the apostle or spokesperson for Christ and the church. The conversion is initiated and superintended by the Spirit, but there is a human mediator who witnesses to Christ (often through the Scriptures): Philip for the Ethiopian, Peter for Cornelius, Ananias for Paul, Paul for Lydia, and Paul and Silas for the Philippian jailer.

There is another fascinating side to this human factor. We might well expect that someone speaks on behalf of God and proclaims the good news as an act of generosity and service to the one who is invited to respond to Christ. Yet there is also an interesting subtheme, that of house and home and sometimes of meal hospitality. Lydia did not just have her heart opened to listen; she also opened her home to Paul and his colleagues. The Philippian jailer insisted that they come to his home, where he gave Paul and Silas a meal (he knew what kind of food or lack of food was theirs in the jail!); indeed, the theme of food appears in Paul's conversion as well. Acts 9:19 mentions a meal after his sight was restored. In all of this, one wonders if we have an echo of Jesus not only announcing the kingdom to Zacchaeus but also declaring that he would be eating in his home that very day (Luke 19).

4. There is a baptism. Water baptism is mentioned in each of these conversion narratives. As we shall see, Acts 2:38 indicates that the appropriate response to the preaching is repentance and baptism; thus it should come as no surprise that baptism appears in each of these accounts. Indeed, baptism apparently was seen to be a matter of course; it was taken for granted, as we read in verse 8 of Acts 18: "many of the Corinthians who heard Paul became believers and were baptized."

5. Also, we note that joy marked their experience of coming to faith in Christ. The affective dimension is a thread that runs throughout each of these narratives. The Ethiopian continued on his way "rejoicing." The Philippian jailer "rejoiced," we read (16:34). These are but part of the recurring emphasis that begins early in the description of the apostolic community as one of deep gladness and joy.

Chapters in the History of the Christian Understanding of Conversion

With the book of Acts as a backdrop, I will now consider a diversity of perspectives on conversion, five in all. From distinct periods in the history of the church, both the experience itself and the key voices of each of these "chapters" provide critical reflection on the idea of conversion:

1. Ambrose, Augustine, and the catechumenate of Milan and North Africa.

2. The Rule of Saint Benedict and the monastic vision, from Saint Anthony through Saint Bernard and up to the sixteenth-century Reformation.

   Then chapter 4 opens with some observations arising from the sixteenth-century Reformers Luther and Calvin before I consider the Anabaptists and three additional chapters in this history of the idea of conversion.

3. The evangelical vision of conversion that emerges in the seventeenth and eighteenth centuries, leading up to and including the Great Awakening.

4. The nineteenth and twentieth centuries and the rise of the Holiness-Pentecostal movement, with its emphasis on the sensible awareness of the gift of the Spirit.

5. The global expansion of the church in the twentieth and twenty-first centuries, and the experience of conversion outside the Christian West, using conversion from Islam as a sample in this chapter.

This is not a comprehensive survey; several noteworthy chapters are not included here. But this will give us a good profile of the diversity of perspective on conversion that comes from different eras in the history of the church.

1. Conversion in the Early Church: Ambrose, Augustine, and the Catechumenate of Milan and North Africa

When we consider the influence of the early church on the understanding of conversion, the most powerful voice is surely that of Augustine of Hippo (354–430). His influence is twofold: both in the testimony to his own experience through his extraordinary spiritual autobiography, *Confessions*, and through the practice of mediating conversions through intentional ritual formation, in the catechumenate of the diocese of North Africa.

There is a notable link between the two. The approach to conversion in the catechumenate emphasized the interplay between intellectual conversion and moral conversion, and as is well known, this is precisely the abiding tension in the conversion experience of Augustine. What seemingly drove the conversion experience of Augustine was his persistent resolve to face what was essentially both an intellectual and moral predicament: how to explain and come to terms with the phenomena of evil in the world (the intellectual challenge), but just as strongly, how to deal with the problem of evil in his own body (the moral challenge). What strikes one in reading Augustine's narrative is that the two are intimately linked. The challenge of conversion for Augustine was not merely intellectual; it was not simply a question of coming to terms with the problem of evil. It was also a deeply moral question.

Augustine's upbringing was not Christian per se. He was born and raised in North Africa, studying in his place of birth, Tagaste, then later in Carthage, and eventually becoming a teacher of rhetoric. His pursuit of an answer to the problem of evil led him first to Manichaeism and eventually to Neoplatonism—as he made his way to Rome and in time to Milan. But along the way his mother, Monica, was an abiding Christian voice. In Milan he was in contact with a number of notable Christian intellectuals, including Ambrose (d. 397), the bishop of Milan, and his successor in that office, Simplician (d. 400), who became a personal mentor to Augustine (as he was also to Ambrose), urging him to read the Letters of Paul and passing on conversion narratives that provided inspiring examples of journeys of faith.

Indeed, he was reading Paul's Epistles when he heard a child, at play outside his window, saying, "*Tolle, lege* [pick up and read]," and as he turned back to what he was reading, he was struck by the power of the words in Romans 13—impressed not merely intellectually, but also through his whole body. Light flooded into his heart; doubt was gone. But more, he felt an immediate release and freedom from the power of sin. In Milan, he joined other candidates for baptism and sat under Ambrose's Lenten instructions and preparations for baptism. Then, on the eve of Easter, he was baptized at the cathedral of Milan by the bishop.

He published his *Confessions* in 401 and, as noted, it is clear that his conversion is not merely a matter of resolving intellectual and moral dilemmas. What "drives" the conversion is the yearning of the heart; a dominant theme in the *Confessions* is the image of finding home, as the soul finds its way to the one to whom it belongs and where it finds rest, in God. The opening paragraph expresses this with its dramatic and compelling doxology: "You made us for yourself, and our heart is restless until it finds rest in you." Through conversion one finds God, comes home to God. Neither reason nor morality ultimately defines what it means to become a Christian; rather, it is the yearning of the soul, the desire for the highest object of desire, God.

Conversion is not about the triumph of reason; neither is it ultimately about moral reform. Yet it cannot occur in either an intellectual or a moral vacuum. The movement of reason—in Augustine's case from paganism to Manichaeism to Neoplatonism to Christian faith—needs to be complemented by the enabling of the will, by grace, to live in the light. Thus we note the influence of Ambrose, whose preaching seems to have established the intellectual landscape for Augustine's faith journey, and the urgings of Simplician that Augustine read Paul. There is no doubt that Augustine had to resolve a moral predicament: his sensual propensities. But these are the context and the tracks, one might say, on which the conversion moves. In the *Confessions* narrative we are caught up by the movement of the heart, not so much the active intellect, as the turning of the heart that is drawn to God by God himself.

Yet, as Rowan Williams rightly insists, more is happening here. Augustine's conversion is a beginning, not merely a noteworthy event. Augustine found God, the object of his desire and thus his true home. Williams observes that for Augustine, in conversion one enters into a journey of faith: a walk of humble dependence on the grace of God amid a tumultuous world.[8] This is so, in part, because through conversion one identifies with the cross and the pain of the world. Conversion brings one into a keen awareness of the evil of the world. There is no place for complacency about the forces of darkness. As Williams puts it, echoing the language of Augustine, "The Christian needs to have more, not less exposed nerves than others to see the world with honesty enough to grasp its appalling cruelties."[9] And one "survives" by following the example of Christ, by identifying with the crucified and suffering Christ. And thus through conversion one enters into the way of the cross. Yet one always lives by faith, by radical dependence on God's grace.

What would be patently evident to Augustine, then, is that no one can manipulate or choreograph a human conversion. This is something that by its very nature is transacted between an individual and God. Yet this does not discount the role of the community or the church in providing the necessary context, the landscape, for this pursuit of God. To the contrary, the experience of Augustine highlights the need for intentionality: conversion is the fruit of God's initiative. But the church is called to provide the setting, the context, the tracks on which the work of God in the human soul can run.

It is fascinating to consider the catechumenate of the early church, the practice by which these faith communities initiated women and men into Christian community. Several authors have highlighted the way in which the catechumenate found expression in North Africa under the bishopric of Augustine. My comments here are largely a summary of the observations of three authors: Thomas M. Finn, L. Gregory Jones, and Alan Kreider.[10]

Jones and Kreider observe that for the early church, conversion was a journey, or perhaps better a *pilgrimage*. It was not so much a moment or event as rather an extended period of intentional formation that (normally) took two or three years. Though it was an individual experience, the whole of the journey to faith was located within the liturgical life of the church, mediated by the life and rhythms of Christian community. And it typically included four distinct stages. Thomas Finn stresses that what Augustine learned from

8. Rowan Williams, *The Wound of Knowledge: Christian Spirituality from the New Testament to Saint John of the Cross* (London: Darton, Longman & Todd, 1979), 73–74.

9. Ibid., 81.

10. Thomas M. Finn, *From Death to Rebirth: Ritual and Conversion in Antiquity* (Mahwah, NJ: Paulist Press, 1997); L. Gregory Jones, "Baptism," in *Knowing the Triune God: The Work of the Spirit in the Practices of the Church*, ed. James J. Buckley and David S. Yeago (Grand Rapids: Eerdmans, 2001), 147–77, esp. 152–61. Jones summarizes the work of two scholars: Thomas M. Finn, "It Happened One Saturday Night: Ritual and Conversion in Augustine's North Africa," *Journal of the American Academy of Religion* 58, no. 4 (1990): 589–616; and William Harmless, SJ, *Augustine and the Catechumenate* (Collegeville, MN: Liturgical Press, 1995). See also Alan Kreider, *The Change of Conversion and the Origin of Christendom* (Harrisburg, PA: Trinity, 1999).

experience, under the tutelage of Ambrose in Milan, and then translated into formal practice in Hippo is the transforming value of the catechumenate as a ritual process, with baptism as the pivot point of this experience.

The first stage of the pilgrimage to faith was a period of instruction: two years of learning but also of personal testing. It was an opportunity for those interested in Christianity to be welcomed into a learning community and to be taken seriously as learners. They were then instructed in the ways of the Christian faith, with a focus on doctrine, ethics, spirituality, and particularly Scripture. As Greg Jones observes, "Augustine recognized that people might show interest in Christianity for a variety of reasons, including fear or as a consequence of a dream. Whatever the reason that brought people to interest in Christianity, Augustine sought to transform their desires through nourishment from Scripture."[11] They were not only told about the Christian faith; they also had opportunity to observe Christian behavior. As Kreider puts it, "The candidate seems to have learned about Christianity by observing the Christians in action and by doing what they did."[12]

Each of those who entered into the catechumenate was assigned a sponsor, who acted as a model and mentor. The relationship was not merely with this one person but also with the whole community; indeed, Kreider insists that as critical as anything to this process was a sense that a person belonged to the community and that the transformation of belief and behavior came through a catechetical process anchored within the network of relationships that make up the church. All of this reflects Augustine's own experience. He was welcomed into a learning community in Milan, with patient teachers, guides, and spiritual mentors who allowed him to move to faith at a pace that they did not choreograph. That pace nevertheless reflected their active participation, leading up to the summer of 386, when he wrote to Ambrose about his intention to be baptized.

The second stage of the pilgrimage was a time of baptismal preparation; this typically took place during the season of Lent. If a person demonstrated in their behavior a quality of life and commitment to embrace the faith, they were then invited into this season of formal testing and prayer. During the forty days, they experienced focused spiritual formation that called for a wholehearted transfer of allegiance. They were called to a renunciation of sin and evil. (Kreider observes that this often included exorcisms.) And they were instructed in the Creed and the Lord's Prayer. What we see, then, is a dual concern for both doctrine and ethics, for both understanding and moral reform.

The third stage was the actual experience of baptism. This came early on Easter morning, after an evening vigil. This was the "nodal point of conversion," the climactic event of the conversion process. As Finn puts it, for Au-

11. Jones, "Baptism," 154.
12. Kreider, *Change of Conversion*, 104.

gustine, "baptism, not his experience in the garden in Milan, established his conversion and regeneration."[13] The baptism, witnessed to and celebrated by the whole church community, involved (1) specific renunciations of the devil and the "pleasures" of the world (facing west); (2) affirmations in the pledge of allegiance to Christ (facing east) and the declaration of belief in the Triune God; (3) a triple immersion; and, vital to the whole process, (4) the anointing and chrismation, the rite by which the new convert is immersed in the life of the Spirit, so that it is clear and explicit that the life of the Christian is strengthened by the power of the Spirit. With baptism, a person was now welcomed at the celebration of the Eucharist.

The fourth and final stage in the pilgrimage was the *mystagogia*, a one-week period of postbaptismal instruction. This mystagogy introduced the new convert to the mysteries of faith, most notably the meaning of the Eucharist, which would now be a centerpiece of their Christian experience.

This process of conversion has captured renewed attention today, particularly with the way in which the Rite for the Christian Initiation of Adults has essentially become a contemporary version of this ancient practice. This process, adopted by the Roman Catholic Church, is clearly adapted from this early church understanding of the experience of conversion. What catches our attention is, at the very least, two things: (1) the interplay of understanding with behavior—both are vital to the experience of conversion—and (2) that the experience is moderated and mediated by the church, particularly by its liturgical life. As Kreider says, the process is "ritually articulated" by the community of faith.[14] Baptism, in this instance, is then the nodal point of conversion.

For the early church, conversion thus was a process—better put, a journey or *pilgrimage*, and a specific kind of pilgrimage: a catechetical, or learning, process. Furthermore, what is also clear is that for the early church, conversion could not be separated from discipleship. The catechetical process was intensive and focused on both understanding and behavior as those who were coming to faith learned what it meant to live in obedience. Finally, we should not miss that for the early church, conversion occurred within the faith community and was mediated by the community—specifically by the liturgical life of the community, with baptism as the pivot on which the whole journey to faith rested.

Before moving on to the next chapter in the history of the idea of conversion, an observation needs to be made about the early church's practice of linking water baptism with "chrismation," the ritual anointing of the convert with oil, at baptism, as a sign of the filling or baptism in the Spirit. The link made by Augustine in North Africa, reflecting his own experience under Ambrose, in Milan, likely arose through the influence of the Christian community in eastern Syria.

13. Finn, *From Death to Rebirth*, 230.
14. Kreider, *Change of Conversion*, 7.

Baptism and the reception of the gift of the Spirit were clearly linked for the church of the book of Acts, with baptism in the Spirit occurring either before or after water baptism (thus suggesting that though the two are linked, it is not a causal link). In the second century a number of documents attest to how the early church profiled this association between baptism and the gift of the Spirit. Tertullian, for example, speaks of the intimate presence of the Spirit at baptism: the Spirit hovers over the baptismal waters much as the Spirit is described as present in the birth of creation in Genesis 1; the person was readied for the gift of the Spirit through the cleansing waters of baptism; and the baptized one was then anointed with oil, chrismated, much like the anointing of Aaron. This included the laying on of hands with the prayer that the baptized one receive the gift of the Spirit.[15]

Students of second-century Christianity frequently cite the *Apostolic Tradition*, by Hippolytus of Rome. Though it is a third-century document, its author speaks of seeking to preserve the practices of the "apostolic tradition" of the previous century, and thus gives us a guide to a number of such practices, including baptism, about which he provides specific instructions. Baptism was to follow a long period of instruction, scrutiny by the community, exorcism, and then water baptism, which in turn was to be followed by the anointing with oil. The bishop would lay hands on those who had been baptized and pray: "Lord God, you who made these worthy of the removal of sins through the bath of regeneration, make them worthy to be filled with your Holy Spirit, grant them your grace, that they might serve you according to your will."[16]

Essentially, this perspective assumed that the anointing of oil, representing the gift of the Spirit, essentially confirmed what had been represented in baptism. And in time, over centuries, these two could and would be separated, so much so that by the late Middle Ages confirmation became a separate rite, theoretically linked to baptism but often separated by years. This practice was reinforced by the rise of infant baptism as the primary means of Christian initiation, and the increasing logistical difficulty for bishops to be present at each baptism—on the assumption that only the bishop could confirm.

But not so in the East, by which I mean the ancient Christian east of Antioch, Syria, and Turkey, often spoken of as the Syrian tradition. Postbaptismal anointing was practiced, but it was also assumed that the Holy Spirit was given through both water and the oil.[17] This insistence on linking the two is clearly a reflection of another Eastern orientation: that the primary source

---

15. Thomas M. Finn, *Early Christian Baptism and the Catechumenate: Italy, North Africa, and Egypt*, Message of the Fathers of the Church 6 (Collegeville, MN: Liturgical Press, 1992), 185–86.

16. Kevin P. Edgecomb, trans., *The Apostolic Tradition of Hippolytus of Rome* 21.21, http://www.bombaxo.com/hippolytus.html.

17. Thomas M. Finn, *Early Christian Baptism and the Catechumenate: West and East Syria*, Message of the Fathers of the Church 5 (Collegeville, MN: Liturgical Press, 1992), 22.

of the baptismal rite is the baptism of Jesus, which included the reception or anointing of the Spirit.

The question I will raise later in this book is the following: should the contemporary Christian community recover a rite for the incorporation of new Christians into the church, a rite that would need to include baptism, and should this rite include the anointing of the newly baptized, representing the gift of the Spirit? Could it be that this pre-Christendom understanding of the ritual articulation of conversion would have particular relevance for the church in a post-Christian world?

2. The Rule of Saint Benedict and the Monastic Vision of Conversion

There is one factor that more than any other was a catalyst for the understanding of conversion in the Middle Ages, a factor that shaped not only this period but is still pertinent in many contexts today: the conversion of Constantine and the fact that Christianity became legal in AD 313 and then the official religion of the empire in 389.

The outcome of this was that it became possible to become a Christian in name only. Everyone was Christian. Citizenship and one's faith identity became one and the same. To be baptized a Christian meant that one was a citizen of the empire; one's baptismal papers were the documentation of one's national identity. The effect was huge and its impact lasting, right up until the twentieth century. The three-year process of initiation that was expected in the early church in time became a ten-day event before Easter. Eventually it was not required at all. *Christendom* had arrived. And conversion was neither expected nor called for: you were born a Christian, you grew up a Christian, and you died a Christian.

Yet the call for conversion, though perhaps muted, was not lost. It only found a different expression, most notably in the monastic movement. In many respects the father of monasticism, the defining visionary, is Bernard of Clairvaux. Yet we cannot appreciate his vision except against the backdrop of earlier figures, most notably Anthony of Egypt and Benedict of Nursia.

Though monasticism is fundamentally a medieval phenomenon, there is a premonastic figure who over the centuries was an abiding symbol, a kind of icon, to the special character of the monastic movement: Saint Anthony. He was part of a generation of Christians—actually, many Christians through the third and fourth centuries—for whom the desert was the symbol of their spiritual aspirations. For them, there was a one-to-one connection between the desert and their commitment to discern and follow the will of God.

First, there is a sense in which the desert captured the spiritual ideals of Christians in the third and fourth centuries. The desert fathers uniquely embodied the spiritual aspirations of the church. Their willingness to forgo material comforts was linked to a commitment to discern and follow God's will. This desire led them to abandon the comforts of civilized city life. Instead, reacting against what they felt to be compromise with society in the church of their period, they chose to live in isolation and solitude and devoted themselves to prayer. Included in their understanding of the Christian life was the conviction that the body is evil, that physical desires are wrong, and that the desire for material or physical comfort is detrimental to the spiritual life. For them, a rejection of material comforts and self-denial, particularly of physical and sexual appetites, was synonymous with true spirituality.

There were extremes. Simon Stylites is famous for little other than his thirty-seven-year stay on top of a stone column. But Christians of all generations and traditions recognize in Anthony (ca. 251–356) a spiritual master of great significance. His biography, attributed to the great theologian Athanasius, describes a man of simplicity, inner strength, and peace, with deep love for Christ and others. Anthony of Egypt viewed his life as a direct response to the command of the Lord: in his late teenage years, at the celebration of the Eucharist, he heard the words: "If you want to be perfect, go, sell your possessions, and give to the poor, and you will have treasure in heaven." He took it literally and sold all, retreating initially to a disused fort and eventually to a secluded mountain near the Red Sea. His spirituality was that of a hermit, but he had countless visitors who came for counsel and spiritual direction. His successors eventually formed small colonies of monks, precursors to monasteries.

Critical to the uniqueness and genius of Anthony and the other desert fathers was their remarkable relationship with the desert itself. They recognized that the desert is an important biblical motif for encounter with God. The desert was significant in the life of Moses, the Israelites, the prophet Jeremiah, John the Baptist, and for Jesus himself. It was the sphere where spiritual sensitivity was most acute. It was a place of renewed commitment as the external comforts and nonessentials of life were cut away, as the emotional, physical, and spiritual crutches that sustain people were left behind, and consequently where God could be met in an unprecedented manner. The desert fathers saw their flight to the desert as an encounter with their own identity that would refine their dependence on and commitment to God. They viewed it as a time of intense temptation and willingly faced up to the reality of sin and the evil one. But more, the desert represented for them an opportunity for a renewed awareness of God and his will. The desert, they believed, tears away personal masks and emotional crutches and tests the authenticity of a Christian's faith.

The modern city-dwelling Christian would do well to recognize the value of the desert motif. The city breeds superficiality, and we need to retreat, possibly within the city itself, to a place of quiet, a place of few distractions. The noise of radios and traffic needs to be replaced by the stillness of God's presence. We are embodied souls, and there is consequently a direct correlation between our inner space and outer space. We need to find quiet. In the desert, Anthony found the ingredient he considered essential to true spirituality: solitude. The quest for holiness was dependent, he believed, on personal solitude. For the desert fathers, solitude did not mean that a person was alone. The Christian is never alone, for one is with God. When we are alone with God, we can be silent before him, hear his voice, and be most keenly aware of divine mercy. The noise of the city and of a busy human community creates a spiritual distance for the soul from its Maker. We need silence before God, solitude in his presence, to properly know God and discern his will. It is only as we learn solitude that we can confront the deep loneliness of our hearts and face up to the darkness and secret sins that lurk within us. There is no substitute for this baring of the soul before God.

Solitude then is a prerequisite for Christian community. Recent writers have appropriately stressed that the church is the body of Christ, and thus we should live in vibrant community. But this emphasis on community should never undermine the complementary call to being alone with God. The desert fathers remind us that solitude is an essential dimension of authentic spirituality. We need to return again and again to the "desert" and maintain a rhythm between silence and communication, between solitude and community.

As Rowan Williams stresses, this was essentially a protest movement. The rejection of the city was at heart a denial of its values, but more, a rejection of the nominal Christianity found in the city. Williams puts it this way: "The flight from the City, the deliberate isolation of oneself from the social order, from family and civic life and financial transaction, is a statement of the belief that Christian possibilities cannot be exhausted by life in the city."[18]

Thus, for Anthony, conversion was essentially an embrace of a life that confronted head-on the forces of temptation. He accepted that this engagement was part of the very character of the spiritual life and that temptation is faced through a baring of the soul, solitude, and silence—things realized more acutely against the backdrop of the desert. The only "crutch" would be God. But solitude should not be viewed as a denial of community. To the contrary, solitude enabled one to truly love the other, to genuinely live in community. And community, in turn, enabled one to grow in love and humility, two essential marks of Christian identity and maturity. In this regard, the Christian life was viewed as the "imitation of Christ," which is the title of the work that will be highlighted at the conclusion of this section on monasticism.

The monastic traditions of Eastern Christianity eventually had counterparts in the West, largely through the influence of John Cassian (360–435). Benedict of Nursia (480–547) is the source of the most influential document in the history of monasticism, the Rule of Benedict. It provides definition and focus to the monastic vision of the Christian life. Just as Anthony of Egypt was appalled by the degenerate life of the city, which was corrupting the spirituality of the church, Benedict fled urban life and set up small monastic communities, bands

18. Williams, *Wound of Knowledge*, 94.

of men who could strive for holiness in community. He drew up a guide—now known as "The Rule of St. Benedict"— designed to govern this common life around the principles of discipline and simplicity.

The monks who joined Benedict were simple laypeople, peasants. The Rule directed them to live as a family, with an abbot as father. Each monk was responsible not only for his own spiritual development but also for that of his companions. The Rule provided for learning to enhance their devotional reading; then also, it discouraged idleness by providing routine and discipline. Most of all, Benedict sought to provide a guide for monks to live in the presence of God and eventually know the life of heaven. At least three dominant concerns reflected in the Rule are relevant to the twenty-first-century Christian. First, the Rule affirmed a spirituality of community, on the conviction that spiritual growth toward maturity was to take place in community. This was not a denial of the value of solitude but a recognition that the hermit's life in itself was not an authentic spirituality.

Second, Benedict called for a rhythm and balance in the routines of daily life. The daily life of the monk was remarkably ordinary. Rather than seek the miraculous and the spectacular, the monk was to delight in the mundane. His routine included both the active and passive, from prayer, contemplation, meditation, and study of Scripture to such activities as work in the monastic gardens and fields, education, preaching, and works of charity. Our daily routines may have different components, but we have much to learn from the order and simplicity of the monk's daily life.[19]

Although there is no doubt that the central focus of the monastic communities was their own spiritual growth, in community, it would be wrong to characterize the entire movement as focused on self. Indeed, out of the movement emerged three commitments: apostolic service, scholarship, and care for the poor. When Gregory the Great desired to send missionaries to England, the group he looked to was the Benedictines; a group of them, including the one who eventually became Augustine of Canterbury (d. 604), set off to evangelize England and Ireland and eventually most of northern Europe.

When it comes to scholarship, we must recognize that all of the great European universities arose out of the monastic movement. The monastic movement was also characterized by a profound and active concern for the poor and underprivileged. The neglected of society throughout the Middle Ages found

19. Daily life in the monastery consisted of a routine and rhythmic balance of three elements: liturgical prayer, manual labor, and *lectio divina*. Liturgical prayer consisted of the daily office sung in choir. A major segment of the Benedictine Rule addresses how the daily office is to be sung. Manual labor consisted especially of farmwork—not as "apostolic work" per se, but as part of daily life. *Lectio divina* was quiet, prayerful reading of sacred Scripture. It was meditative reading that turned into prayer and contemplation. The order and routine were viewed not as an end in itself but as a means to enable each monk while in community to grow in love, humility, and obedience to Jesus Christ.

shelter, food, and medical care in the monasteries. This was particularly the case with the mendicant monastic orders, notably the Dominicans, founded by Dominic of Osma (1170–1221), and the Franciscans, founded by Francis of Assisi (1181/2–1226). They affirmed the principle that true spirituality cannot ignore the reality of poverty.

While Anthony and Benedict were key figures in establishing the monastic vision, the true "father" of monasticism is surely Bernard of Clairvaux (1090–1153). While hundreds of communities throughout Europe adopted the "rule" in various forms, from the sixth century onward, it is the Cistercian reform at the end of the eleventh century and into the twelfth that established the Rule as the guide to the common life of monks. Through the influence of Bernard, the monastery became a place of conversion in the midst of a compromised world. The emphasis in Bernard is the love of God: God's love for us, but then also, our love in response. The monastic community was designed intentionally to foster this end: perfect love for God and others. Conversion is essentially a decision to choose the way that leads to this end, perfect love. This is known and experienced in a community that seeks conversion daily, in the routines and rhythms of work, prayer, and study, though never at the expense of solitude, which remains a vital dimension of the Christian life.

Later monastic and mendicant orders were marked by the threefold vows of poverty, chastity, and obedience (the Jesuits added an additional commitment of obedience to the pope). The Rule itself, though, is first a call to community that devotes itself to prayer, the study of the Scriptures, and daily domestic work. In later monasticism, there were two kinds of monks: those who devoted themselves to the choir and the liturgical life of the monastery, and those who focused their attention on manual labor. The latter, who were laypersons, were called the *conversi*, those who were thought of as having converted from the world. But the original vision for the monastic life did not make such a sharp distinction or assume that some would be devoted entirely to liturgical prayer and others to manual labor.

Further, the fundamental mark of the monastic life was humility and obedience. What this suggests is that conversion is fundamentally interior, marked by a humility that recognizes the need for God (a rejection of self-reliance), an attentiveness to God (the spiritual discipline of *listening*), and then a life of deference to the will of God (expressed in obedience to the abbot). But all of this pointed to a particular end: that the monk mature in faith, hope, and love. Conversion was essentially an act by which a person chose the way of conversion. This perspective remains within contemporary Roman Catholic perspectives on conversion and Christian life. The Catholicism of our generation is much more inclined to use the language of conversion to speak of an extended process of change, such that the whole of the Christian life is an experience of conversion.

While I am seeking to make the case that there is a distinct primal Christian experience, an identifiable beginning to the Christian life, what the monastic heritage profiles and what must be maintained is that any conversion so understood is really nothing more than the beginning of a life of ongoing conversion. Indeed, the whole purpose of conversion, as I am using the language, is that we would enter into a manner of life that would enable us to grow in faith, hope, and love. For the monastic tradition, this would mean that a convert is one who joins a disciplined community that, through intentional practices, lives with a common objective marked by an ongoing conversion.

Rowan Williams provides a most cogent summary of this vision: "The Rule epitomizes the monastic rationale: here are persons attempting to create, by grace, the likeness of Christ, forming themselves and each other in a shared life."[20] Williams stresses that the relational character of monastic life profiled something crucial: this common life meant that Christianity was not a private experience and that the relational dimension was not merely what *occasioned* maturation, but was the actual *form* that it took. This monastic vision may seem ancient, and it is, but it has notable contemporary expressions, including that found in the most famous monk of the twentieth century, Thomas Merton, who lived out his monastic calling at the Abbey of Gethsemani, in Kentucky. Merton describes his journey to faith in his best-selling autobiography, *The Seven Storey Mountain*. While the whole of this work is essentially the account of his journey to faith, he speaks in this way of the particular realization of where he was on that journey:

> As November began, my mind was taken up with this one thought: of getting baptized and entering at last into the supernatural life of the Church. In spite of all my studying and all my reading and all my talking, I was still infinitely poor and wretched in appreciation of what was about to take place within me. I was about to set foot on the shore of the foot of the high, seven circled mountain of a Purgatory steeper and more arduous than I was able to imagine, and I was not at all aware of the climbing I was about to have to do. . . . The essential thing was to begin the climb. Baptism was that beginning, and a most generous one, on the part of God.[21]

Later in this very same chapter he speaks of how ordinary folks are not expected to be saints, to be holy, which is the specific calling of the monk. This vision of the Christian life dominated almost a whole millennium of the history of the church, informing the spiritual vision of Saints Dominic, Francis, and Thomas Aquinas. Aside from Bernard, the definitive text of monastic spirituality and thus of this vision of the converted life is likely the *Imitation of Christ*, attributed to Thomas à Kempis.

20. Williams, *Wound of Knowledge*, 105.
21. Thomas Merton, *The Seven Storey Mountain* (New York: Harcourt Brace, 1948), 221.

4

Chapters in the History of an Idea

Part 2

While evangelical Christians are increasingly coming to an appreciation of the full scope of their Christian heritage, it is also essential that they make some sense of their own heritage and spiritual roots. In other words, what we might advocate is that we be thoroughly evangelical without being sectarian: we recover our own heritage while appreciating the insights that come from those of other theological traditions. In so doing, we start with the sixteenth-century Reformers who, while not providing a theology of conversion per se, nevertheless established the theological sensibilities that have shaped the contours of the evangelical vision of the Christian life.

The Sixteenth-Century Protestant Reformers Martin Luther and John Calvin

In coming to the experience and thought of the magisterial Reformers, it is important to state from the outset that we look in vain to either Martin Luther or John Calvin to find a particular theology of conversion; they did not give focused attention to the genesis of Christian experience.[1] It thus is essential that contemporary Christians not try to superimpose on their narrative such things as Luther's so-called tower experience, producing an anachronistic perspective on a concept of conversion experience that really emerged with the rise of evangelicalism in the eighteenth century. Nevertheless, both the

---

1. Luther and Calvin are representative of only two streams of the Protestant Reformation. The Anabaptists and Menno Simons are another, and I will describe their contribution to this discussion at a later point.

experience and the thought of the Reformers are of vital interest in developing the idea of conversion in the church's history.

We can only appreciate the contribution of Luther (1483–1546) to the idea of conversion when we view his perspective against the backdrop of the great sweep of the monastic movement out of which he emerged. For over a millennium, the idea of conversion in the Western church could be thought of as the beginning of a particular way of life. In many cases, this was not just figurative but tangibly expressed in the act of becoming a monk. Conversion meant joining a monastic community: a renunciation of the world and a resolve to pursue the way of holiness, through a life of penance. Viewed in this way, what really counts is not so much the initial decision but the pursuit: the focus was on the Christian pilgrim seeking salvation.

This was the world in which Martin Luther was immersed. As a young man he became a novice of a chapter house of the Hermits of Saint Augustine, much like any novice would have done, seeking salvation. He pursued theological studies and was ordained a priest in 1507 and eventually, following extended studies, was given a teaching appointment at the University of Wittenberg.

Yet through all of this, he lived with a crushing tension. On the one hand, he struggled to find resolution for his own ongoing sense of guilt. He was deeply struck by the righteousness of God and that he could not appease or satisfy this righteousness. He felt (not just in the abstract, but deeply in his own tormented soul) the horrors of hell, the spiritual and moral hopelessness of humanity. He spoke of this as an experience of hell, that the righteousness of God was a black cloud threatening his life.

Conversely, as an Augustinian monk, Luther was immersed in Scriptures both in his personal study and in his academic work as a teacher. He was also reading Augustine of Hippo, John Tauler, and other medieval mystics. But the primary influence in his thinking and development was the Scriptures. Amid this inner tension between the holiness of God and his own guilt, while he was lecturing on Psalms and Romans, he gradually came to the realization—in what has often been called the "tower experience"—that the cross was the demonstration of God's love that delivers humanity from the feared "threat," guilt, and horrors of hell. Indeed, Lutheran theology would then always be a theology of the cross. From this vantage point, the cross would also be the perpetual reminder of the inability of humanity and of the glory of God revealed in the cross.

There is some debate as to whether this experience was itself a conversion; as noted earlier, we must not backdate a later evangelical idea of conversion and superimpose it on what happened to Luther. Yet there is no doubt that this period in his life was significant in his coming to a mature faith in Christ; at least it was one of a series of events in which he came to three critical understandings: (1) the righteousness of God is central to God's salvation, (2) God grants faith to the believer, and (3) in justification there are no works, only faith. In Luther's view, humanity is impotent, and human actions are useless in the face of sin. The work of salvation for Luther is unilateral, by God alone: humanity is passive in the face of the cross and the grace of God. God grants faith, and believers receive this grace with thanksgiving.

The Lutheran vision is thus a reaction to the monastic idea of conversion and its emphasis on the deliberate, intentional actions by which one is formed in faith, hope, and love. For Luther, the Christian does not *become* righteous but rather accepts the imputed righteousness of Christ, imputed on the basis of our faith (which is also a gift from God). There is nothing to be done per se; there is no work by which a person appropriates salvation. Faith grows, certainly, but growth in faith is but a deeper awareness that it is all of God and that the Christian is free in Christ.

Luther's experience profiles some fundamental themes that emerge in the three major streams of the Protestant Reformation: Lutheran, Reformed, and Anabaptist. While there were significant differences among the three distinct theological and spiritual traditions, the points of convergence are a distinctive benchmark in the history of the idea of conversion. This convergence is noteworthy at two major points and with a significant secondary theme. More could certainly be said or offered at this point, but these two major points and one secondary point cannot be left unsaid.

First, what marked all the Reformers was their emphasis on justification by faith. For Luther, Calvin, and others, justification was an act of God by which the repentant believer experienced forgiveness for sin and freedom from guilt. One appropriated this forgiveness (or justification, for they are virtual synonyms for Calvin and Luther) by faith, by which they meant a radical dependence on the grace of God. This experience of justification was not, for the Reformers, focused on one defining event: a punctiliar conversion experience. The link between a momentary conversion and justification arose in later Puritan and evangelical thought. For the Reformers, instead, justification was more a process, as one increasingly learned what it means to live by faith in the justifying grace of God. Neither Calvin nor Luther attached much significance to the beginning of the Christian life.[2]

Many of the themes in Luther are also found in Calvin. But worth emphasizing in Calvin's perspective on justification is the critical place of repentance in this understanding of the Christian life and conversion in particular. In Calvin, repentance is indeed almost synonymous with conversion, as we see in one of the headings of the *Institutes*: "Our Regeneration by Faith: A Discourse on Repentance" (bk. 3, chap. 3). Repentance is the heart of the matter. For Calvin, repentance is a turning from dependence on the "flesh," turning from self-dependence to a true dependence on God. This is faith, specifi-

---

2. See Pete Wilcox, "Conversion in the Thought and Experience of John Calvin," *Anvil* 14, no. 2 (1997): 113–28.

cally, "justifying" faith. Thus justification is the fruit of repentance. Taken together, the Reformers would affirm that conversion begins in the depths of one's heart with the realization that apart from God's justifying grace, there is no hope. In turning to the cross, one in faith finds unmerited grace in the crucified Christ.

Second, the Reformers' emphasis on justification by faith was complemented by their affirmation of the Scriptures as a means of grace, indeed as *the* means of grace. For the Reformers, especially Calvin, regeneration is by Word and Spirit. Thus the experience of conversion is intimately linked with the Word; the Word actually brings about a conversion. In Calvin, the reign of Christ is established, and hearts are aligned with the kingdom by and in response to the preaching of the Word. Thus repentance is an inner change that is effected by the Word and the Spirit (in tandem, most notably in tandem through preaching). It begins in the interior self, in the heart and the mind, and then finds expression in outward works (which, especially for Calvin, are a necessary complement to inner faith and repentance). What made this possible, then, was something central to Calvin's own experience: a *receptiveness* to Word and Spirit. In his commentary on Acts, Calvin speaks of his own experience and indicates that we know the salvation of God when our heart "is marked by a docility to teachableness."

These two major themes are complemented by a significant secondary theme, also vital to their understanding of conversion. The Reformers rejected the vision that regarded the Christian vocation as essentially monastic (or "religious"). If the monastic vision of conversion was one of leaving the world to pursue the salvation of God within a monastic community, the vision of the Reformers insisted that the Christian vocation and call to holiness could and indeed must be pursued in the world and that the calling to religious work or service was one of equipping all Christians, through the ministry of the Word, to live out their Christian identity in every sphere and sector of society.

The monastic vision emphasized that conversion is a beginning of a journey in pursuit of God's salvation; to the contrary, heirs of the Reformation insist that through the justification of God, the Christian can rest in the knowledge of God's work of salvation. One does not pursue justification but rather accepts the justification offered by God. One is not so much active as passive in the experience of salvation. Further, the critical element in this experience is the Word, received in faith, and the fruit of this experience is one by which the Christian is equipped to fulfill one's vocation in the world.

Many contemporary Christians, including heirs to the Protestant Reformation, are wondering if they need to choose between these two visions. Can we not eagerly appropriate the monastic vision for spiritual growth and vitality, in community, but then also insist that this corporate, disciplined life flows from and is grounded in a dynamic vision of God's prior love and justifying grace? The voice that perhaps most brilliantly captures this dynamic is that of Dietrich Bonhoeffer, who in his exquisite spiritual guide, *Life Together*,[3] effectively anchors the life of the Christian in the grace of God while insisting that this is not a "cheap grace" but rather a grace that sustains and empowers the disciplined life. He does so by drawing on many of the guiding principles of the monastic movement.

Chapters in the History of an Idea—Continued

Now that I have considered the impact of the Reformers on the idea of conversion, we can look at those especially Protestant and evangelical, Holiness and Pentecostal influences of more recent centuries. With Augustine and the early church as the first chapter and monasticism as the second, we come now to a third chapter.

3. The Puritans, the Pietists, and the Eighteenth-Century Rise of Evangelicalism

While the roots of evangelicalism certainly precede the eighteenth century, it was through such voices as Jonathan Edwards and John Wesley that the movement came to maturity. And in particular, it was these voices, along with others, that interpreted the evangelical experience in the light of the inherited theological heritage from the Reformation.

JONATHAN EDWARDS AND THE PURITAN VISION OF CONVERSION

Many factors shaped the emergence of evangelicalism in the late eighteenth century, including Continental (European) pietism. Most noteworthy is the Puritan movement, which had theological anchors and roots in the Reformation. Two factors shaped the emergence of the Puritans: one was a theological conviction, the other their experience of conversion.

The theological conviction reflected the influence of Luther, Calvin, and the other Continental Reformers. Puritanism arose within and in reaction to the Church of England, following the break between the English church and Rome. Those who had been influenced by the Reformation on the Continent did not believe that the church of England had become truly Reformed. Many sought to bring a fully Calvinist reformation to the Church of England, seeking government support for their efforts. Others, Separatists, no longer regarded the Church of England as the true church and with their followers

---

3. Two editions could be mentioned: Dietrich Bonhoeffer, *Life Together*, trans. John W. Doberstein (San Francisco: Harper & Row, 1954); and idem, *Life Together*, trans. Daniel Bloesch and James H. Burtness (Minneapolis: Fortress, 1996).

formed independent congregations—in many respects, the forerunners of today's Baptists.

The other defining feature of the Puritans was their common insistence on a conscious experience of conversion. Mark A. Noll observes that the experience of early evangelicals was paradigmatic: their experience established a model of expectation for what conversion would look like and feel like.[4] Puritan preachers effectively demonstrated the possibilities of grace—the potential for radical transformation through conversion. They repeatedly emphasized that conversion was supernatural in origin; they affirmed the priority of God's grace. But they also insisted on the potential for transformation: conversion could and would lead to a holy life.

By the late eighteenth century, two figures—representing later Puritanism—embodied this Puritan vision in complementary ways: Jonathan Edwards in America and John Wesley in England. They took the best from this Puritan heritage and formulated an understanding of conversion that reflected both their theological convictions and experience, drawing on their experience and that of others.

The particular genius of Jonathan Edwards (1703–58) was, at one and the same time, to provide critical theological reflection complemented by astute observation of the religious experience of his contemporaries. He was a student of both theology and experience, and so was highly influential in defining the standard, the basic expectations of a Christian conversion. Noll writes of Edwards's study of the 1737 revival in Northampton, the "Faithful Narrative," that "it was the exemplary exposition of revival, the paradigmatic evangelical event."[5] It thereby established what Noll calls a "model spiritual life for all converts."[6] It described conversions and provided theological commentary and reflection on the experience.

From this and other sources, we observe the following regarding Edwards's perspective on conversion. First, Edwards, with the whole Puritan heritage, insisted on both the necessity and possibility of conversion. This was and is the only way that spiritual transformation would occur. Transformation is God's work; it is not the fruit of human endeavor or self-fulfillment. Edwards writes:

> The doctrine of conversion, or the new birth, is one of the great and fundamental doctrines of the Christian religion . . . because [conversion] is by Christ's express declaration absolutely necessary to their salvation.[7]

4. Mark A. Noll, *The Rise of Evangelicalism: The Age of Edwards, Whitefield and the Wesleys* (Downers Grove, IL: InterVarsity, 2003), 74.
5. Ibid., 91.
6. Ibid., 90.
7. Jonathan Edwards, "The Reality of Conversion (1740)," in *The Sermons of Jonathan Edwards: A Reader*, ed. Wilson H. Kimnach, Kenneth P. Minkema, and Douglas A. Sweeney (New Haven: Yale University Press, 1999), 83.

Thus the voice of reason, Scripture and experience, and the testimony of the best of men do all concur in it, that there must be such a thing as conversion.[8]

The Puritan conviction about the necessity of conversion was a cognate to their doctrine of sin. Conversion is the only possible response to the depth of the human predicament, and this was complemented by the conviction they held regarding the possibilities of divine grace. Since this is the only possible way in which a person can experience transformation, it is essential. For them, a personal radical conversion is a benchmark of authentic religious experience. It is the indispensable first experience of all genuine Christians.

Second, this conscious awareness of conversion was for them the basis for assurance. A Christian is a person who has been converted. This is what it means to be a Christian: one has had a conscious and specific conversion experience. Without such an experience, one cannot be certain that one knows the salvation of God. The Puritans were deeply concerned about *assurance*; indeed, some argue that their emphasis on conversion itself was but part of a broader concern to delineate the character of assurance of salvation.[9] In their view, a true child of God can know without any doubt that the self is saved. In this they are heirs to Luther and Calvin. A person has this assurance because one has had an authentic and conscious conversion experience. One is admitted into church fellowship on the basis of a conversion narrative; indeed, it is the capacity to witness to a conversion experience that gives that experience credibility and authenticity.

Third, the Puritans generally assumed that conversion would be a protracted experience, a process or series of events. Though Puritan preachers generally agreed that conversion is an extended process, they exhibit much variety in characterizing these events and identifying the stages or moments of a Christian conversion. Richard Lovelace summarizes different perspectives: William Perkins insisted on eight stages, four before regeneration and four afterward. William Ames argued for four, which was typical: hearing the law, conviction, despair, and evangelical humiliation.[10] Others, such as Cotton Mather, were inclined to downplay a standardized conversion scheme, recognized that it would be an extended process, and merely insisted that there was more than one way in which the Spirit might bring someone to Christ.[11] Despite this diversity, all agreed that conversion was not an immediate experience and would take time, potentially a long time. Further, it was often marked by a season of prolonged introspection as one waited for the gift of grace that would come from God.

8. Ibid., 89.
9. See, e.g., Richard F. Lovelace, *The American Pietism of Cotton Mather: Origins of American Evangelicalism* (Grand Rapids: Eerdmans, 1979), 94–95.
10. Ibid., 76.
11. Ibid., 78–79.

Fourth is something basic to the Puritan vision of conversion: the experience of conversion comes in response to the initiative of God. For the Puritans, the primary means by which God initiates is through the preaching of the gospel. For example, John Wesley, to whom we will come, was convinced that conversion is the fruit of preaching the Scriptures, particularly the doctrine of "justification by faith."[12]

Fifth, though God was the initiator, it was still possible and indeed essential to *pursue* conversion—in the words of Edwards, "earnestly to seek conversion."[13] And so, Edwards in a sermon declares to the potential convert: "Don't put off waiting for the Spirit of God to awaken you and stir you up to seek salvation. . . . The way for you to have the needed influences of the Spirit of God is for you to be [in] the use of all appointed means, and to watch at wisdom's gates, and wait at the posts of her doors (Prov. 8:34)."[14] Conversion is definitely a human activity; yet there is no sense of admitting self-salvation. Hence, conversion is both a response to God and an act of utter dependence on the mercy and grace of God. Edwards writes, "Take heed that you don't trust either in anything that you have done or can do for, when you have done all, you have done nothing, nothing that can make any atonement for the least of your sins or that [is] worthy to be offered as a price for the least of God's favors."[15] Edwards is keen to outline what a person must do in order to experience the grace of a Christian conversion, but this does not mean that he views these activities or events as actually enabling the conversion: they are but a way that one appropriates the grace of God, which then remains grace, freely given. And so he concludes: "If you follow these directions, in all probability you will be converted."[16]

What can the potential convert do to foster or encourage the process? Edwards counsels: "Reading and praying and attending ordinances are not a means of conversion by any virtue or power in those duties, but because they are the appointed way in which God will be sought and waited upon and will bestow his grace and blessing."[17] Thus, while conversion is an act of response to the initiative of God and not something that can be forced or manipulated, the potential convert is not entirely passive. Indeed, the Puritans' preaching apparently assumes that this eagerness to receive is a precondition for receiving the grace of God.

Sixth, it is clear that for the Puritans conversion is costly, not easy. Edwards observes that many wish the way of the kingdom to be easy: "They love ease. It is very cross to them to comply with hard and constant labor in the busi-

---

12. Noll, *Rise of Evangelicalism*, 139–40.
13. Edwards, "Reality of Conversion," 90.
14. Ibid., 91.
15. Ibid., 103.
16. Ibid., 92.
17. Ibid.

ness of religion."[18] The costly character of conversion is first and foremost a matter of addressing the presence of sin in the penitent's life. Conversion includes a reformation of life, an act of radically turning from one way of life toward the way of holiness, so much so that for the Puritans, conversion is fundamentally a penitential pilgrimage.

Seventh, the Puritans, and especially Edwards, recognized the possibility of counterfeit spiritual experience. He insists, "Scripture teaches us that men are often deceived concerning themselves and others." Edwards uses this language of "counterfeit"[19] conversion and adds this fascinating observation: "When any person sets about this business [of conversion], the devil is wont to be exceeding busy with him."[20]

Eighth, conversion leads to transformation. Some Puritans so exaggerate the importance of conversion that everything after that is anticlimactic, so much so that, as Richard Lovelace puts it, the rest of the Christian life is a "quiet epilogue."[21] But the dominant theme for the Puritans is the importance of a lifelong pilgrimage, a penitential journey, toward sanctification. The costliness of conversion is linked backward to the depth of the human predicament, needing radical spiritual surgery, yet also linked forward, to the "narrow way" in the pursuit of righteousness.

JOHN WESLEY AND THE RISE OF METHODISM

It is this commitment to holiness or transformation that is so compelling in the spiritual writings and preaching of John Wesley (1703–91). Wesley's Puritan roots—his parents were Puritan dissenters, and the family's devotional reading included Puritan divines such as Richard Baxter and John Bunyan—nurtured within him a deep commitment to holiness, so much so that during his Oxford years as a university student he took an active role in giving leadership to the so-called Holy Club. This was reinforced by his readings during that time, including such works as Jeremy Taylor's *The Rules and Exercises of Holy Living and Holy Dying*, and later, William Law's *A Serious Call to a Holy and Devout Life*.

This passion for sanctity would be central to Wesley's understanding of conversion. Indeed, for Wesley this was the very purpose of conversion: one's "perfection." Wesley's early adult conversion reflected this deep commitment, and no doubt something was missing: his awareness of God's grace and the response of faith. Yet when Wesley discovered the deep wellspring of divine grace, it did not invalidate this vision for Christian sanctity. To the contrary: in discovering the deep assurance of forgiveness, he also entered into the only possible foundation for authentic spiritual maturity.

18. Ibid., 94.
19. Ibid., 91.
20. Ibid., 100.
21. Lovelace, *American Pietism of Cotton Mather*, 74.

Although Wesley was deeply influenced by the best of early Puritan theology and spirituality, he also drew heavily on high Anglican theology and piety as well as the spirituality of the continental Moravians. It was perhaps this broader influence that allowed him to build on the best of his Puritan heritage but also incorporate elements from other streams of Christian spirituality. The net result was an understanding of conversion that affirmed human responsibility as a response to divine initiative. Thus he consistently challenged the theology of predestination held by his contemporary, George Whitefield.

Further, for Wesley the commitment to holiness or sanctification was matched by a deep awareness of the integration of intellect and affections in authentic religious experience. Conversion, if it was a true encounter with the living God, would lead to sanctity, to moral reform. But Wesley also insisted that there would be a transformation or reordering of the affections, and the critical sign of this transformation for him was joy.

The spiritual theology of John Wesley is deeply marked by the conviction that conversion is an experience of joining a community, most notably a community committed to intentional formation and spiritual growth, with a vision for a common experience of spiritual perfection.

Sidebar: Anabaptist Perspectives on Conversion

1. The Experience of Menno Simons (1496–1561)

Menno Simons is not the founder of the Mennonites, as, say, Luther was to Lutheranism or Calvin to Calvinism; neither was he the most influential theologian of the movement. However, he was a key player in helping the struggling movement sustain an identity.

Menno was born in Witmarsum, Friesland, and spent his early adult years in a monastery. He was ordained a priest in 1524 at twenty-eight years of age. While serving as a parish priest, he was increasingly uncomfortable with some aspects of his Roman Catholic practice, especially the understanding of the Lord's Supper (partaking of the literal flesh and blood of the Lord). In his discomfort he went to the Scriptures; he speaks of reading the Bible every day. He also read Erasmus and Martin Luther and Thomas à Kempis (of the Brethren of the Common Life). He might have become a Lutheran; he recognized the priority of faith. But he was increasingly convinced that baptism was to be experienced on the basis of one's *personal* faith. Menno was initially attracted to the Münsterite movement, a protest that affirmed many of the things he was coming to believe. But the movement became increasingly more violent, and he began to actively oppose its teachings and practices.

Then in 1536, after more than ten years of inner wrestling, Menno left the priesthood and went into hiding for most of a year. He speaks of this year as a time of "quiet

72

training" in the Scriptures, a period of solitude, study, and writing.[22] Then, in 1537, he was called to ministry and leadership among a group of Anabaptists. He was rebaptized and reordained. Later he married and had two daughters.

Menno's writings continually stress repentance. Though he gives prominence to the role of the Scriptures and faith, conversion is essentially a matter of true repentance, beginning with contrition: a deep awareness of one's own imperfections and weakness, matched by a thorough submission to the teaching of Christ. It is marked by a hatred for sin and a love for holiness.

For Menno, this resolve had a distinctly costly character to it. His decision to leave the Roman Church and accept the call to provide pastoral leadership for early Anabaptist communities meant a life marked by suffering. When one became a Christian, one accepted the way of the cross; for the early Anabaptists, it inevitably meant significant suffering.

2. Early Anabaptist Perspectives on the New Birth

Early Anabaptist authors, especially Menno Simons, tended to speak of conversion as the accumulation of many spiritually significant experiences, or, as one commentator has put it, experiences on different levels (emotional, moral, volitional, and intellectual). But the heart of the matter was a commitment to renounce the (sinful) past and devote oneself to Christ's agenda. Anabaptists were not inclined to use the language of justification as much as did the Lutherans and the Calvinists yet nevertheless stressed that salvation is a gift. The central features of their understanding of conversion included the following:

Each person can become a disciple and appropriate a new life in Christ in an act of personal conversion made possible through the grace of the Spirit. This is a gradual process: one hears the Word preached. This in turn leads to repentance, which is followed by the regenerating work of the Spirit. The consequence is that by faith one is now "in Christ" (52–54).

This new faith necessarily has expression in good works; indeed, they insisted on obedience as the fruit of faith and offered criticism of other Reformation groups who did not emphasize the need for behavioral change (53).

Baptism follows repentance. The means of rebirth is the Scriptures, the Word of God, and then baptism ensues from this experience of new birth (54–55).

3. Nineteenth-Century Anabaptist Perspectives on Conversion

Nineteenth-century Anabaptists emphasized that conversion is personal and experiential. John Toews speaks of several key aspects in their understanding of how the Christian life begins.[23]

22. Cornelius J. Dyck, trans. and ed., "The Conversion of Menno Simons," in *Spiritual Life in Anabaptism* (Scottdale, PA: Herald, 1995), 49; following in-text references are to this work.
23. John B. Toews, "Patterns of Piety among the Early Brethren (1860–1900)," *Journal of Mennonite Studies* 12 (1994): 137–55; following in-text references are to this work.

as a protest against a Christianity that seemingly tolerated a lack of radical transformation in the life of the Christian. The leaders of these movements were convinced that, however appropriate it might have been to speak of conversion as belief and repentance, this was clearly not the whole of the Christian life and not the foundation or springboard for the life of the Christian and the witness of the Christian in the world. It was, at best, preliminary.

Holiness preachers of the nineteenth century were struck by a contrast: "dead orthodoxy," which characterized the churches of which they were a part, and the dynamic experience of the Spirit, as described in the book of Acts. Almost as a single voice, they were convinced that the genius of this dynamic was the experience of Pentecost: though the disciples were clearly authentic followers of Jesus before Pentecost, they were not ready to live out the full demands of the Christian life or to be witnesses for Christ in the world. For those of us raised in this tradition, Peter was consistently profiled as a case in point: a follower of Jesus, certainly, but at the trial of Christ lacking the courage of conviction that he later had on the day of Pentecost. Thus, as the preachers of this tradition were wont to emphasize again and again, the disciples were told to wait—or rather, since they would be using the King James Bible, they were to "tarry"—until, as it turned out, they experienced the powerful baptism of the Spirit on the day of Pentecost.

Yet they went further and noted the small aside that perhaps was not incidental: Peter stresses in Acts 2:39 that "the promise is for you, for your children, and . . . everyone whom the Lord our God calls to him." It was this promise that became their mantra: they were convinced that every Christian could experience this transformation. Each could have his or her own "Pentecost," their own baptism of the Spirit. The key to transformation and dynamic witness in the world would be this "second blessing." Just as the original disciples needed their Pentecost, so the church and indeed all Christians can receive this promised gift.

Those within the Wesleyan and Methodist movements insisted that this second experience, as a complement to "conversion," was specifically the enabling of God to bring the perfection or sanctification of which they were preaching. Some even went so far as to speak of this experience of the Spirit as one in which the power of sin, which is the "flesh," is broken, thus making Christian perfection possible. John Wesley himself did not teach this and indeed argued to the contrary; rather, this perspective came from a colleague, John Fletcher (1729–85), who taught that "adult perfect Christianity . . . is consequent upon the baptism of the Holy Ghost, administered by Christ himself."[25]

The most prominent contemporary expression of this doctrine is found in the Wesleyan, Free Methodist, and Nazarene Churches; for example, the Naza-

---

25. Quoted from the works of John Fletcher by Roland Wessels, "The Spirit Baptism, Nineteenth Century Roots," *Pneuma* 14, no. 2 (1992): 131.

rene Church's current doctrinal statement, article X, paragraph 13, indicates that "entire sanctification is that act of God, subsequent to regeneration, by which believers are made free from original sin . . . and brought into a state of . . . the holy obedience of love made perfect." Further, it states that this is "wrought by the baptism with the Holy Spirit" and specifies that this happens instantaneously.[26] This is the classic perspective of the Holiness movement built on the specifically Wesleyan foundation, or perhaps better, the Wesleyanism of John Fletcher.

In contrast, those of a more Presbyterian background—most notably D. L. Moody (1837–99), and R. A. Torrey (1856–1928)—were not convinced that one could speak of perfection in this life. Charles Finney (1792–1875) preceded them on this score, being convinced that baptism of the Spirit is not so much for sanctification as it is a matter of empowerment for service. Moody did not deny that at one's initial experience of "conversion" one has the Spirit; he admitted that the Spirit dwells within the new Christian "in some sense and to some extent," but he also insisted that the Spirit does not dwell in the Christian "in power."[27] However ambiguous this might seem, it did galvanize a generation of Christians to seek a second experience wherein they would know the grace of God's enabling for service in the world.

This set the stage for the influential R. A. Torrey, who concurred with Moody and Finney that the baptism of the Spirit is about empowerment for service; and yet, he went further and spoke of the manifestation of diverse gifts. He raised the matter of evidence: how do we know that we have experienced the baptism of the Spirit? And in response, he pointed to glossolalia, speaking in tongues, as perhaps the evidence of something that could not be explained as anything other than the presence of the Spirit in the believer's life. Though he did not actually indicate that this would be the defining evidence, the Pentecostal movement arose in the early twentieth century with precisely this conviction, claiming that "tongues" is indeed evidence that one has been filled with the Spirit. But still, the orientation for the Pentecostal movement was not so much sanctity or perfection as empowerment for witness and service.

Hence, on the one hand, we have those within the Wesleyan heritage who affirmed that the Spirit baptism is oriented toward sanctification; on the other hand, we have those within the Finney-Moody-Torrey-Pentecostal stream for whom the "second blessing" was fundamentally about empowerment for service.

There is also a distinct and third stream of the Holiness movement, which emphasizes what was typically called the "higher Christian life" or, actually in some cases, the "deeper Christian life," including such proponents as Wil-

26. See http://www.nazarene.org/ministries/administration/visitorcenter/articles/display.aspx.
27. Quoted by Wessels, "Spirit Baptism," 149.

liam Boardman (1810–86) and A. B. Simpson (1843–1919). Typically the focus here was more christological—without missing the enabling for sanctification and empowerment, but seeing these as derivative of another grace, the experience of Christ himself. Roland Wessels captures it well: "They taught that one entered the higher Christian life not through an experience eradicating original sin, not through a change of nature, but through becoming aware of Christ within as the Sanctifier, an illumination experience, coupled with an act of commitment, yielding oneself to Christ's control."[28] Yet it was still an experience of the Spirit: it was the grace of the Spirit that was encountered in a definite moment or "crisis" subsequent to conversion.[29]

For those outside of these movements, the typical response to the Wesleyan, Nazarene, Alliance, Pentecostal perspective is that the whole idea of a two-step or two-stage entrance into the transformed and transforming Christian life has little if any exegetical justification. They are inclined to observe that this argument is based on experience rather than on the clear witness of the Scriptures, and that when those within these traditions have sought to justify the "second blessing," they have had to force the Scriptures to say things that are not clearly there. Indeed, many within these movements have come to a similar conclusion: they cannot sustain their conviction regarding the two steps on the basis of their exegesis.

However, there is something from this chapter in the history of conversion and religious experience that should not be lost, two things in particular. First, we must sustain a deep appreciation of the vital call to holiness as the goal and indeed as the expectation of authentic Christian living—as long as this holiness is defined and described as life that is rooted in Christ. Second, this heritage also affirms the deep pastoral value that comes with a marker, a benchmark, wherein the ministry of the Spirit is represented through symbolic action—perhaps, for example, the laying on of hands and the request for the filling of the Spirit. Something of the intent of the book of Acts has thus been sustained by the teaching of this theological tradition. For a huge segment of the Christian community worldwide, without a sensible confirmation of the presence of the Spirit in their lives, believers will consistently doubt that they have indeed received this gift. If the purpose of Christ is explicitly that the Christian would receive the gift of the Spirit, they argue that surely this has to

---

28. Ibid., 133.

29. A. B. Simpson was the founder of the Christian and Missionary Alliance, whose doctrinal statement retains this feature: the crisis. Article 7 reads: "It is the will of God that each believer should be filled with the Holy Spirit and be sanctified wholly [citing 1 Thess. 5:23], being separated from sin and the world and fully dedicated to the will of God, thereby receiving power for holy living and effective service [Acts 1:8]. This is both a crisis and a progressive experience wrought in the life of the believer subsequent to conversion [Rom. 6:1–14]." I am quoting from the doctrinal statement of the C&MA in the United States, http://www.cmalliance.org/about/beliefs/doctrine#cite22; the C&MA in Canada no longer has this reference to a "crisis subsequent to conversion."

be represented and experienced through the grace of a Christian conversion. I will probe the implications of this more fully when I speak of the relationship between baptism and the gift of the Spirit in chapter 8.

5. The Twentieth and Twenty-first Centuries: Global Expansion and the Encounter with Islam

At least four things mark the perspective on conversion that emerges from the twentieth century.

First—at least for evangelicals, but the impact has been felt widely—the revivalism that arose in the nineteenth century was institutionalized, notably through the powerful influence of parachurch and mission organizations. By institutionalized, I mean that the language of revivalism became so ensconced in the vocabulary of the typical evangelical that it was unconsciously assumed to be "biblical" language.

Second, the twentieth century is without doubt the Pentecostal-charismatic century in the history of the church, with the growing global presence and influence of those who identify themselves as affiliated with this stream of the Christian tradition. In many countries, especially in Latin American and Africa, Pentecostalism is the mainline church and the dominant Christian presence. Since the mid-twentieth century, the influence of Pentecostalism has been felt in every sector of the globe and within virtually every Christian tradition; now one can speak of charismatic Roman Catholics and charismatic Anglicans. In 2006 the Pew Forum on Religion and Public Life conducted a survey and concluded that fully one-quarter of the estimated two billion Christians in the world identified themselves as Pentecostal or charismatic and that this is the fastest growing sector of world Christianity.

Third, one of the defining events of the twentieth century, especially for Roman Catholic Christians, but with significance for Christians of all traditions, was the Second Vatican Council, 1962–65, and the groundbreaking and revolutionary actions of the Roman Catholic bishops. Pope John XXIII called the college of bishops together to discuss the church's understanding of the gospel, the nature of the church, and the relationship of the Roman Church to other Christians as well as to Jews and people of other religious traditions.

A significant outcome of Vatican II, one that was not fully felt or appreciated for a generation, was the call for a revised rite for the incorporation of adults into the Christian faith. The Rite for the Christian Initiation of Adults will be discussed more fully in chapter 10.

Fourth, the twentieth century is also the century of the expansion of the church, not just global expansion, but also a dramatic shift in the defining center of Christianity, which is no longer the West, but rather the South and the East, with the huge and influential presence of the church in Africa, Latin

America, and increasingly, Asia. Hence, the definition of what it means to be Christian and what it means to *become* a Christian will undoubtedly be deeply shaped by the reality of post-Christendom in the West and the emergence of dynamic Christian movements outside of the West. The understanding of Christian conversion will be shaped by the experience of those who come to faith from a background in one of the other major religions of the world. As an example, it is surely fruitful to consider the experience of those who are coming to Christian faith from a Muslim background.

Muslim conversions to Christ are worth considering in part because of the growing international presence of Islam in the world; it is the fastest-growing religion of the early twenty-first century and will increasingly be a global and influential presence much as Christianity has been in the twentieth century. But also, there is a growing body of literature on the character of Muslim conversions to Christian faith, both conversion narratives and critical theological reflection on the experience of those who tell about their becoming Christian.

One Muslim conversion narrative has perhaps been circulated more widely than any other: the story of the journey to faith in Christ by the Pakistani woman Bilquis Sheikh, as recounted in her book *I Dared to Call Him Father*.[30] Sheikh, in her midforties, was living in the small village of Wah, Northwest Pakistan, after being immersed in the cultured circles of the diplomatic and governmental elite of her country. Following the untimely death of her parents and then abandonment by her husband, she had returned to the village of her youth and with her only grandson stayed in relative isolation on her large estate, waited on by numerous servants.

She loved her garden and found much solace there. But she was also troubled by the seeming presence of haunting spirits, and she longed for some measure of emotional and spiritual settledness. Since she had been raised a Muslim, her natural inclination might have been to read the Qur'an and seek out the local mullah. But she found this to be unsatisfying.

Ms. Sheikh was aware of the Christian alternative, perhaps because of her international travels but also because she had Christians on her staff: one of her closer servant girls and her driver. She was also aware of the persecution of Christians, especially of Christians who had been killed for converting. Nevertheless, a yearning developed within her to know more about the Christian faith, and finally she persuaded her driver to get her a copy of the Bible. She began to read, at random, and the impact was immediate. The Qur'an taught that Jesus was a prophet; her first impression on reading the Bible was that he was more than that.

---

30. Bilquis Sheikh and Richard H. Schneider, *I Dared to Call Him Father* (Lincoln, VA: Chosen Books, 1978).

Then one evening she had a dream where Jesus came and ate with her; later in the same dream, she met John the Baptist, who she thought might lead her to this Jesus. Three days later, she had yet another dream, this time one in which she was immersed in the aromas of glorious perfumes. She linked this to the beauty and the aromas of her garden. Ms. Sheikh wondered about the meaning of the dreams and felt that perhaps a young Christian missionary couple who lived in her village could help her, a couple on assignment with TEAM.[31] She visited them under cover of darkness. The couple offered her hospitality, explained the meaning of John the Baptist, and also suggested to her that the delightful experience of aromas may be understood in the light of 2 Corinthians 2:14, which speaks of God spreading his knowledge throughout the world like a lovely perfume.

This deeply moved her, and she continued in the coming days to immerse herself in the Scriptures. At one point, her grandson became ill, and while at the local Roman Catholic hospital she met a nun, a medical doctor from the Philippines. Ms. Sheikh was reading her Bible when the doctor came into the room. When she was asked about this, she said she was searching for God, so the doctor urged her to seek God and indeed to call on him as her Father. Back at home, in the privacy of her prayers, she realized that the sweet comfort of her garden, particularly a sweet Presence in its aromas, was indeed the same Presence she felt in reading the Bible.

She continued to immerse herself in the Scriptures while all along reminding herself that in Pakistan it was no small thing to become a Christian. There were regular reminders of what it might mean for her in terms of either being socially ostracized, rejected by her extended family, or even killed. Yet she persisted; when she was most struck by what it would cost to become a Christian, she came upon the text of Revelation 3:20, saying that Jesus is at the door, eager to come in and eat with her. Suddenly she recognized the link to her first dream. She knew there was no going back.

As a Muslim, she was aware of the Christian "heresy" of three gods, the so-called Trinity. Yet now, her pilgrimage had led her first to the living presence of Christ and then to the Father. As she continued in her reading, she was struck by the words of Acts 1:5 and the promise of the Holy Spirit. On her own she prayed for this gift and found that the room and her body were filled with wonder and awe and, most notably, joy. With this, she returned to the missionary couple and announced: "I am a Christian now! I have been baptized with the Holy Spirit!"[32] From then on, she joined a fellowship of Christians that met weekly.

During the following weeks, she had a growing sense that she should be baptized; yet she was also deeply conscious of the potential implications of

31. The Evangelical Alliance Mission, http://www.teamworld.org.
32. Sheikh and Schneider, *I Dared to Call Him Father*, 58.

baptism and the ostracism of her family. But she was still increasingly convinced that this was demanded of her, and so she finally insisted that the local Anglican minister baptize her. This became the flash point with her extended family: any rumors about her movement toward Christianity were confirmed with the baptism. She found herself systematically pushed to the social margins, and at times she actually had her life threatened. Eventually, despite being able to find ways to make a significant Christian witness in her community, she felt it necessary to leave the country, and she immigrated to the United States.

As mentioned, there is a growing body of critical literature that has provided some fascinating analysis of the experience of conversion for Muslim-background Christians.[33] What these studies of the last twenty to twenty-five years have demonstrated is that while the conversion narrative just recounted is unique, it does reflect some common themes in the experience of those who convert from Islam to Christ.

First, it is common for those who are searching to speak of their disillusionment with contemporary Islam, and this is consistently matched by a fascination with the Christian Scriptures.[34] Students of these conversion experiences routinely speak of the significant place that the Bible has played in the pilgrimage of those coming to faith. As in the case Ms. Sheikh, it is not uncommon for seekers to have an insatiable appetite for the Scriptures.

Second, Pieter Pikkert reports that one of the most common elements in a Muslim-Christian conversion is the desire for a personal encounter with God, a longing for something immediate and intimate.[35] For example, in the Bilquis Sheikh narrative, one is struck by how the capacity to call God "Father" was a dramatic turning point in her whole faith journey, as she accepted the idea that a person could have this level of intimacy with the living God.

Third and also significant, these conversion narratives often include references to unforgettable and defining dreams. Muslims take dreams seriously and typically seek out their meaning. One study of Muslim conversion narratives

---

33. In the comments that follow, I am particularly indebted to Jean-Marie Gaudeul's book *Called from Islam to Christ: Why Muslims Become Christians* (Crawborough, East Sussex, UK: Monarch Books, 1999). Gaudeul considers the experience of Muslim-born Christians, some of whom became Roman Catholic and others of whom became Protestant; and to Pieter Pikkert's "Protestant Missionaries to the Middle East: Ambassadors of Christ or of Culture?" (ThD diss., University of South Africa, 2006, http://etd.unisa.ac.za/ETD-db/theses/available/etd-02192007-141439/unrestricted/thesis.pdf); also as *Protestant Missionaries to the Middle East: Ambassadors of Christ or of Culture?* (Hamilton, ON: WEC Canada; Scotts Valley, CA: CreateSpace, 2008; distributed by Amazon.com). Pikkert's work is an inquiry into the cultural dynamics that influenced conversions and the strategies used by missionaries from the West. His observations about the clash of civilizations—European Enlightenment versus the Ottoman Empire, the West versus pan-Arab nationalism, and the more immediate confrontation between the postmodern West and the resurgence of Islam—are particularly insightful.

34. Pikkert, "Protestant Missionaries," 261–63.

35. Ibid., 267–68.

observes that the most common figure in three or four of the dreams referenced in these narratives is Christ; in other cases, it is John the Baptist; in others Mary, the mother of Jesus. Also, Christians often play a key role in interpreting and making sense of these dreams. The Muslim may have a dream and not be sure of its significance but then either seeks out or crosses paths with a Christian, who then interprets the dream in the light of the Jesus event.[36]

Fourth, many converts to Christian faith from a Muslim background appreciate the love, acceptance, and warmth of Christian fellowship. In addition, Pikkert reports that in some cases it is specifically Christian fellowship in the context of the church's liturgical life. He notes that two of three converts speak specifically of their positive experience of individual Christians and the church.[37] Pikkert goes on to observe that the church is most effective when its approach to mission within Muslim settings is intentionally "church centered" (over against an outreach heavily dependent on parachurch agencies).[38] He further insists that the approach must not be polemical, but winsome, as in a Christian community that witnesses to the person of Christ as much as anything by the grace of Christian character and community. Yet he insists that mission approaches must be specifically designed for Muslim-background Christians and thus not be based in homes but in spaces officially designated for worship.

Fifth, nothing is so significant in the typical Muslim-Christian conversion experience as a fascination with Jesus Christ. Sometimes, indeed often, it begins with the references to Christ found in the Qur'an; in many cases, there is a distinct sense in which the coming to faith is in direct response to the call or command of Christ.

But what of baptism and its implications for a connection with one's own social context and environment? The question of baptism has been a matter of significant consideration and not a little debate for church leaders and theologians for church groups in Muslim settings. It is commonly observed that in a Muslim setting, a Christian baptism is the make-or-break point: it is both the rite of initiation into Christian faith and the act of definitive break from one's Muslim circle of family, friends, and neighbors.

Many who read the Bilquis Sheikh account notice that her baptism meant that she was shunned by her family, and then eventually her positive influence within her community was lost by her departure to the United States—a legitimate and understandable departure, but one that disconnected her from her social context. So some ask, "Was this necessary? Does baptism need to be an act of defiance against one's own culture and setting?" Some see no

36. Some have observed that the frequency of reporting dreams and visions seems to have increased notably in the last twenty years; see D. Jones, "Dreams of Christ Awakening Muslims to Newfound Faith," *World Pulse*, March 10, 1995.

37. Pikkert, "Protestant Missionaries," 267.

38. Ibid., 270–80.

alternative; they insist that baptism is essential. Others wonder if there is an alternative that would allow the new Christian to sustain a meaningful network of relations within a Muslim context. "Is baptism absolutely necessary?" some ask. "Or if it is, can it be done in secret or at least in a form that is not so offensive to the Muslim world?" Phil Parshall, for example, was asking this question in the late 1970s. He observes that for Muslims to participate in the rite of baptism means being a traitor against the social, political, legal, and economic structures of Islamic culture. One desecrates oneself through idolatry, in that one has chosen to affirm three gods in the perceived explicit denial that God is one, a cardinal truth for Muslims.[39]

Some who question the need for baptism wonder if it is truly so essential to a Christian conversion; others fully recognize its need but suggest that it is not inherently necessary to a Christian that it be done in public and thus in a way that would be so offensive. The answer to this dilemma is surely one that will be resolved in large measure by a new consideration of the place of the sacraments and the church in Christian experience and especially in conversion.

Finally, another emerging theme in the reflections on the nature of Muslim conversion is the recognition that such experiences do not tend to rest or pivot on a decision or a particular act of acceptance. Rather, it has been well documented that these conversions are slow and incremental. Further, there is a growing recognition that nothing should be forced, that Muslims who are coming to Christ do so through a process of learning and discovery that will typically take many years. Even if baptism is affirmed as necessary, there is no reason to press for baptism prematurely or in a way that unnecessarily creates antagonism with family and social systems.

Conclusion

We come then to the conclusion of this overview of the history of an idea, a sampler of distinct ways in which the church has given critical and focused attention to the character and meaning of the conversion experience. Surely each of these has profound relevance for the contemporary Christian community, including but not limited to the following:

- From Augustine and the catechumenate of the early church, we appreciate that the tracks on which conversion runs will be both intellectual and moral reform, but that conversion is not a triumph of reason or moral reform but rather the experience of the soul that finds its true home in

39. Phil Parshall, "Contextualized Baptism for Muslim Converts," *Missiology* 7, no. 4 (1979): 502.

God; the church is uniquely positioned to guide this process through its own liturgical life.

- From Bernard and the monastic movement, we appreciate afresh that conversion is a beginning and that through conversion one joins a maturing community.

- From the Reformers, we see the fundamental way in which conversion is only an authentic beginning if it is rooted in the love and acceptance (the justification) of God, in Christ; this is a gift that is mediated to the new Christian by Word and Spirit, received in faith.

- From the Puritans and Wesley and the Anabaptists, we consider how conversion is a fundamentally penitential experience that ultimately leads to transformation.

- From the Holiness and Pentecostal movements of the last two centuries, we affirm that conversion is indeed only authentic if it leads to transformation but that this experience of transformation is necessarily linked to a conscious experience of the Spirit.

- And finally, from contemporary conversions of those from a Muslim background, we appreciate that conversion is ultimately an experience of Christ that is mediated by the Word on the one hand and the Christian community on the other, and that this coming to faith in Christ cannot be choreographed.

Our reflection on the meaning of conversion will surely take account of the wisdom of previous centuries but also insist that such experience and wisdom are appreciated most through a critical reflection on the language and thought of the New Testament.

5

To Be a Saint

Conversion and Spiritual Maturity

Many would concur that the finest Graham Greene novel is the hauntingly telling book *The Power and the Glory*, published in 1940. This extraordinary account of a priest takes place in a Mexican state that has outlawed the church, calling it the source of greed and corruption. Priests are arrested and shot, except for this one, who is known as the "whiskey priest."

He is on the run. But each time he might get to safety, he is held back by a sense of vocation, even though he is deeply aware that he is unworthy to perform his religious duties, especially presiding at the Eucharist. His sense of duty keeps hounding him. In what has been called a "theological thriller," toward the end we have a remarkable statement, which surely captures something integral to Graham Greene's understanding of the Christian life. And I wonder if it is not something profoundly true about the Christian life as a whole. When the whiskey priest comes to the end of his strength and wonders whether it was all worthwhile, all the effort and the pain, we read: "He knew now that at the end there was only one thing that counted—to be a saint."[1]

Though it is a troubling novel, a remarkable portrayal of the ambiguity of life and of religion, this line is actually a still point in the portrayal of the priest's sojourn; it gives us something to grasp amid so much else that is uncertain. More to the point, Greene is right. The one thing that counts is to be a saint. This is the fundamental purpose of life. This is what it means to be a Christian, to mature in faith, hope, and love and in so doing to experience the righteousness of God. To be a saint. One might well say that the only tragedy in life is the failure to be a saint. Consider this against the witness of the New Testament and human longing in its manifold expressions.

1. Graham Greene, *The Power and the Glory* (New York: Viking, 1940), 253.

87

The Christian Life and Sanctification

As is demonstrated by the Letter to the Ephesians, our theology of conversion needs to be located in two particular connections. First, we need to consider the relationship between conversion and discipleship. Second, we need to consider the relationship between conversion and the church, both the historic and apostolic church, and the visible and local congregation. This chapter is a consideration of the first of these, the relationship between conversion and discipleship, locating the experience of becoming a Christian within the whole of the Christian life. Conversion is initiation; we therefore only have a credible understanding of conversion when we are clear on what it is to which one is being initiated.

What is clear from the New Testament is that the structure of the Christian life includes a beginning; a middle, with an identifiable character that includes nurture and growth; and an end, a particular goal or objective. This vision for the Christian life is not a passing reference in the New Testament; rather, it is clearly central to a biblical understanding of salvation. In other words, it is taken as a given that conversion, as the beginning of the Christian life, is specifically that: a beginning. It is fitting to speak of conversion as the appropriation of the justifying grace of God, but the assumption of the Scriptures is that the Christian will be sanctified. This is the will of God for the community of faith (1 Thess. 5:23). This is clearly an *experiential* holiness; it is a personal and radical transformation enabled by grace and evident in the life quality of the individual and the community.

Thus, for example, 1 Peter 1:22–2:7 uses the image of infancy: a new Christian is compared to a newborn. Then the text recalls the obvious assumption that a baby grows up, and this is a reflection of health. In my preaching, I find it helpful to explore this image and observe that a newborn child is something of extraordinary beauty. But what is beautiful in a newborn is a source of great concern if weeks and months later the child is not gaining weight, responding to the environment, and in due time learning to speak. Similarly, what might be delightful in a teenager is simply pathetic when the same behavior is found in a middle-aged man. Yet we often seemingly tolerate this in the church: a person comes to faith, but no one is surprised when years later there is no appreciable change in understanding, behavior, and emotional maturity. It is not built into the very fabric of our understanding of and approach to conversion to assume that this is but a beginning. Indeed, if maturity and transformation do not follow, something is terribly wrong. My point here is that maybe the source of the problem is our approach to conversion in the first place.

In the autobiographical portion of the Letter to the Colossians (1:24–29), the writer provides a complementary perspective to that found in 1 Peter. Assuming for the moment that this is the apostle Paul writing, we notice that he speaks of his suffering, his calling to preaching, and his personal passion.

88

What strikes us is that all three are oriented toward a clearly articulated and unambiguous objective: "*so that we may present everyone mature in Christ*" (1:28, emphasis added). Paul speaks of his suffering as completing the sufferings of Christ. He counts his preaching as having this objective, this ultimate goal. And then he speaks of "struggling" for the Colossians and the believers in Laodicea. In other words, while Paul is clearly an evangelist, what he speaks of as his passion is the perfecting of the believers in these congregations.

Thus we come to the obvious conclusion and logical deduction: since the apostle is suffering, preaching, and struggling to this end, he naturally writes, "As you therefore have received Christ Jesus the Lord, continue to live your lives in him, rooted and built up in him and established in the faith, just as you were taught, abounding in thanksgiving" (Col. 2:6–7). "As you therefore" needs to catch our attention. It is clearly flowing directly out of what Paul has just outlined: the passion, purpose, and focus of his own ministry. His suffering is not an end in itself; rather, that suffering is clearly oriented toward a particular purpose: completing the work of Christ. Not, surely, in the sense that there was some insufficiency in the cross but rather that the cross is not "complete" until it is complete in the people of God, until the full benefits of Christ's death result in transformation, the very goal of Christ's death.

Paul also speaks of his preaching and specifically of "the commission God gave [him] to present . . . the Word in its fullness" (Col. 1:25 TNIV). Here too, he could not be more explicit about the purpose of preaching, or at least of *his* preaching: the completion or, one could say, the perfection of God's people. I fear that often our contemporary translations soften the force of this, as does the TNIV in rendering it "fully mature" (1:28), which seems to be a tautology. Though we rightly fear perfectionism, we miss Paul's intent here if we do not come away with a deep appreciation of the goal of preaching.

We seek transformation. Though preaching is not the only means by which this will happen, it is noteworthy that for the apostle it played a definitive role not only in his ministry but also in the life of the church. Thus we read that to this end the apostle contended, wrestled, struggled (1:28) with all the energy within him. It suggests strenuous, muscular endeavor. Of particular note, then, is that evangelism is a means to an end: Paul proclaimed the gospel not merely so that women and men would become Christians but specifically so that they would enter into a pilgrimage of faith and obedience that would lead to maturity in Christ.

Yet this objective, transformation, will only be a meaningful expression of the life of the church if it is reflected in evangelism. If it is not, if evangelism is not integral to discipleship, then the great danger is that evangelism is nothing more than a vaccine: it only pricks the surface, does not really infuse the whole, and does not lead to transformation. What this means is that conversion is but a beginning yet only a good beginning, an authentic beginning, if it enables the outcome for which it is intended: maturity in Christ. It follows, then, that we will only have a clear understanding of conversion if we have a clear conception of the goal of the Christian life. Our theology of conversion is bundled with our theology of the Christian life, our understanding of the goal of the Christian life (the doctrine of sanctification), and our understanding of how the Christian life is sustained and nurtured.

This takes us back to the propensity in evangelical circles to use the word *saved* to speak of conversion. Is it time, because of our one-dimensional misuse of this word, to pronounce a moratorium on using this word unless we do so with equal attention to the full perspective on salvation found in the New Testament? Instead of the language of "being saved," we can more appropriately speak of becoming disciples, using *disciple* as a noun, or talk of coming to faith in Christ or becoming a follower of Christ. Perhaps we need to recover the monastic ideal of conversion as an act of choosing a particular way, entering into a beginning on the way of the pilgrim. We would long for and hope for a gradual but incremental growth in faith, hope, and love, with the assurance that what God begins God will complete (see Phil. 1, esp. v. 6; Rom. 8:29–30). We need to recover precisely this dynamic orientation toward spiritual growth and maturity, so that we are comfortable with other dimensions of the word *salvation*, comfortable enough to urge one another to "work out . . . [our] salvation with fear and trembling" (Phil. 2:12–13). In our common daily speaking of God's salvation, our primary manner takes conversion as but a beginning; the passion of our lives is this growth in Christ.

The Need for a Compelling Theology of Sainthood: The Mature Christian Life

If we speak of the need for spiritual growth and maturity and completion, and if we speak of the tragedy if in this life we are not enabled to become saints, then we need to ask about the *content* of this vision of the Christian life. If conversion is but part of a whole, part of the total experience of the saving grace of God, then what constitutes this "whole"? The apostle makes it clear that his suffering, his preaching, and his personal ministry are all oriented toward one end, one *telos*, so it follows that we need to profile this end, this completion of the Christian life. If we go back to the language of Philippians 1:6, that Christ will complete what Christ has begun, what will this "completion" look like? What will it feel like? We need to consider this with enough clarity and definition so that we know that what we have before us is a saint. We need some sense of the contours and content of mature religious experience, enough clarity about this so that we can speak of it in our pulpit, celebrate it in our hymns, and most of all, practice an approach to spiritual formation that will enable us to know this end.

What we are after here is a compelling and accessible vision for spiritual transformation. One of our challenges at this point, especially if we come from an evangelical theological and spiritual tradition, is that we have relatively little to build on. This vision of transformation, of the mature Christian life, of what it means to be a saint, is a theme that evangelical theologians have not developed well. I suspect that this is due in part to the fear of perfectionism, moralism, or legalism, which is surely death to the Christian life. We certainly need to recoil at articulations of the Christian ideal that are nothing more than perfectionism or legalism. But have we missed something in our legitimate fear of this heresy? There is, further, an ambivalence in this regard within the spiritual traditions that are heirs to the Reformation, particularly where there is a theology that is properly conscious of the depth of the human predicament and the power of sin. Those from this heritage are rightly skeptical about the Holiness traditions that speak of the possibility of sinless perfection in this life.

These legitimate theological instincts should not lead us to discount the importance of holiness and the possibilities of grace in this life and thus to fail to articulate the Christian ideal that can inform our lives, individually and corporately, and give us hope and clarity amid the challenges of living faithfully. Living more and more into holiness and grace should be an objective that inspires us and encourages us to persevere and not become cynical in the face of sin and setback. The goal of spiritual maturity is thus not an impossible burden that oppresses us, but a vision of freedom in Christ that we hold on to as a faith community that refuses to be victimized by sin.[2]

The lack of a distinctly evangelical theology of spiritual maturity means that in a sense what follows can only be a preliminary contribution to a conversation—a proposal, a way, perhaps, that those within the evangelical tradition might think about this vision for spiritual transformation. What we are after is a vision that has the following characteristics and qualifiers:

1. It needs to be a vision that can incorporate both individuals and corporate dimensions of the Christian life, so that we can speak of an individual as a mature Christian but do so in a way that only makes sense in community, and then conversely also speak of a maturing community that only makes sense as its individual members are growing in faith, hope, and love. We seek a vision

2. As I write this, I sit on the Commission on Accreditation of the Association of Theological Schools (ATS) in the United States and Canada. The ATS approach to accreditation has made a substantive change in recent years that mirrors what I am suggesting here. The "standards" of accreditation are no longer the bare minimum for a school to offer an approved degree. Rather, the standards are an ideal of what makes for a good theological school. And accreditation is not a regulatory function of verifying if the school has met the minimum standard. Rather, accreditation is granted to a school that sustains the vision of good theological education and gives evidence of a plan to offer good theological education. In the same way, it is not so much how mature you are, but rather, do you have a clear vision of spiritual maturity that is informing your practices, disciplines, and routines as a Christian believer?

of the Christian life that we can embrace together; we affirm that we cannot know the grace of God in isolation from Christian community.

2. It needs to be a vision of the spiritual life that clearly and self-evidently emerges from our reading of the Scriptures, both the ancient Hebrew text and the New Testament, and yet it will also be one that allows this biblical vision to be informed and sharpened by the historic witness of the church and the wisdom of the church's spiritual masters.

3. It will be a distinctly *theological vision* of the Christian life such that even if the vision that emerges draws on the social sciences and other perspectives, it remains an essentially theological understanding of what it means to be mature, unapologetically so.

4. It will be a perspective on the Christian life that can with reasonable ease be translated into approaches to formation and disciple making and spiritual practices. Thereby a person and a community can seek and embrace this vision in a way that integrates the whole of life, each dimension of life and work, of being in the world and in retreat from the world. They can do this in a way that integrates the whole of what it means to be a faith community so that each aspect or dimension of congregational life has meaning in light of this vision.

5. It will be a perspective that is congruent with a biblical understanding of creation and reflects the beauty, simplicity, and complexity of what God intended in creation, which then finds fulfillment through the redemptive work of God: to what end did God create and redeem us?

6. As this vision emerges, it also needs to be one that is clearly an understanding of the Christian life that is transcultural, not a vision that arises within one culture or social context and is then transported and artificially imposed on the church in another setting, so that we end up with so-called purpose-driven churches scattered throughout Brazil. In other words, when this vision is incarnated within a cultural and social setting, we will not have any sense that something is being franchised. I should also add here that there will be an extraordinary diversity between two mature Christians (no two Christians are identical), and the mature expression of the church in each culture and society will be remarkable for its diversity. Thus Thomas Merton rightly observes that holiness is never generic; it is always particular to this person, in this place, at this time, and for the particular vocation to which this person is called.[3]

7. Finally, while what follows will seek to be consistently and thoroughly evangelical, it will also be ecumenical. It will be evangelical in that all theological reflection is located within a tradition and context, yet ideally, not in a manner that is sectarian but that intentionally draws on the wisdom emerging from the whole range of the Christian spiritual heritage. A Roman Catholic

---

3. Thomas Merton, *Life and Holiness* (New York: Herder & Herder, 1963), 293.

or Orthodox theologian could do the same, developing an essentially Catholic vision yet drawing on the insights of Christians of other traditions. A Baptist and a Lutheran will have distinct visions of the Christian life; what we need is a theology of mature Christian faith that can be translated into diverse theological and spiritual traditions.

The end result will be a vision of the Christian life that, though located within specific contexts and social environments, will intentionally turn from cultural or conventional associations of civility or what it means to be acceptable and respected people. It will have vigor and substance to it; it will call forth our deepest hopes and aspirations, our longings to be all that we are called to be as individuals and as communities and indeed as nations. We deeply long to transcend any idea that we want to form our children into nice little Christians. Instead, we do better to seek a vision of substance and passion that can inform what it means to raise our children in the faith, what it means to be faith communities, and how we foster Christian maturity within organizations pursuing an explicit part of our institutional mission.

In this latter regard, I am thinking especially of theological schools that as part of their mandate accept the formation of women and men for religious leadership. The common consensus is that such ministry formation needs to incorporate intellectual formation and understanding, training and competence, and this very dimension: formation toward spiritual maturity. While we might legitimately challenge this threefold approach, all theological schools recognize the call to soul formation. But what is the vision of the Christian life that informs this agenda and the curricula? What I am suggesting is that our vision of the Christian life must find expression within such contexts as theological schools.

And then, as a bottom line, we need a vision of the Christian life that is clearly not a human project or construct, an accomplishment of the church, or yet another form of human self-perfection or achievement. It must be clear that this is God's work, through the grace of the Spirit. Hence, this vision will be matched and complemented by a focused conversation on the means of grace: if this is the grace we seek, then it only follows that we ask what the means of this grace might be.

This point is crucial and must permeate this whole discussion: preaching is not about urging hearers to work harder, try harder, and do more so that they are more faithful. They cannot do so; the depth of the human predicament makes this impossible and thus futile and (rightly) results in much cynicism about the Christian life—better put, it is cynicism about a false conception of the Christian life. Rather, preaching is about drawing the people of God into the grand accomplishment of Christ in the cross and the resurrection so that they can participation in this life, rest in the wonder of the gospel, and know the transformation that comes through the ministry of the Spirit.

Yet in this they are not passive! Rather, they need to be involved in active response comparable to one who attends to the subtle yet sure movements of a lead dancer. We need a vision of the Christian life that gives substance to the call to Christians to take responsibility for their lives, to exercise adult accountability for how they respond to the grace that is offered them in Christ Jesus.

The Christian Life as Union with Christ

A theologically consistent vision of the Christian life will be trinitarian: we are called to the Christian life by the Father, who is the creator of all things; we speak of the sanctified life as the life for which we have been created. And, as will be stressed below, the fullness of the Christian life is effected in the life of the Christian by the Spirit's grace. Yet, though our vision must be trinitarian, there is no avoiding that it is also *christocentric*: the life of the Christian is caught up in the life of the risen and ascended Christ. To be a Christian is to be in Christ, and our holiness, or righteousness, is one that we can only speak of or experience by virtue of our identification with the cross of Christ and our participation in the risen life of Christ.[4]

This identity of the Christian in Christ is dynamic, not static. It is not uncommon for the New Testament to use the metaphor of growth. We have it in 1 Peter 1–2 and also in Ephesians 4. In Ephesians, this growth is distinctly christocentric. We grow up into Christ, our head. Similarly, in Romans 8:29 we have reference to being transformed into the image of Christ Jesus. This perspective also comes up in Colossians 2:7, where those who have come to faith are urged to be "rooted and built up in [Christ]." It is a first and fundamental orientation for Christians: a biblical understanding of the goal of the Christian life is distinctly oriented toward Christ Jesus.

This is not a static experience; it is not an identification with a concept or a principle; instead, it is a dynamic union of being in Christ as Christ is in the Christian, such that in Colossians 1:27 we read, "Christ in you the hope of glory." The clear sense of an ideal or goal of the Christian life comes through in John 15, when Jesus speaks of his longing for his disciples: that they would abide in him even as he abides in them. When the rich young ruler comes to Christ, he is portrayed as one who has lived faithfully under the old covenant,

---

4. In the current debates within evangelical circles on justification and the imputation of Christ's righteousness, I find it most helpful to affirm that through justification we become participants in the righteousness of Christ, rather than to speak of righteousness as something that is distinct from Christ and thus something that can, in a sense, be "imputed" to another apart from this participation in the life of Christ, which is really the heart of the matter. God's grace in Christ is not a commodity but Christ himself given to us, Christ himself, in whose life we live and move and have our being.

but Jesus says, "You lack one thing; . . . come, follow me" (Mark 10:17–22 pars.). Though our vision of the Christian life must draw on the whole of the biblical witness and affirm points of continuity with the Old Testament, the heart of the matter will be the New Testament witness to the person of Christ Jesus.

There is no doubting, then, that the telos of the Christian life is a transformation into the image of Christ, which comes through an actual dynamic and perhaps even mystical union with Christ. Christ becomes the beginning and the end and the means, as we see in Colossians 2:6–7. Indeed, each dimension of the Christian life that I will address in the coming pages is derivative of this encounter and this union with Christ.

It is vital that when we speak of the *telos* of the Christian life we sustain this distinctive christological character. We can and certainly will use such theologically rich words as *righteousness* and *holiness* in speaking of what makes a mature Christian. And yet, when we think of these words, the crucial element is Christ Jesus, and thus our affirmation must always be that our righteousness or holiness is found in Christ. Without this central dynamic—the person of Christ, the "Christ in you, the hope of glory" (Col. 1:27)—the Christian life is oppressive and an impossible objective. We are left with nothing but preaching that calls for personal reformation but does not truly anchor that reform in what enables transformation: union with Christ.[5]

Hence, I am deeply sympathetic with the ancient ideal that I discovered through the spirituality of Ignatius of Loyola: to know, love, and obey Christ. Here is what it means to be a Christian. This experience of Christ is located within the church and is mediated to us through the grace of the Spirit. These are two crucial qualifiers to our understanding of life in Christ. This identity in Christ is not found in isolation but within and through the faith community. Further, this identity and experience of Christ is "charismatic" in that the union with Christ and the grace that is experienced through this union is mediated to the Christian by the Holy Spirit. But in the end it is all about Christ Jesus.

This is what it means to be in Christian community: it is only a Christian community if our sense of identity, purpose, and what it is that sustains us is all deeply oriented toward Christ. If not, the church is nothing more than a religious project or club. This is what it means to be or walk in the Spirit: it is only truly an experience of the Holy Spirit if it is a spiritual dynamic that draws into and enables us to live more fully in Christ. This vision of a Christian life is then marked by the cross of Christ and by radical dependence upon Christ crucified: we are justified by faith in Christ; and we are sanctified by faith in

5. Richard Lovelace puts it this way: "Ministries that attack only the surface of sin and fail to ground spiritual growth in the believer's union with Christ produce either self-righteousness or despair, and both of these conditions are inimical to spiritual life" (*Dynamics of Spiritual Life: An Evangelical Theology of Renewal* [Downers Grove, IL: InterVarsity, 1979], 214).

Christ; we grow in faith, hope, and love through and in radical dependence on God. Our faith is in Christ and in the work of Christ.

Finally, this union with Christ also means and must mean an alignment with the purposes of Christ in the world. The Christian learns to live life toward the glory and reign of Christ, rather than toward oneself. A mature Christian is one with a deep desire and capacity for service that is offered to Christ for the sake of others. Prayer is the primary means or practice, the principal form through which union with Christ is sustained. It is the worship of the church and the prayers of the individual Christian that sustain the communion and thus the union with Christ. We learn holiness, then, by learning to pray. Nothing is so central to the practice of spiritual formation as teaching the people of God how to pray.

This core focus of the Christian life cannot be overstated. Even though I am going to offer a more nuanced definition below, nothing that is added can in any way take away from the focus and simplicity: we want to know, love, and serve Jesus. In one very real sense, it is not more complicated than that, and nothing else that is said can undermine or qualify it or distract us from this central and defining vision. Without this vision of Christ as the focal point of the Christian life, particularly that the Christian life is one of participation in the life of Christ, any call to righteousness, maturity, or sanctity is but an oppressive and impossible burden. Without Christ, the law is oppressive; in Christ, it is the wonderful guide and teacher that leads us to freedom. The Christian life begins and ends with Christ. Its defining energy is one of immediate and intimate union with Christ.

With this as a baseline, we can ask: What are the elements or dimensions of this union with Christ? What does it mean to be transformed into the image of Christ? What is the content of this new identity? Taking the abiding witness of the Scriptures, and reading this through the lens of the church's history and faith, a good place to begin is to affirm that this content has the following elements. (I stress that this is at most a good place to begin.) To be mature in Christ is to know the grace of

- sapiential holiness: to know the truth and to live in the truth with wisdom;
- vocational holiness: to know oneself and to live out one's vocation in the world in a manner congruent with one's identity in the crucified and risen Christ;
- social holiness: to love others with courage and generosity;
- emotional or affective holiness: to know the ordering of the affections and the grace of living with joy in a fragmented world.

96

What I see here is an ideal of the Christian life that takes the church beyond the current fad as I write these words: the "purpose-driven life." Surely we need a vision that is not so simplistic. In response, it seems helpful to think in terms of these four elements (listed above). They are distinct yet ultimately inseparable, and they, hopefully, pick up the central threads that emerge in the Scriptures, but which then also surface in the teachings of the spiritual masters of the Christian heritage. Further, any vision of the Christian life needs to be, in some sense, something that we can expect, by the grace of God, to experience. Though perfection may not be possible in this life, the objective we seek should be translatable into meaningful approaches to spiritual formation that, in turn, allow a person to experience genuine growth in grace.

Wisdom as Sapiential Holiness: To Know and Do the Truth

This first dimension and expression of Christian holiness must undergird everything else in the Christian life; to be a Christian is to know and do the truth; it is to walk in the light. Intellect and volition are intimately linked, each informing the other. This is wisdom, and wisdom is an essential dimension of holiness. As Bruce Waltke observes, the law of Moses is refined and expounded in the proverbs of Solomon,[6] and thus Waltke concludes that we cannot speak of righteousness without speaking of wisdom. If a person is righteous, that person is wise.

The Christian vision of holiness, sanctity, and spirituality is captured by the twofold vision of Jesus's own ministry: teaching (toward understanding) and obedience. Knowing and living the truth is really nothing more than the ancient vision of wisdom so beautifully reflected in the Wisdom literature of the Old Testament, found in the book of Proverbs but not exclusively there. Transformation comes by the renewal of the mind (Rom. 12:2); it is the truth that sets us free (John 8:32). But it is the truth lived, embraced such that the truth forms and reforms lives and enables us to walk in the light. It is the Christian mind together with a Christian conscience. It is a holiness that is rooted and grounded in the truth. It is light to the mind and heart and then light to the feet, the hands, and the tongue. Thus wisdom is equated with light in the Scriptures, notably in the Pauline Epistles, where the apostle enjoins his readers to "live as children of light" (Eph. 5:8).

When we use the language of wisdom, we highlight that this dimension of holiness includes knowledge and understanding. The way of darkness is the way of ignorance (Eph. 4:18); light represents truth and knowledge as an essential element of wisdom and thus holiness. There is no wisdom without knowledge, and there is no wisdom without study and purposed, disciplined

6. Bruce K. Waltke, "Righteousness in Proverbs," *Crux* 44, no. 4 (2008): 16–18.

engagement of the mind. Though there might be knowledge without wisdom, there is no wisdom without knowledge. Hence, the Christian spiritual tradition has always given teaching and learning a central place in congregational life and spiritual formation.

When we use the language of wisdom, we stress that it is not merely cerebral; it is knowledge that is lived, truth that is obeyed; it is light to the mind and to the feet so that we walk in the truth as we walk in the light. It must be both. The test of authentic faith is not knowledge, but obedience. We call for the renewal of the mind, a renewal that is not just cerebral but also experiential. One lives in the knowledge of God and has comprehension of the purposes of God in the world. A disciple is one who knows the truth and does the truth; a disciple is one who obeys, eagerly and willingly. Jesus could hardly make this clearer: "If you love me, you will keep my commandments" (John 14:15).

Thus, to be wise is to live faithfully in time, doing good, knowing and doing the will of God. Wisdom then integrates the knowledge of God and of God's will (Col. 1:9–10); it implies the integration of understanding and practice. These are one because in the end they cannot be separated. Behavior and actions are informed by understanding, and understanding is expressed in behavior that is congruent with this understanding. This is surely the basis for the catechism of the early church, with its assumption that the coming to faith would be on two rails: understanding and moral reform. This twofold commitment was and remains the only way we can be formed in wisdom.

Consequently, there is no wisdom (and thus no holiness) without education; indeed, this is precisely what education is. Education is spiritual formation precisely because it is formation in wisdom. One of the urgent needs of our day is to recover an appreciation of the power of education and learning for the Christian life.[7] Education is an inherently deeply Christian act, and few things are so empowering to life as learning; the church by its nature is a teaching-learning community. Learning opens the mind, frees the heart, encourages the disheartened. We are animated (ensouled) by learning. Though education surely includes classrooms and libraries, the wise are deeply attuned to the rhythms of God's creation: they understand, from the inside out, what it means to see and live in the truth (thus work in the library is complemented by work in the garden).

If this learning leads to wisdom, it leads equally to humility. Knowledge in itself "puffs up" (1 Cor. 8:1). The only understanding or learning that leads to transformation is that which is marked by humility: the humility of the

---

7. I say "education and learning" because, unfortunately, we cannot assume that they go together; yet we must actively seek ways to affirm the vitality of learning, the very goal of education.

child, the humility of teachableness, a willingness to learn from our teachers, from our children, from those who differ with us, from those of other cultures and traditions.

This humility is evident in our actions. We live in the light; thus the way of wisdom incorporates integrity in speech, sexuality, and finances—as is so evident in the book of Proverbs. But it also speaks of doing good, or as the Revised English Bible aptly translates Colossians 1:10, a person who knows the wisdom of God will demonstrate an "active goodness of every kind."

Having affirmed the priority of wisdom, we need to add some important caveats:

1. This vision of holiness will always be social; we are wise *together*, and this wisdom is something that we share and "pass on" (thus the critical place of community and of intergenerational conversations).

2. Further, the experience of wisdom comes slowly and incrementally. It is the fruit of a lifetime of growth in understanding, along with a lifetime of myriad choices. Yet, though it comes slow, it does require formation and intentionality. We seek wisdom; we are formed in wisdom. The faith community can be a venue for intentional formation in wisdom.

3. The call to wisdom is always, implicitly, a challenge to both the pragmatist and the sentimentalist. A wise person has a deep love of the truth and a passion for seeing life through a theological lens. This suggests that the wise person is never content with merely knowing what works or what feels good.

4. The Christian vision and wisdom are always shaped by the contours of God's creation. Further, they are always embodied; we are only wise in the body. It is not a cerebral or ethereal wisdom but a wisdom that is earthly, physical, and tangible. It finds expression in the care of the body, living with grace within the limits of our bodies, and the capacity to work with our hands; the wise person is both thoughtful and handy. Wisdom is not ultimately about ideas and concepts but rather about living with insight, yes, but insight that takes form in and through our bodies.

5. It is a vision of wisdom that is thoroughly christological. "All the treasures of wisdom and knowledge" are found in Christ (Col. 2:3). The church consequently has no patience with the *appearance* of wisdom, which in the apostle's words is no wisdom at all. Rather, wisdom finds its anchor and compass in Christ—incarnate, crucified, and risen. One is united with God through Christ, and this union with God provides a fundamental vantage point (or worldview) by which one lives; it is a knowledge of God's will.

6. Finally, this wisdom is found in the Spirit; to live wisely is to live in the Spirit. The apostle's language in Ephesians moves easily from the call to wisdom (5:15) to the call to "be filled with the Spirit" (5:18). Thus we cannot separate life in the Spirit from a life marked by wisdom. The Spirit *is* the mediator of wisdom, the very one who empowers believers to both know and live the truth.

99

We must add that a mark of wisdom is surely the yearning for wisdom. One longs for wisdom as one longs to live, and in the process one develops a deep distaste for foolishness.

Vocational Holiness

The Christian ideal for life in this world will include the capacity to be in the world in a way that is congruent with the purposes of God. It will mean an alignment of one's life with the reign of Christ in the world—to walk humbly, in justice and mercy (Mic. 6:8). It will include, surely, that one does the work to which one is called by God. We cannot conceive of the holiness of Christ without reference to Christ's work in the world and to the call of Christ on our lives to be witnesses to this work in word and deed.

Eugene Peterson aptly speaks of "vocational holiness," the holiness of doing what God calls us to do.[8] We are struck, for example, by how Christ is able to offer to the Father the observation that he has completed the work that had been given to him to do (John 17:4). Vocational holiness, maturity in Christ in this regard, means two things simultaneously: (1) that one is engaged in the world in a way that is congruent with what God is doing in the world and (2) that one is engaged in a way that is consistent with one's own identity and calling and does the specific work to which one is called. The challenge here is to affirm that indeed we must speak of vocation when we speak of spiritual maturity, but then we must not reduce spiritual maturity or holiness to doing good work. We seek a vision of vocational holiness that is anchored in wisdom and is more complex and multidimensional than the typical pragmatism of American popular piety, which virtually reduces the Christian life to behavior. Again, the current popular literature speaks of the "purpose-driven life" as "letting God use you for his purposes." Yes, our maturity in Christ will include our identification with the purposes of God in the world. And yes, it will mean that we will respond to the purposes of God for our lives. But we urgently need a fuller appreciation of vocational holiness, one that is not a mere echo of the pragmatism of our culture.

Without doubt the heart of the matter is what Hugo Rahner, the Austrian theologian (brother of Karl), called an "undaunted readiness to serve," which he spoke of as the evidence of an ordered life.[9] Philippians 2 calls us to have this mind, the mind of Christ, with whom we are united, who gave himself in radical service and did not grasp for rights or privileges but simply gave

8. See Eugene H. Peterson, *Under the Unpredictable Plant* (Grand Rapids: Eerdmans, 1992); and Gordon T. Smith, *Courage and Calling: Embracing Your God-Given Potential* (Downers Grove, IL: InterVarsity, 1999).

9. Hugo Rahner, *The Spirituality of St. Ignatius Loyola: An Account of Its Historical Development* (Westminster, MD: Newman, 1963), 64.

himself for the sake of others. From this baseline, Christian maturity will include, at the very least, the following:

1. Vocational holiness means having a knowledge and love of the purposes of God in and for the world: a heartfelt and deep longing that God's reign would come, that the will of God would be fulfilled on the earth as it is in heaven. We seek and yearn for the kingdom; this is our prayer and this is the focus of our mental and physical energies. We "seek first" the reign of Christ—eagerly, joyfully acknowledging one Lord (so that the "lord" is not us, and we are not seeking to build our own "kingdoms").

2. Vocational holiness also means self-knowledge: to be holy is to know oneself and to accept oneself. In the language of Teresa of Avila (and Catherine of Siena), this is humility. Such holiness and humility will be at least partly evident in knowledge of one's calling, having clarity about what one is called to do. We know who we are and choose to live not by pretense or by wishing we were someone else but in humility. We know ourselves and accept who God has made us to be and what it is that God, who alone is the potter, has called us to do. We turn from envy and wishing we were someone else with their gifts and opportunities. Hence, vocational holiness is not about doing everything or even trying to do all we can do; we leave it to Christ to be the "Messiah," and we graciously recognize and accept our part in the kingdom work of Christ. It is about doing that and only that to which we are called. It is the grace of living in a way that is faithful to the reign of Christ and consistent with the truth of our own identity; this is humility, living without pretense. It is about living faithfully in space and time without anxiety and with no need to run about frenetically.

3. Vocational holiness will include the courage to be one's self and to act in the world in a way that is marked by this courage rather than fear (2 Tim. 1:6–7). This courage is complemented by perseverance and patience in the face of setback, difficulty, and even persecution, which suggests that all vocations are marked, as was that of Christ, by the cross.

4. Vocational holiness will include, by implication, the capacity to say no, to discern not only what one is called to do but also the freedom to say no, to discern and accept what one is not being called to do. This means having peace, in other words, regarding where the Christian can decline opportunities and challenges that are not what God is calling one to do.

5. Vocational holiness also means observing Sabbath. It is about knowing how to be thoroughly engaged in the world in response to the call of God, to work with diligence and creativity, in the arts, in business, in education, in religious ministry, in the care of children and the making of home—whatever the call! But it is also about knowing when to disengage, when to rest, when to step out of the fray and celebrate and live in the work of God. One of the signs of failure on this front—the call to vocational holiness—is frenetic business or overwork. The counterpart to this is that we see our work as but

a participation in the work of God; hence, we do not overwork ourselves but rather trust God with the work of God and contribute as we are called, with a rhythm between work and prayer, between work and rest, between work and recreation. Nothing so speaks to this as the observance of Sabbath rest. Sabbath means a day in seven, but it represents more. It characterizes us as persons and communities deeply engaged yet knowing that there is more to life than work. Our vocation is compromised when we break the Sabbath or fail to be faithful to our fundamental relationships—notably to one's spouse if one is married, to one's children if one has a family, but for all, the fundamental joy and privilege of human friendship.

6. There is also an intimate connection between vocational holiness and joy: we are called to be in the world as those who know that Christ is on the throne of the universe and thus brings joy to the world. Vocational holiness means that we live and work in a fragmented and discouraging world, but also with a deep and pervasive joy. More will be said on joy below (under the ordering of the affections), but here, in specific connection with vocational holiness, we must affirm and recognize that there is an affective quality that sustains this dimension of sanctity. We do not engage the world with anger, cynicism, or fear but with a joyful courage, for our hope and confidence ultimately rests not on our accomplishments or our capacity to overcome or not overcome obstacles, but in the ascension.

7. Further, vocational holiness is always communal. It is an engagement in the world that is always (yes, always) done in partnership and cooperation with others. And thus one of the key indicators of vocational holiness is the capacity to work with others. Vocational holiness thus includes the capacity to submit and defer to others, to live under constituted authority, to listen well as one who knows how to work with others, to depend on the capacity and strengths of others, and to work with an eager desire to empower others to fulfill their vocations.

8. Then also, a key sign of vocational holiness is that we have the grace to let go when it is time to "retire." This begins when we are younger and learn that we are not married to our work or ultimately defined by our work, but in our senior years, it means that we now entrust to others the work that had been given to us, and we leave it now in the hands of others. We let go, for whatever work we have is always only given to us for a time, for a season. Indeed, I wonder if one of the crucial indicators of vocational holiness is that one is able to let it go when the time comes to let it go.

9. Finally, vocational holiness includes the capacity to do our work in obscurity. It means that we have learned to do our work, with a commitment to excellence, away from the affirming public eye, with minimal if any thanks and affirmation. It means that we do not need recognition or acclaim or even thanks. If affirmation comes, good; we graciously receive it. We learn to do our work with some attention to affirmation and critique, but we are not

crushed by criticism, and our heads are not inflated by praise. As necessary, we do our work without affirmation and thanks. We do what we do "for the Lord" (Col. 3:23).

Most of all, vocational holiness is the act of being in Christ even as we are in the world. Our engagement with the world, our work at home or in the marketplace, in the church or in the world—all are derivative of our union with Christ. We are in the world as those who are in Christ, not in a formal, mechanical, or merely forensic sense, but as the very dynamic that informs life and work. Many would concur that there is hardly a more compelling vision of vocational holiness than that sustained by the heritage of Ignatian spirituality, as captured by the wonderful expression "the contemplative in action."

The sixteenth century was surely revolutionary when it comes to the Christian conception of holiness. We hear its deep affirmation—both from Protestant reformers such as Calvin and Luther and from Roman Catholic reformers, including Ignatius of Loyola—that our Christian identity takes us into the marketplace and that consequently religious work is not inherently more sacred than domestic work (the management of home and family) or the work of business or the arts or education (in the world). Furthermore, here Ignatius has particular significance: our being in the world is both derivative of and an essential dimension of our union with Christ.

Ignatius of Loyola is the founder of the Jesuits, the Society of Jesus, an apostolic order rather than a monastic order. Hence, the spirituality of this tradition is oriented not to retreat from the world but rather to actively engage in the world, yet with an engagement that is rooted in the contemplative life. This becomes the crux, the crucial dynamic that sustains our vocation and enables our work in world to be, specifically, a dimension of our sanctity. This contemplative vision of Christ enables our work in the world to be discerning (we do what we are called to do), accomplished with patience as we bear the cross of Christ with joy, courage, imagination, and creativity. Christ calls us not only to be his servants but also to be his friends (John 15:12–17). This is a reminder that our work in the world is always derivative of our relationship with Christ and our communion with him.

Social Holiness: To Love as We Are Loved

We must speak of holiness as also having a distinctly social dimension. Actually, each dimension of the Christian life has a social dimension. We need to resist the propensity (also part of our revivalist heritage) to regard the Christian life as being about an individual transaction with God, either at conversion or in the process of transformation. It is necessarily a life lived in community. The Christian vision of life is anchored in relationships—specifically, in relationships that are marked by love. Jesus puts it simply and clearly: "I give you a new commandment: . . . Just as I have loved you, you also should love one another. By this everyone will know that you are my disciples, if you have love for one another" (John 13:34–35).

Thus it is so important that we articulate the meaning of love and what this means for the Christian life, giving it this content. We insist that it is so much more than just being nice: our love for the other is a reflection of God's love for us and derives from our experience of the love of God. This love has substance, content; there are specifics to what it means to love another. The Scriptures provide us with this content, including the recurring references to love in Romans 12–16, for example. The apostle celebrates the richness of diverse relations and friendships in Romans 16, but this is set up by his call to love and his call to live at peace with others in the preceding chapters. The call to love seems to be reflected in three distinct acts:

1. God calls us to welcome the other (Rom. 15:7) in the radical hospitality of accepting the other, receiving the other, and not demanding that the other conform or change or be likable or be agreeable before they are received. A crucial sign of this hospitality is that we listen to the other—which surely is an act of service (indeed, for Dietrich Bonhoeffer it is the first act of service).[10] It will mean that we have learned how to differ graciously with the other on "disputable matters," as Paul puts it in Romans 14:1 (NIV), and to continue to welcome the other even when (perhaps particularly when) we have marked differences of opinion.

2. To love another is to serve the other, to respond to the needs of the other with generosity (and not calculation). We cannot meet the needs of all; we cannot be all things to all people. We are not the one through whom everyone we meet will know the love of God. Nevertheless, love is marked by service, by a generous response of giving, in word and deed, of our time and energy for the other.

3. To love the other is to live in harmony with the other. This means a number of things, but we must begin with the line of Paul in Romans 12:18, where he calls us to live at peace with others "so far as it depends on [us]." In other words, good people may well have conflicted life situations, whether at home or the office or the church. But the key is that if we love the other, we will do all that is within our power to live at peace; we will take personal responsibility for our side of the relationship. This includes that we forgive the wrongs of the other, though it is always forgiveness that seeks justice, not as revenge, but as the basis for authentic reconciliation.

A sign of holiness is the capacity to build peace, at home, in the church, and in the world: we need to be an instrument of peace. But it is crucial that peace is not merely about easing conflict or making people feel good. Rather,

10. Dietrich Bonhoeffer, *Life Together and Prayerbook of the Bible*, trans. Daniel W. Bloesch and James H. Burtness (Minneapolis: Fortress, 1996).

there is no love without wisdom. The sequence here is intentional: love is an expression and dimension of wisdom. Further, there is no love without justice. It is a false love, a sentimentalized notion of love, that does not take wisdom and justice seriously.

Thus the call to wisdom and to vocational holiness in one sense precedes the call to love, as seems to be implied by the order of Romans 12, where the call to wisdom comes first (v. 2), followed by the call to vocational integrity: "think of yourself . . . with sober judgment" (v. 3), which in turn is followed by the call to love (v. 9). Our love for the other is grounded in truth and wisdom. It is only an authentic love if it is a discerning love. Further, we can only truly love the other if we do so in a manner that is congruent with our own identity.

This dimension of holiness is obviously communal, yet we also need to stress that we learn how to love the other by *being* in community. We learn to love by living in a community that is resolved to learn how to love the other. The call to love begins at home and moves out in concentric circles. For those who are married, it begins with spouse and, if there are children, with the love of daughter or son; then we move to church and society; in time we begin to think globally and ask How and in what ways am I being called to love the people of Iran, Indonesia, and Ireland?

Finally, the call to love finds expression in spiritual friendship: the companionship of another with whom we have a foretaste of what all relationships will be at the consummation of the kingdom. Indeed, without friendship there is no holiness, no spiritual maturity. One of the marks of a holy woman or holy man is the quality of friendships that they have.

Emotional Holiness: The Ordering of the Affections

Spiritual formation necessarily includes the ordering of the deep loves, desires, and longings of the human soul; indeed, if this does not happen, all other aspects of our spiritual growth will be stunted and one-dimensional. Emotional holiness is the vital complement to growth in understanding and wisdom, to the cultivation of vocational holiness, and the fostering of our capacity to love and to receive the love of others. We can count this as growth toward emotional maturity. While emotional maturity (and intelligence) is not all that is implied by the ordering of the affections, it will surely include this. As the most definite expression of what it means to be holy, the ordering of the affections will be evident in our capacity for and experience of joy.

A holy person is a happy person; there is an intimate connection between sanctity and joy. Various writers have persuaded me of this; most notably, the works of Alexander Schmemann have reinforced my conviction that Christianity is supremely a religion of joy.[11] In Christ we find that our joy is made complete and that this joy is nurtured by all the gifts of God, most notably through worship and within worship specifically by the joyous celebration of the Lord's Supper. In worship the joy that is given us is the capacity to know even more that the deepest longings of our souls are met in Christ Jesus. Christ is always sufficient for us. Always! In a very real sense, our capacity for joy is not limited by the circumstances of our lives, for Christ's presence to us is not limited by them. The older we get, the more this becomes a defining mark of our lives: we become older and wiser and, quite simply, happier. We do not become grumpy old people: we become sweeter and sweeter and, indeed, more joyful into our senior years. This is, indeed, a mark of spiritual maturity.

Spiritual formation, then, orders the affections by ordering the mind, cultivating a love for truth and for delight in the good, the just, and the pure. This includes that we learn what it means to be honest about what we are experiencing emotionally—to name the reality of anger, fear, or mourning and to insist that we will grow in our capacity to be angry but not sin in our anger, to be afraid when we feel our vulnerability but not to become fearful people (for we know how to cast our anxieties upon God, who cares for us; 1 Pet. 5:7). We know how to experience loss but then consistently come back to the center, to the Christ whom we cannot ultimately lose. We learn to get angry at the right things, to be angry about what makes God angry. Further, we get angry without losing our temper, our even emotional keel. It means we can be honest about what is happening to us emotionally—be it anger or fear, for example—but do so in a way that enables us to grow in faith and hope, to be angry and not sin, to be afraid but not to *camp* there, as a friend once put it.

As explained above, the sequence between these marks of holiness is intentional. Joy is the fruit of wisdom and integrity; we are governed by wisdom. Yes, we long for joy, but we also recognize that this joy is the fruit of wisdom. Thus comes the link between sanctity and joy. Joy is the fruit of wisdom, of a life well lived, knowing the truth and doing good. Further, joy is found in doing good work, specifically, the work to which we are called. "For the joy set before him, [Jesus] endured the cross" (Heb. 12:2 NIV). Thus, joy is found not in an escape from the world, but specifically in the lives of those who are engaged with and in the world, in but not of the world, fulfilling their vocations but not overcome by them. Then also we must stress the joy that comes from a rhythm of work and rest, of engagement and Sabbath disengagement.

Joy inevitably is found through the grace of authentic relationships: the joy of married love, the company of children and grandchildren, but most of

---

11. See, e.g., Alexander Schmemann, *For the Life of the World: Sacraments and Orthodoxy* (Crestwood, NY: St. Vladimir's Seminary Press, 1998), 24–25; idem, *The Journals of Father Alexander Schmemann, 1973–1983*, trans. Juliana Schmemann (Crestwood, NY: St. Vladimir's Seminary Press, 2000), 137.

all, the grace that we know through friendship. In this, we do not discount the grace of joy that comes through solitude; but rather, we must affirm that human joy is ultimately something shared and mediated to each one through the grace of community. There is almost a sense in which joy is contagious: we catch it from others and have to share it. All religious traditions recognize that people in remarkably difficult circumstances sustain a vibrant joy largely because they are not alone.

Fundamental to this ordering of the affections is the central most crucial disposition of Christian piety, the heart of the identity and response of a disciple of Christ: thanksgiving. For the Christian spiritual tradition, thanksgiving is the crucial expression of faith: faith is expressed in gratitude to God, who is the source of life, who is creator, redeemer, and sustainer. Thus, the ordering of the affections is the completion of faith. Joy is rooted, ultimately, in a trust in God that finds expression in thanksgiving.

It is essential for us to affirm that this joy is fully rooted in and expressive of the Christian life: it is the fruit of wisdom, of vocational holiness, and of just and generous relationships marked by love. Most of all, it is the fruit of a relationship with Christ.[12]

Life in the Spirit

Wisdom, vocational integrity, love for others, and joy—each is not an end in itself but rather a dimension of what it means to be in Christ. Each is part of giving focus or content to what it means to be in Christ. And each is specific enough, something we can teach and preach and call one another to. It is vital for us to recognize that the goal of the Christian is simply impossible; it is beyond us. It is also essential to stress something else: each is also but another dimension of life in the Spirit. Life in Christ is mediated to the Christian by the Spirit, the Third Person of the Triune God. The New Testament vision of the Christian life cannot be spoken of without reference to the vital dynamic of life in Christ: the Spirit.

Two things need to be stressed here. First we must affirm that the Christian life is one of being indwelt by the Spirit. The Holy Spirit dwells in each Christian, and the Spirit dwells in the church, the faith community, the gathering of the people of God. What this suggests is a crucial interplay between Christ and the Spirit. It means that there is no experience of Christ that is not mediated by the Spirit. We do not have Christ, we do not follow Christ, we do not reside

12. In words attributed to Bernard of Clairvaux (ca. 1150):
    Jesus, Thou Joy of loving hearts!
    Thou fount of life! Thou Light of men!
    From the best bliss that earth imparts,
    We turn unfilled to Thee again. (Trans. Ray Palmer)

107

in Christ *except* by the grace of the Spirit. We cannot speak of Christ except by speaking of the Spirit. Each dimension of life in Christ is mediated to the Christian and to the church by the Spirit: the fullness of divine wisdom, the vocational alignment with the reign of Christ, the love for others that flows from "God's love . . . poured into our hearts through the Holy Spirit" (Rom. 5:5), and the joy of God, which is the fruit of the Spirit. But the converse is also true. We cannot speak of the Spirit unless we speak of Christ. The only spirituality that is truly of God is mediated to us, to the church, and to the world by Christ. Any experience of spirit that is not mediated through the person and work of Christ is inherently suspect.

Second, this New Testament trinitarian vision is a reminder that the Christian life is not self-constructed. We do not become Christians or mature as Christians by pulling our act together, by sheer dint of our effort, or as a human accomplishment. It is fundamentally an act of response to the Spirit and of personal alignment with the purposes and movement of the Spirit in our lives and our world. When we speak of human actions, we mean what we must do if we are to know the salvation of God. But we must always do so with reference to our response to Christ in the Spirit; we must speak of the church as the fellowship of the Spirit.

We want to ask, If this is the goal of human existence (in this life), what will enable this to happen? The answer to this question has two parts. First, it will require a good foundation, a good beginning; indeed, it will mean a radical conversion. Second, it will require an intentional process of formation—a process (there is no quick fix) and, further, an *intentional* process. We will be able to identify specific practices by which we foster our union with Christ and each dimension of Christian holiness.

My focus here is the first of these: spiritual maturity is the fruit of a good beginning, a dynamic point of departure. Evangelism will not be merely an act of helping people cross some kind of border, getting them in the door. It will rather be an invitation to a particular life, according to a specific vision of human life and existence. It is a life that is lived under the reign of Christ. Hence, evangelism is an invitation to become a saint. We make no promises that this will come quickly; indeed, in becoming a Christian, one enters into a pilgrimage that will be long and, potentially, arduous. But still, evangelism at its best will hold out a specific vision of the Christian life, a vision that is theologically consistent, with biblical and theological coherence, and compelling as an authentic vision of what it means to be mature in Christ.

This vision will not be equally compelling to all people. Some will be drawn to the dimension of wisdom while others perhaps are drawn to the experience of joy or the Christian vision of love and community. But still, evangelism will ultimately profile the whole Christian doctrine of sanctity, or at least each dimension, and (this is most crucial) evangelism will be the practice of leading women and men into a conversion experience that will inaugurate for them a pilgrimage, a journey, to Christian maturity.

It is appropriate to ask, then, What will conversion look like if it is a good beginning? What implications will this have for our approach to evangelism? Logically, we turn to the early church and ask: What conception of conversion defined the life and witness of the church described in the book of Acts? What implications might that have for the church in our generation?

Here is a final word before we examine the character of conversion. The objective of the Christian life, perfection in Christ, should immediately leave us recognizing that we cannot do it. The call of Christ is beyond us. Each time we are once more confronted with the call and demands of the gospel, it should lead us again to anchor our lives in Christ: in the knowledge of God's forgiveness and cleansing in the cross, in the grace of the Spirit by which we are empowered to be in union with Christ and the fellowship of God's people. We do not walk this road alone and cannot be expected to do so. As I will stress, each of these—union with Christ and then also forgiveness, the grace of the Spirit, and the fellowship of the faith community—is testified to through the rite of water baptism.

6

The Contours of a Christian Conversion

✠

Establishing the Question

Thus far I have considered the following:

- The language of conversion, and specifically the problem of the language of revivalism (chap. 1)
- The theological framework for an understanding of conversion, considered through the lens provided by the Letter to the Ephesians (chap. 2)
- The idea of conversion in the history of the church, beginning with the book of Acts (chaps. 3–4)
- The critical question: To what end? What is the ultimate goal for conversion? (chap. 5)

With these matters considered, we come to the heart of the matter: What is a Christian conversion? What makes a conversion Christian? What are the elements of this kind of religious experience? We are asking a discernment question, acknowledging that not all religious experience is Christian but further that not all who confess that they are Christians are truly followers of Christ. Inauthentic religious experience is possible.

It always merits mention that when we ask this question, we are asking one of the most fundamental questions of all; few things call forth such emotion from the depths of the human soul as the inquiry What must I do to be saved? We long for life; we long for the salvation of God. We know that there is no self-salvation and that in the depth of our human predicament, our only hope is that God intervene and grant us salvation and life.

111

So we ask, what must we do to know the grace of God and thus the life and salvation of God?

Posed in this manner, the question affirms unequivocally that God is the Savior, and that the only hope for humanity is the gracious initiative of God. But we can and must nevertheless ask the question from the human perspective of response: What must *we* do to know this salvation? How is humanity to respond to the salvation of God, and appropriate the offer of life that is given through Christ Jesus?

I offer two preliminary observations. First, we can and indeed must affirm that no two conversions are alike and that the work of the Spirit is wonderfully diverse, thus having different manifestations not only for each person, but also in distinct geographic, cultural, and social settings. Hence, we are looking for the contours of a Christian conversion, not the specific content, and we are seeking to delineate these contours in a way that would make sense of each person's experience and, further, allow for an authentic conversion to take place in any cultural soil.

Further, we affirm that we are not looking for a minimalist response to the question: not what must we do to be spared the horrors of hell? but rather what must we do to know the transforming grace of God? We are looking for a good beginning, an experience of justifying grace that is integrated with the purposes of God for our lives. We want to begin the journey of faith well, on a good foundation; we seek a genesis to the spiritual life that will, as God enables, lead to the full experience of God's transforming grace.

Some protest this fundamental approach and insist that we need to know the bare minimum; we need to determine the least that a person needs to do in order to know that they are "saved." But this minimalism inevitably leads to a truncated gospel, one-dimensional and ineffective. Further, this minimalism is a relatively recent phenomenon in the history of the church. It has led to the emphasis on the idea of a punctiliar conversion, which is not consistent with either the biblical witness or the actual experience of Christians.

Therefore, we are looking for an answer to the question what must I do to be saved? that will take account of the rich and complex character of Christian experience and acknowledge the diversity of experience while simultaneously being clear on what it will take to know the transforming grace of God through an encounter with Christ Jesus.

The Significance of Acts 2:38

In Acts 2:38 we have one of the most cogent replies to the question what must I do to know the salvation of God? On the day of Pentecost, the apostle Peter preaches his sermon and declares that the one who has been crucified is indeed the Lord and the Christ. We read that those who hear this word are struck by the message and in response ask, "What should we do?" (2:37). Peter replies, "Repent, and be baptized every one of you in the name of Jesus Christ so that your sins may be forgiven; and you will receive the gift of the Holy Spirit" (v. 38). Then he continues, "For the promise is for you, for your children, and for all who are far away, everyone whom the Lord our God calls to him" (v. 39).

What follows in this chapter and, essentially, in the rest of this book is an explication of this verse, an attempt to let it carry the freight when we ask the question. While there is certainly more to the experience of conversion than these two acts—repentance and baptism—as I have explained above, could it be that in this twofold response we have the heart of the matter and that Peter's response in Acts 2:38 can provide us with the essential point of departure?

The question what must we do to be saved? is certainly asked elsewhere in the New Testament in a variety of forms. A variety of answers are given, explicit or implied. We find answers in the dramatic encounters with Jesus, such as that of the rich young ruler, who asks what he needs to do to inherit eternal life. We also have it implied in the multiple ways that the apostle Paul references the experience of coming to faith in Christ. But what makes this particular text, Acts 2:38, significant for the church is precisely that now the question is being established *for* the church, and it comes precisely in that book of the New Testament where the experience of the church is being described. Now the church is being asked what it means to be saved after the ascension of the risen Christ, after the fulfillment of the promised sending of the Spirit, and now that the community of faith, in the Spirit, has been established as the new Israel. Now the church is responding to the promise of Christ that they will be witnesses (1:8).

In the book of Acts, as we have already observed, there are numerous conversion narratives, and these conversion narratives are, without question, instructive for the church and significant in informing our understanding of the Christian doctrine of conversion. Why then do we focus on Acts 2:38 as the paradigmatic text in Acts on conversion? The answer is straightforward: the other conversion narratives are descriptions of what happened, whereas Acts 2:38 is a specific proclamation of *what needs to happen*. This does not minimize the place of the other conversion narratives; it merely means that they play a different role in informing our understanding of the conversion. The other narratives draw on the experience of the church; the Acts 2:38 account provides a theologically normative outline or program. Richard N. Longenecker puts it this way:

> We should understand Peter's preaching at Pentecost as being theologically normative for the relation in Acts between conversion, water baptism and the baptism of the Holy Spirit, with the situations having to do with the Samaritan

113

converts, Cornelius, and the twelve whom Paul met at Ephesus . . . to be more historically conditioned and circumstantially understood.[1]

Acts 2:38 and following, then, is a vital text for understanding the New Testament vision for a Christian. This, at the very least, is what we observe: two distinctive dimensions of human responses are identified: "Repent, and be baptized." In response to a promise, we have a call, and it is a call that incorporates two movements: one that is interior with external manifestation, and one that is exterior with an internal manifestation. The internal movement of repentance is a call to personal responsibility. In one sense it is necessarily personal: no one can repent for another. It is both individual and personal.

The external movement, "Be baptized," is inherently social; it is mediated by the community. Even as one cannot repent for the other, so the converse applies to baptism: there is no such thing as a self-baptism. Thus the twofold movement of repentance and baptism incorporates a dynamic interplay between the individual and the community. I will examine both of these in more detail, but for now I will highlight that this dual movement is identified as the human response to the grace of God. I hope to demonstrate why both are crucial to the process and why they are crucial *together*: each side of this equation needs the other.

In a quick overview of the text, we also recognize that while repentance and baptism are given prominence in terms of the actions of response, this is clearly not the whole of what it means to be a Christian convert. The text of Acts 2:38 is part of a narrative. This call follows the experience of hearing the preaching of the apostle, and the text also speaks of the experience of forgiveness, reception of the gift of the Spirit, and incorporation into congregational life. Though there is more to conversion than repentance and baptism, this text profiles these two actions—or perhaps better put, this *dual* action—as pivotal to the conversion experience.

We are struck by the energy that emerges from this twofold action. It has immediate impact: Christian community is formed, a dynamic community that devotes itself to teaching, fellowship, and worship, a community marked by a deep and pervasive joy that sustains their witness in the face of persecution. But the impact is also intergenerational, with the promise that their response on that day, their response in repentance and baptism, will have implications for their children and their children's children.

Finally, it is clear that conversion is but a beginning. Those who responded that day were launched on a journey, together, as together they devoted themselves to the teaching of the apostles, to each other as a faith community, and "to the breaking of bread and the prayers" (Acts 2:42). It seems fair to say that

1. Richard N. Longenecker, "The Acts of the Apostles," in *The Expositor's Bible Commentary*, ed. Frank E. Gaebelein (Grand Rapids: Zondervan, 1981), 9:285.

these are activities that necessarily follow and complement the experience of conversion. Conversion is not an end but a beginning. One wonders if one may conclude that the conversion is authentic only if it is followed by these very acts to which they devoted themselves.

Hence, we are drawn back to the simplicity and power of the twofold character of their response to the preaching: "Repent, and be baptized." Can we speak of these two acts together—the one interior and the other exterior, the one the interior act of the individual and the other the exterior act of the community—as the contours of a Christian conversion?

The Character of Religious Experience

It is helpful to appreciate the simple force of Acts 2:38 against the backdrop of contemporary philosophical reflections on the nature of authentic religious experience. This is particularly instructive when we consider how religion and religious experience are understood within our social context and environment. It is my impression that though Acts 2:38 insists that repentance and baptism are two inseparable acts, the social context, notably of Western society, insists on pulling these apart.

Particularly instructive in this regard is the work of the Canadian Roman Catholic philosopher Charles Taylor. In 2002 he published *Varieties of Religion Today: William James Revisited*.[2] As is obvious, Taylor is taking on William James, who published the seminal and groundbreaking study in 1902, *The Varieties of Religious Experience*. William James made a crucial distinction and insisted that religion is either personal or institutional. Religion is either subjective and interior, or it is institutional—which for James included rites and rituals, dogmas and creeds, and the organizational side of religious life.

For James, the only religion that counts is the first: personal religion, heart experience, interior spirituality. He discards the second—institutional religion with its creeds, forms and structures, rites and rituals—as derivative, or what one might call "secondhand" religion, dependent on tradition and having no authenticity in its own right. He emphasized the interior and effectively rejected the institutional, and he viewed the church as institutional. In so doing, he was on a restoration project, responding to if not actually rejecting what he viewed as empty forms in order to stress the inner, subjective nature of authentic experience; contemporary language often calls this "spirituality." James counts the inner experience as authentic, while the church is *just* religion. For James, there is a necessary division between the two, between spirituality and religion.

2. Charles Taylor, *Varieties of Religion Today: William James Revisited* (Cambridge, MA: Harvard University Press, 2002).

James published *Varieties* in 1902; by the end of the century, the split was taken for granted in much of Western society. In 1995–96 a survey of Americans discovered that one-third of the respondents affirmed that because people have God, they do not need the church. The church is superfluous. Or as a student put it confidently and boldly in a class I taught in the fall of 2004, "Nature is my church!" She went on to insist that she would meet God in nature and so did not need the "church." Indeed, for this person the church was an actual obstacle to her "spirituality," not merely superfluous but actually something to be rejected.

In some ways, we must be sympathetic. Many of us can only describe our own coming to faith in Christ as one that included a season of disillusionment with the church—whether it is the weight of a burdensome legalism, or the proclivity toward unresolved conflict and power politics, or the accommodation of church authorities to wealth and/or government leaders. With good reason, many have been cynical about the church. A recent popular book on the spiritual life draws on this heartfelt desire for spirituality without all the encumbrances and sheer bother of church dogma, structures, and problems: "For those who want to be spiritual without being religious," the jacket cover reads. And it sells; it taps into the spirituality of the current era, a longing for interior, spiritual, expressive experience, with no external religious structures. It echoes the sentiments of John Lennon when he sings, "Imagine . . . no religion," which he lumps together with war and all manner of social evils.[3] It is William James gone to seed.

"Institutional religion" is easy to disparage: the abuse of power, the stifling of creativity, the propensity to view the institution as an end in itself. But does this mean that we can just toss it out and pursue a religionless spirituality? Charles Taylor responds to James, a century later, and questions this split, this preference for personal religion that discounts the need for the church. He claims that it is essentially a false polarity and that the two, the subjective and the institutional, must be held together.

James located religious experience in "feeling" rather than cognition and discounted the importance of doctrine and dogma as incidental; what counted was experience. But as Taylor points out, "All experiences require some vocabulary, and these are inevitably in large part handed to us in the first place by our society, whatever transformations we may bring on them later." The critical fact is that the vocabularies of religious experience "are never those simply of an individual." Inner religious experience needs a common vocabulary by which it can be discerned as authentic, shared, and then strengthened. For Taylor, the idea of purely subjective experience is conceptually absurd;

3. Another example: Bruxy Cavey of the "Meeting House," based in Toronto and Oakville, Ontario, has published a book in which he speaks of the "end of religion," and he markets his church to those who "aren't into church."

there must be some kind of theological formulation on one hand, and shared communal experience on the other. When we have faith, we have faith in something, and that something is both identified and transmitted by the community and actualized in common practices.[4] In other words, it is conceptually absurd to say, "For those who want to be spiritual without being religious." It is simply not possible. All authentic inner experience will find expression within religious dogmas and shared rituals.

In his reflections on Taylor's work, Robert Bellah puts it this way: "Personal religion, then, is not in any ultimate sense personal, but is the product of a certain kind of society, which, like all other kinds of society, imposes itself on individuals."[5] True religious experience is certainly personal and subjective, but it is also necessarily social and communal, and the social-communal is necessarily institutional. Authentic religious experience is always both/and: personal and subjective, and institutional and sacramental.

The two are inseparable. Religious experience is located within the human heart. William James was right, that authentic religious experience is found in the interior movements of the human heart and that this is where we find passion and faith. We can certainly affirm that if it is *not* interior and subjective, it means nothing; the exterior forms become nothing but structures, empty rituals, relics perhaps of a previous dynamic spirituality, but having no meaning today or capacity to sustain faith.

But in speaking of religion as, essentially, a matter of the heart and no more, James created a split, an unnecessary and potentially devastating bifurcation. Religion today has become largely personal and private. Sustained commitments to the church are few. Even if people "go to church," they go as consumers, then move on as soon as this particular church no longer meets their "felt needs." Religion has merely become another item for sale at the mall, so much so that some church groups have actually sought to echo the mall in their church architecture! And the forms of worship in these situations are consistent with the ethos of the mall.

Even when contemporary spirituality finds expression in communal practices and worship forms, in twentieth-century evangelical circles worship is dominated by songs about the personal, the subjective, the expressive, with little if any theological content. All that seemingly counts, if one is to have a worship event that will draw the young and will enable one's church to grow, is a series of songs that have one single bottom line: they are about "me" and about "my" feelings.

Taylor notes that the Jamesian view of religion negates the Catholic appreciation of the church as a "sacramental communion," a necessary means

4. Taylor, *Varieties of Religion Today*, 26–27.
5. Robert Bellah, review of Charles Taylor, *Varieties of Religion Today*, *Christian Century*, May 22–29, 2002.

by which the life of God is experienced. If religion is both interior and institutional, subjective and communal, it is communal specifically in its sacramental actions. Its sacramental actions make it communal. And so, Taylor observes, Protestantism in particular was vulnerable to the emphasis on personal religion because it had already emphasized the priority of the Word in the liturgy (and deemphasized the sacramental). In other words, Protestant (and by implication evangelical) forms of religious experience, by emphasizing the "Word" in worship, have already leaned strongly toward interiority. They insist that the sacramental is optional not essential; by leaning away from the sacramental toward the subjective, Protestants have, perhaps unwittingly, reinforced the split—even if this is done collectively!

Could it be that Taylor's Catholic sensibilities raise a question that all Christians need to appreciate? If the split between interior subjectivity and external forms (rituals, sacraments, shared practices) is to be resisted, will it be resisted not so much through Protestant structures and proclivities, but specifically through the Catholic insistence on the sacramental? It is so easy for Word-oriented Christian traditions to just go along with the Jamesian view and unwittingly affirm the interior and subjective, even when it is done collectively. So much Protestant and evangelical worship is personal and subjective, even when the songs are sung together and the preaching is heard together. Nothing can cut this nerve, this attempt at pure subjectivity, quite like the sacraments: baptism and the Lord's Supper.

It is not enough to just do religious things together to make the experience communal. We can sing the songs and hear the Word, and even though we are together, it is still no more than subjective expression. It is not true religion, not truly shared, and most critically, if it is not shared, it is not transforming. Each one is on their own, singing the songs and hearing the Word. Though the connections made are no doubt meaningful, they are no more significant than those one would find in a social club. Thus Taylor calls for common faith that is *sacramental*. Rightly so, as we shall see.

Acts 2:38 Revisited

Conversion is a complex experience. Elsewhere I have suggested that it is helpful to think of conversion as having seven distinct threads, each of which is essential to making a Christian conversion truly Christian.[6]

Four of these were identified as the internal actions of the Christian convert:

• The intellectual component points to belief and the change of mind.

6. Gordon T. Smith, *Beginning Well: Christian Conversion and Authentic Transformation* (Downers Grove, IL: InterVarsity, 2001).

- The penitential involves repentance and deliberately turning from sin to righteousness.
- The affective includes the intentional appropriation of God's forgiveness and also the experience of joy.
- The volitional leads to the reorientation of one's life to live in the truth and in intentional response to the call of God.

The other three dimensions of a Christian conversion were identified as supporting and enabling a person to come to faith, yet they are still inherent to the experience:

- The sacramental notably includes water baptism.
- The charismatic means the conscious appropriation of the gift of the Spirit.
- The communal views conversion as necessarily including incorporation into the faith community.

Each is part of what it means to come to faith in Christ such that there is a good beginning, a good foundation for the experience of being a Christian.

In the chapters that follow, I will give focused attention to two of these elements: repentance (or the penitential) and baptism (the sacramental). I do so in a way that takes account of the philosophical consideration of the nature of religious experience, which gives us a fascinating lens by which to view the simple statement and call of Acts 2:38: "Repent, and be baptized."

Charles Taylor's response to James is not some new and novel way to think about religious faith and experience. Rather, Taylor is actually affirming ancient wisdom that is deeply biblical and consistent with the nature of authentic human and religious experience. It is both/and, or it is not at all. In the end, the faith community will test these insights against the witness of the Scriptures. Yet, could it be that what Taylor is talking about is found, simply and forcefully, in this verse? The call is there: if you want to know the forgiveness of God, then it is both/and. Repent. And be baptized.

Could it be that in these two acts, repentance and baptism, we have the hub or locus of a Christian conversion? Could it be that this is the twofold pivot on which the whole experience hangs, and by which the experience becomes a true and good beginning to the Christian life and ultimately to the experience of the transforming grace of God? The evangelical community recoils at this suggestion that it is both. Yet in our secular, post-Christian, postmodern, pluralist social context, we urgently need to reconsider what it means to speak of a Christian conversion. This reconsideration will take us back to the ancient text, and we will find guidance for our day. When it comes to conversion, the biblical witness is but an echo of the fundamental nature of authentic religious experience.

Yes, there is more to conversion than repentance and baptism, but philosophical reflections on the nature of religious experience and the simple witness of Acts 2:38 suggest that something pivotal happens in these two acts. Thus *both* merit our consideration and reflection; I devote a chapter to each. Yet, while considered separately, what I hope to demonstrate is that for the New Testament they were, in the end, inseparable, even though in the two chapters that follow, they will be considered on their own.

Here is the thesis: If we are going to truly treat conversion seriously, as a deep turning that in turn establishes a person for growth toward the transformation of the whole person—then we need to embrace the biblical understanding of conversion that has, as its two benchmarks, the interior experience of repentance and the exterior experience of baptism. These two have the capacity to be the pivot on which the conversion experience hangs and from which we then live as Christians. Repentance is the heart of the matter, virtually equivalent to conversion: conversion, as we shall see, is fundamentally a matter of a turning of the heart, a reorientation of the inner person toward Christ and toward the reign of Christ. Baptism will be presented as the necessary counterpart to repentance, the outward expression of this inward reality. As Ambrose, the bishop of Milan (d. 397), is said to have observed, there are two conversions for those who come into the church: "there are water and tears: the water of Baptism and the tears of repentance."[7]

But more needs to be said. If it is true that one comes to faith by first entering into fellowship with a faith community—if one indeed needs to "belong before one will believe"—then it follows that what is needed is for people to join themselves with communities that have two defining marks. One of the two marks is *penitential*. They are communities where the Word is preached as the announcement of the kingdom and the people embrace this Word; they live out what it means to respond to the call "Repent, for the kingdom of heaven has come near" (Matt. 4:17). They are continually seeking the Word that announces the kingdom, reveals the kingdom, and calls them to live in light of the inbreaking of the kingdom. Thus they are continually turning, they are penitential, they are seeking fresh alignment with the kingdom.

The other mark is *sacramental*. These communities will be marked by the fact that they take baptism seriously; indeed, they take the whole sacramental life of the church seriously.

The evidence that persons are truly penitential and sacramental is, at the very least, that they live forgiven and live in the life of the Spirit. For, as Peter

---

7. See the United States Roman Catholic Catechism, par. 1429, http://www.scborromeo.org/ccc/p2s2c2a4.htm, quoting Ambrose, *Epistles* 41.12, http://www.ccel.org/p/pearse/morefathers/ambrose_letters_05_letters41_50.htm#Letter41.

in Acts 2:38 puts it, "Repent, and be baptized . . . so that your sins may be forgiven, . . . and you will receive the gift of the Holy Spirit." I say "at the very least" for there will surely be other marks or signs, including Acts 2:42, their devotion to teaching, fellowship, and the prayers. But the energy of an authentic faith community will surely be one in which this is a central dynamic: a deep awareness of the gospel and that we are forgiven people, and an equally marked awareness that we live in the grace and power of the Spirit.

The Means of Conversion

As mentioned, I will consider at length the two sides of the dual act of conversion: both repentance and baptism. But it is important to pause and insist that in a very real sense, these two acts do not convert; they are the *acts* of conversion, but not the *means* of conversion. They are the essential human responses to the offer of salvation, but they do not "save." Often evangelicals want to insist that baptism does not save us. Fine! But neither does repentance! We must, in a sense, insist that there is no human action that in and of itself is salvific. Rather, both are in response to the saving initiative of God; both, together, are the pivot of the human act by which one might know the salvation of God. What I hope to demonstrate is that both are essential. And yet, they are still a *response*.

Response to what? They are the act of response to the salvation offered by God, in Christ, through the ministry of the Spirit. But, more specifically, what is the *means* by which the salvation of God is offered? In reply, we turn to the theological tradition that more than any other has sought to insist on the appropriate response to the question: the insistence of the Reformers, and particularly John Calvin, that the means of grace and of the salvation of God is Word and Spirit.

But in consideration of this principle, we begin not so much with Calvin as with the day of Pentecost itself, with the events that lead up to Acts 2:38. It is no coincidence that what sets the stage for the call "Repent, and be baptized" is the twofold event that precedes it in Acts 2: the outpouring of the Spirit and the preaching of the Word. This suggests that the means of God's salvation is God's very self: The Father is surely the originator of the salvation of God, Christ is the mediator, and the one who executes this salvation in the world and in the lives of converts is the Third Person of the Trinity, the Holy Spirit. John 14–16, for example, could not be clearer: Jesus returns to the Father and sends another, who is then described as the very one by whom the purposes of Father and Son would be effected in the world.

Yet the Scriptures continually testify to the role of the Scriptures—read, taught, preached, received, and lived. It is not the Bible as letters on a page, but as *living* Word, the Word of God. All things are created by the word: Genesis 1 witnesses to the marvel that God spoke, and all things came into being. Similarly, all things are redeemed and made whole by this same word.

Thus in James we read of being born again "by the word of truth" (1:18). And in 1 Peter 1:23–25 we have a similar idea, the word as "living and enduring" and the very means, "seed," by which new life emerges. It is not merely the Word here in 1 Peter; it is the Word "preached," which again is a reminder that we are not speaking here of letters on a page, as though the Bible in and of itself is "living," but specifically of the Word as preached—*broadcast*, to build on the image of Jesus in Mark 4:1–9, where he speaks of the seed and the sower.

As we speak of preaching, we are reminded that this proclamation is of necessity located within the life and witness of the faith community and, in particular, within the church's liturgy (worship). This is most apparent in Colossians 3:14–16, where the reference is clearly to worship with the mutual call to live "in harmony with one another" and sing songs, hymns, and spiritual songs "with gratitude." As the gathered people, in worship, we have the invitation to "let the word of Christ dwell in [us] richly."

In other words, while we can and must never discount the significance of private reading and study, it is clear that the primary reference or intent is that the Word would richly indwell the faith community. This is what makes the church the church; she is a faith community where the Word is broadcast, heard, received, and lived. The church becomes the living embodiment of the Word; thereby the church is a sacramental entity, living out the life of the kingdom, to which the Scriptures call the world.

What must be recognized is that the Word does not dwell richly among the people of God apart from the ministry of the Spirit. It is by the Spirit that the preached Word is redemptive. This is a recurring theme of the whole of the Scriptures. John 14–16 provides the words of Jesus calling his disciples to remain in him as he remains in them (15:4), and this is all made possible specifically by the sending of the Spirit. It is by the Spirit that the words of Jesus will remain in the disciples. Jesus is stepping away, but he is sending the Spirit, who will remain with them and will be their teacher (16:13).

This interplay between Word and Spirit is demonstrated in the way that the apostle Paul speaks of the conversion experience of the Thessalonians. His description of their journey to faith includes this fascinating line: "For we know, brothers and sisters beloved by God, that he has chosen you, because our message of the gospel came to you not in word only, but also in power and in the Holy Spirit and with full conviction; just as you know what kind of persons we proved to be among you for your sake" (1 Thess. 1:4–5). It is the Spirit who brings about the transforming work of God in the lives of the Thessalonians, but we cannot speak of the Spirit's work without reference to the Scriptures. I need to stress: this is not an appeal for biblicism; it is rather a recognition that the transforming work of the Spirit is intimately linked with the vital place of the Scriptures in the life of the faith community. What enables us to know the transforming power of Word and Spirit is precisely that the grace of Word and Spirit is located within the faith community. It is in the context of the church and particularly the worship of the church. This is the venue of the Word/Spirit, proclaimed, lived, and embodied.

Further, the biblical text cannot be read or preached without reference to some interpretive grid or hermeneutic—not merely the exegetical and theological bent of the preacher, but of the whole community. Thus the genius of great preaching is that each text is preached in light of two things: (1) the grand narrative of redemptive history—creation, fall, and redemption; and (2) the new covenant against the backdrop of the old, so that we only preach both Testaments, each in the light of the other, and that we appreciate how this text that is being preached enables us to enter into the kingdom purposes of God.

We truly do this only when the defining interpretive grid for preaching is the ancient creeds of the church. When preaching is nothing more than verses to substantiate some idea or piece of advice (biblical principles for how to be a good father, perhaps), or when preaching is nothing more than the piece-by-piece, phrase-by-phrase dissecting of the passage of Scripture, or when the interpretive grid is Jungian psychology and preaching is public therapy—it is possible that something of benefit is passed on. But we should not confuse any of these with preaching the Word—the living Christ, who is revealed and known through a dynamic and living ancient text that is read and preached with reference to the ancient creeds and the ongoing witness of the Spirit through the experience of the church. Those creeds anchor our preaching in the triunity of God and the dual nature of Christ, in the confessional heritage of the church.

The Word is transforming when it is received, and it is received by hearing. But it takes root through the twofold response of repentance and the sacramental actions of the church. Thus when the Word is proclaimed—preached or broadcast—we hear and respond through an interior alignment of mind, heart, and will with the gospel (repentance). And the necessary complement to the Word is baptism, for the new convert. And for the Christian, it is the Lord's Supper. Baptism or the Lord's Supper without the Word makes no sense; they are empty, without content. The content is the Word. And yet, the Word without baptism or the Word without the Lord's Supper, while still good in itself, is missing the element or piece that anchors the Word in the hearts and lives of the hearers. Thus in evangelism, baptism always follows the Word and is the means by which the Word is not merely heard but also received. For the maturing Christian, the same principle applies: the Lord's Supper follows the Word. When congregations arbitrarily place the Lord's Supper before the Word, the holy meal is empty of meaning, but when there is word without sacrament, the danger is that we neglect the very act that may well enable the church not only to hear but also precisely to receive and be transformed by this Word.

In all of this, the means of conversion and transformation is Word and Spirit. We can only consider the contours of conversion and the vital place of repentance and baptism if this principle is sustained.

Justified by Faith

What about faith? For Christians who are heirs to the Reformation and to the Great evangelical Awakenings of the eighteenth century, it is simply impossible to speak of conversion and the salvation of God except through Pauline categories—as expressed in the works of the magisterial Reformers. We thus speak of salvation by grace alone and through faith alone: *sola gratia, sola fide*. Using the phrase from the Pauline corpus, one is "justified by faith" (as in Rom. 3:28). Typically this emphasis on faith is pitted against "works," with the insistence that salvation comes only through the expression of heartfelt faith and not through works of the law. Often it is assumed that this was the problem with the so-called Judaizers, who, it is said, sought a works righteousness rather than a righteousness based on faith. Further, many evangelicals think that the Reformers mounted this campaign in favor of faith against the backdrop of a works-oriented Roman Catholic piety.

As recognized in the exposition of the Letter to the Ephesians, faith does have primacy. Though the typical characterizations of the Judaizers of Paul's day or the Roman Catholic Church of Luther and Calvin's day may need to be challenged, what we can affirm is that indeed faith is the vital ingredient in the response of the believer to the offer of God's salvation. On this, Paul could hardly be clearer. The apostle's portrayal of the human predicament is a vivid depiction of the impossibility of human achievement or self-salvation. God alone is the Savior. And the act of God in Christ is one that calls for trust: a confidence in the work of God in Christ for humanity. And this trust—faith, confidence—is precisely the only possible response to the initiative of God. Only as we trust God, in Christ, can we hope to know the salvation of God.

What then of this insistence on the need for a conversion of repentance and baptism? First, at no point can we think of either baptism or repentance as "works," as some kind of human achievement. They are but an act of response, comparable perhaps to the two hands held out to receive a gift, the open hands of a beggar asking for food. Second, when we speak of repentance, it should be evident that this is the quintessential expression of faith. Faith is the act of trust, of turning from self-dependence to dependence on God, to turn from a life oriented toward self to one that is turned toward God. Faith means nothing if it does not represent this radical turning—in other words, repentance. Though faith and repentance are distinct, they are inseparable.

There is no faith without repentance, and faith necessarily finds expression in repentance.

Third, baptism, in similar fashion, is but an expression of trust and confidence in the God of our salvation. When Peter is asked in Acts 2, "What should we do?" he is not preaching a different gospel from that of Paul when he responds with "Repent, and be baptized" rather than "Have faith in God." Rather, the deep assumption is that the only possible response is to trust the Word that has been preached, to trust in the One who has been preached, to believe the good news, that there is indeed hope for humankind. Peter's point is that if one trusts, if one has faith, then the natural and necessary expression of this faith is repentance and baptism. Both repentance and baptism must be understood in this light.

7

The Penitential Dimension
of Conversion

When it comes to the fundamental nature of a Christian conversion, to defining what it is, at it most basic and elemental state, nothing quite captures this as the word *repentance*. Indeed, repentance is so much at the heart of the matter that in many respects it is virtually synonymous with conversion. One could almost say that to convert is to repent. Yet it is not as simple as this. Conversion involves more and is a more complex experience. Further, repentance is so integral to the whole of the Christian life, beyond conversion, that we want to avoid any suggestion that repentance is only about the *initial* experience of coming to faith in Christ. Thus conversion is more than repentance, and repentance is more than conversion. Yet, when we fold back the layers of this complex experience of coming to faith in Christ, we find that repentance is the pivot on which the experience of conversion rests. Baptism, as we shall see in the next chapter, is its necessary counterpart. But for now, consider that the heart and soul of conversion is repentance.

If repentance were so central to conversion (and thus to the whole of the Christian life), one would assume that repentance is therefore central to the way in which Christians speak of conversion and to how they approach the whole question of evangelism. Naturally, it would be evident in the worship of Christians, including evangelical Christians. But such is not the case. To the contrary, the practice of confession has virtually disappeared from the worship practices of evangelical Christians, and the language is reserved for only the most severe judgments that Christians make about non-Christians. It is no

This chapter is adapted from an earlier publication: Gordon T. Smith and Mark J. Boda, "Confession as Essential Practice: An Evangelical Perspective," *Conversations* (Spring 2005): 43–48. For a more comprehensive discussion of this topic, see Mark J. Boda and Gordon T. Smith, eds., *Repentance in Christian Theology* (Collegeville, MN: Liturgical Press, 2006).

longer central and vital in the worship and piety of most of the Christians of this theological and spiritual tradition.[1]

The reasons that one hears for this development are interesting and instructive. Some are more pragmatic in their reasons. They insist that the church needs to be more "seeker oriented" in its worship, which requires the removal of such "discouraging" acts as prayers of confession. Confession is a bit of a "downer"; it is not necessary for the spiritual life and may actually undermine a healthy and positive self-image. These evangelicals would then naturally dispense with such things as Lent and perhaps even the observance of Good Friday in an effort to get to the celebration of the resurrection, the "real" focus of the Christian faith, the "positive" side of the gospel.

Others, though, are more *theological* in their reflections. They say they have dispensed with the practice of confession because they see it to be a violation of the gospel. The argument, put simply, is that we need to confess our sins when we *become* Christians, but not afterward. Why? Because, they say, in Christ a person's sins are forgiven, past, present, and future. These preachers proclaim that to confess regularly is to "nail Christ to the cross again and again." Rather, they urge their followers to "live in the forgiveness they have already received."

Both of these may be understandable responses to the ways in which confession has been practiced and understood—either by other traditions, such as Roman Catholicism, or even by earlier forms of evangelical practice. Even so, to dispense with confession is to lose out on one of the most vital practices of the Christian life. We only truly sustain repentance and confession for conversion if we appreciate that conversion is fundamentally an act by which we enter into the penitential life. There is a deep continuity between conversion and the whole of the Christian life. Repentance is integral to conversion, but this is so because it is integral to the whole of what it means to be a Christian. Confession and repentance are not merely episodic components of the spiritual life—such as when one feels that one has "sinned" and needs to ask for forgiveness, however legitimate that may be. Instead, the penitential is part of the fabric of the spiritual life and is its very rhythm. It is inherent in what it means to be a Christian.

A Scarlet Thread through the Biblical Witness

If repentance is integral to Christian conversion, then we assuredly need clarity about its meaning: what does it mean to repent? In particular, what is the place of repentance in the genesis of the Christian life, in the experience of coming to faith in Christ? Acts 2:38 suggests that repentance was viewed as integral

---

1. For both repentance and baptism, I will address these questions with particular reference to the evangelical theological and spiritual tradition because it is my own context, but also as a case study of the issues being considered.

to Christian experience, at least to conversion, but certainly the contours of conversion also become integral to the experience of being a Christian.

What was the *content* of this call for the apostle Peter when he spoke these words? What did it mean for him to call for repentance? Our response is surely shaped by a consideration of two critical sources: (1) the religious heritage as present to us in the Hebrew Scriptures—the Torah, the Prophets, and the Psalms, indeed in the whole Old Testament; and (2) the words of Jesus, and what he intended when he proclaimed that his hearers should repent, for the kingdom of God was near, at hand, indeed already upon them (Mark 1:15). Jesus's call is that with the kingdom at hand, they are to repent and believe the good news—suggesting that repentance is inherent in belief.

The theme of repentance runs like a scarlet thread through the Scriptures, integral to the dialectic of sin and redemption that arises with the events of Genesis 3 and continues to Revelation 22. This is highlighted, for example, by the sacrificial system. While Christians typically view sacrifice in the old covenant as a "covering" of sin, it is important to highlight that sacrifices were offered out of a penitential disposition. The word typically translated "guilty" (*'asham*) is better translated "feel guilty," suggesting a disposition, specifically the remorse that would follow a verbal admission of guilt. This is showcased on a communal level in the yearly rhythm of the Day of Atonement, when the high priest entered the holy of holies and made atonement for the sins of the people. The ritual on that day included confession of the people's sins (Lev. 16, esp. vv. 6, 11, 21). It is not surprising that such confession is ultimately linked to the agenda for renewal after the anticipated apostasy of Israel, which would bring on exile (Lev. 26:39–41). The people are told that after they had been disciplined, penitential confession arising from a humble heart would be essential to their return to the land and their renewal as the people of God.

The perspective within the sacrificial system is complemented by the book of Deuteronomy, so closely linked with the conclusion of Moses' ministry among Israel and the delivery of his final sermon on the plains of Moab. Israel is poised to enter the promised land, with its many blessings but also dangers. Here Moses calls the people to the core values of covenant relationship and renewal. In similar fashion to Leviticus 26, in Deuteronomy 4 and 30 the people are told that there is a great possibility that one day they will falter and turn away from God, placing their affections on idols. If they do so, God will discipline them, scattering them among the nations. The people, however, are offered a pattern of response: they are to "seek the LORD your God," "search after him with all your heart and soul," "return to the LORD your God, and ... obey him" (Deut. 4:29; 30:1–2). This response is made possible because "God is a merciful God," who "will neither abandon you nor destroy you; he will not forget the covenant with your ancestors" (Deut. 4:31; 30:3).

This twofold perspective on repentance (the priestly perspective of the sacrificial system as complemented by the book of Deuteronomy) is foundational for the perspective on repentance developed in the remainder of the Old Testament. One could even say that at the heart of the ministry of the prophets is the call to "turn" (*shub*). It describes the prophet's message to both Israel and Judah in 2 Kings 17, a passage that recounts the reasons for the exile of the northern kingdom: "Turn from your evil ways and keep my commandments and my statutes, in accordance with all the law that I commanded your ancestors and that I sent to you by my servants the prophets" (v. 13). In the latter prophets, this regular use of the verb "turn" (*shub*) is a constant call back to covenant relationship. Superb examples of this are Hosea's invitation in 6:1, "Come, let us return to the LORD," and Jeremiah's cry in 4:1, "'If you will return, O Israel, return to me,' declares the LORD" (NIV). It was particularly a call to repentance within the liturgical life of God's people. This is evident when we read that God's rejection of their offerings was not a rejection of the offering in itself but rather because their sacrifices were brought without the penitence of faith.

The covenantal character of this cry is exemplified in these two prophetic citations (above): the call of repentance is not primarily focused on behavior, but rather on the relationship with this covenant God. The same emphasis is echoed in one of the final prophetic voices of the Old Testament, the prophet Zechariah, in his summary of the message of the prophets: "Return to me, says the LORD of hosts, and I will return to you" (Zech. 1:3). This surely has implications for our behavior (our obedience), as Zechariah immediately reminds us: "Turn from your evil ways and your evil practices" (v. 4 NIV). But repentance is fundamentally covenantal, *relational*; it is a turning to God.

In other words, the primary point of reference for conversion is a covenant relationship. As Terence Fretheim observes, the call to repentance "stands in the wake of a strong reiteration of the unconditional promises to David ([see 1 Kings] 8:22–26), followed by reference to the promises given to Moses (8:51–53)." Then Fretheim goes further and, building on the work of Walter Brueggemann, observes that the call to repentance is always governed by the faithfulness and graciousness of God. Thus, human repentance is possible because of God's promise. But while it is made possible, as Fretheim observes, it is still a gift that actually fosters rather than negates human responsibility. The gift of repentance is precisely an invitation to the people of God to confess their own unfaithfulness and their own part in the failure to sustain the covenant.[2]

The call to repentance is so fundamental to the prophetic message that it comes as no surprise that the New Testament begins with the ministry of a prophet named John calling the people of God to repentance (Matt. 3:2, 11;

---

2. Terence E. Fretheim, "Repentance in the Former Prophets," in *Repentance in Christian Theology*, ed. Mark J. Boda and Gordon T. Smith (Collegeville, MN: Liturgical Press, 2006), 32.

Mark 1:4; Luke 3:3), as the people await the restoration promised by the Law and the Prophets. So also Christ Jesus is a preacher of repentance (Matt. 4:17; Mark 1:15; Luke 5:32; 13:3, 5; 15:7), a sign that his intention is to usher in the promised kingdom of God, but that the arrival of such a restoration must be preceded by repentance. Indeed, a people does repent, recognizing Jesus Christ as the Lord, whose promised coming would be inaugurated by repentance.

N. T. Wright points out that this call is placed within the context of the way in which the prophets (and John the Baptist) called the covenant people to return to their first love. He observes that in this setting the call to repentance spoke of a "turning to YHWH which would result in restoration, return from exile."[3] It is, then, an eschatological call—and yes, it is also a political call: as Wright insists, it includes a call to believe in Jesus and abandon all other ways by which the "kingdom" of Israel might be restored.[4] So Jesus is calling Israel to repentance and doing so within the prophetic tradition.

Personal repentance, then, as Wright observes, is but derivative of this larger eschatological call for national repentance.[5] But then we must see that this personal act of repentance is located within the experience of the whole of God's covenant people. The primary agenda of Jesus is the announcement of the kingdom. He is a prophet at this point more than he is an evangelist. He is not calling for individuals to give up their "rotten" ways and repent; he is calling for Israel, as Israel, to repent, in light of the inbreaking reign of God. Thus repentance is not merely an act of dealing with one's recent sins; it is first and foremost an act of identification with Jesus as the hope of the world.

From the prophets through John the Baptist and then Jesus, we come to the early church and discover that repentance was the essential component of the gospel cry of the early church as they proclaimed Jesus, not only in Jerusalem and Judea, but also to the ends of the earth (Luke 24:47; Acts 2:38; 3:19; 8:22; 17:30; 26:20; cf. Mark 6:12). Furthermore, for this community of God inaugurated in the Old Testament and now enduring in the New Testament, repentance was an essential rhythm to life in covenant relationship with the Lord. Such repentance was always a response to divine justice as well as grace, qualities expressed climactically in and through the death of Christ on the cross.

As in the Old Testament, such a rhythm of repentance for God's people was to flow from an awareness that God is both just and merciful. The emphasis in the letters of Revelation is clearly on the justice of God's wrath (2:5, 16, 21, 22; 3:3, 19), but the divine voice reminds us in the final letter that "I reprove and discipline those whom I love. Be earnest, therefore, and repent" (3:19). Those who respond have the privilege of covenant intimacy with the Lord:

3. N. T. Wright, *Jesus and the Victory of God*, Christian Origins and the Question of God 2 (Minneapolis: Fortress, 1996), 248.
4. Ibid., 251.
5. Ibid., 256.

"Listen! I am standing at the door, knocking; if you hear my voice and open the door, I will come in to you and eat with you, and you with me" (3:20). In similar fashion the apostle Paul mixes emphasis on God's justice and mercy to motivate believers in Rome to repentance: "Or do you despise the riches of his kindness and forbearance and patience? Do you not realize that God's kindness is meant to lead you to repentance? But by your hard and impenitent heart you are storing up wrath for yourself on the day of wrath, when God's righteous judgment will be revealed" (Rom. 2:4–5). This same balance can be discerned in the invitation of 1 John 1:9: "If we confess our sins, he who is faithful and just will forgive us our sins and cleanse us from all unrighteousness."

I notice two things in particular arising out of this overview of the biblical canon. First, confession and repentance are integral to the liturgical routines and rhythms of God's people. It was not merely a crisis moment or event; it was, rather, a practice that was located within the worship of the faith community. I naturally conclude that in similar fashion, the faith community under the new covenant lives with integrity and provides a setting for those who "seek" only if this community, the church, is a penitential event. The church, to be the church, is a penitential community, for whom repentance and confession are part of the defining rhythms of our lives, authenticating our witness, our invitation to the world. The invitation to join the faith community through conversion is an experience that at its heart is the act of repentance.

Second, the content of this repentance is a personal and corporate alignment with the reign of God in the world, through Christ. This is the message of the Old Testament prophets. If our preaching is to lie in continuity with the prophets—as was that of Peter and the apostles—it will mean that the call to confession as we cultivate a penitential disposition is not something either episodic or incidental but central to the proclamation of the gospel and the whole counsel of God.

This preaching will be an explicit affirmation of the priority of divine initiative, grace, and love; it is a call first and foremost into a covenant relationship with God, a relationship based not on fear but on love. Further, it will be a call to live in response to the Christ event: the life, death, and resurrection of Jesus, but also and specifically the reality of the ascension, so that the faith community is continually asking and seeking to live congruently with the reign of Christ. The capacity to see this and feel it, to sense the lack of alignment and the enabling to be aligned, is given by the Spirit. It is the Spirit who convicts of sin and calls us and empowers the church to live a life consistent with the reality of the ascension.

Thus evangelism is, at its heart, a call and an invitation to enter into this covenant relationship and into a life—evident most obviously in the liturgical rhythms of the church—of grace filled with the reign of Christ and continually in alignment with that reign.

The Evangelical Spiritual Heritage

The clear biblical call to repentance is, in turn, matched by the call we hear through the wisdom of the evangelical spiritual heritage. With the Protestant Reformation, Martin Luther and John Calvin reacted to the Roman Catholic practice of penance and any suggestion that confession somehow makes satisfaction for sin, but they then also insisted that true faith in Christ will always be demonstrated in repentance. For Luther, repentance was the essential means by which a Christian would enter into the grace of baptism, the means by which we renew the faith experience represented by our baptism. While rejecting penance, he still held that repentance is necessary for the spiritual life. Calvin made an even stronger call to repentance, insisting that repentance is not only the fruit of faith but also the *necessary* fruit of faith. Without the inclusion of repentance, for Calvin, "any discussion concerning faith will be meager and defective, and indeed almost useless. . . . Repentance not only always follows faith, but is produced by it."[6] The call to a faith that produces repentance is reflected not only in the way in which one enters into Christian faith; it is also integral to the entire Christian experience, both as disposition and as a practice that we are obliged to cultivate during the whole course of our lives.

Evangelicals are particularly indebted to the wisdom of the Puritans, on one hand, and to John and Charles Wesley, on the other, and this perspective is complemented by the spiritual wisdom of the Anabaptist traditions. The Puritans called for a "mind of repentance." As one Puritan preacher put it, "The vigor and power of spiritual life is dependent on mortification of sin," reflecting the words of the Westminster Confession: "Repentance is of such necessity to all sinners, that none may expect pardon without it" (15.3), and, "It is every man's duty to endeavour to repent of his particular sins, particularly" (15.5). Indeed, for the Puritans the Christian life is a penitential life. A genuine life of faith is evident in a penitential habit of heart, with both the disposition of contriteness and the practice of repentance.

J. I. Packer has ably sustained the Puritan vision of the Christian life, which necessarily includes this dimension, the penitential. In an extended section on spiritual maturity and growth in holiness, Packer insists that (what he calls) "growing downward" is indispensable. The Christian's growth in faith, hope, and love depends on what Packer calls "a life of habitual repentance, as a discipline integral to healthy holy living." He affirms the language of Luther, whom he quotes as saying, "The whole life of believers should be one of repentance."[7]

6. John Calvin, *Institutes of the Christian Religion*, trans. Henry Beveridge (reprint, Grand Rapids: Eerdmans, 1979), 3.3.1.
7. J. I. Packer, *Rediscovering Holiness* (Ann Arbor, MI: Servant Publications, 1992), 121; citing thesis 1 of Luther's Ninety-Five Theses (1517); the next two in-text references are to Packer's cited work.

As with the Puritan spiritual heritage, Packer's call to "continual" repentance is based on a particular understanding of the character of sin. It is the appreciation of the deadliness of sin that undergirds the call to the penitential. Sin is viewed to be an affront to the holiness of God, a violation of the creation and the Creator. It is rejection of the goodness of God, arising from ingratitude. Thus the Christian, Packer insists, instinctively longs to pray with the psalmist that God would search the heart and lead in the way of life (Ps. 139). Packer uses the image of the gardener, who must always be about the task of weeding, knowing that what urgently needs to be eradicated is not only the surface greenery but also the root system (135–37). In so doing, we attend to the health of the soul, attentively viewing spiritual health as a gift from God that we do not take for granted but tend with care as the garden of our souls (149).

The brothers John Wesley (1703–91) and Charles Wesley (1707–88) emphasized that the Christian lives with an assurance of forgiveness, a deep, heartfelt confidence in God's acceptance. But this is not a once-and-for-all experience. John Wesley observed that repentance and faith are commonly thought to be only the "gate of religion," only a time-bound disposition concurrent with coming to Christian faith. He reports that some Christians appeal to the line in Hebrews 6:1 (KJV), "not laying again the foundation of repentance from dead works."[8] Wesley insisted, however, that while faith and repentance are certainly needed in coming to Christ (the experience of justification and regeneration), "repentance and faith are fully as necessary in order for our continuance and growth in grace."[9] He declared that though sin does not "reign" in the Christian believer, it nevertheless "remains" in the heart of the new Christian, thus necessitating ongoing repentance. New believers are always prone to love "the creature more than the Creator" (cf. Rom. 1:25 KJV), to be "lovers of pleasure rather than lovers of God" (2 Tim. 3:4 KJV), and thus comes the need to be watchful and to guard over our life. For Wesley, just as "sin remains in our hearts, . . . so it cleaves to all our words and actions."[10] He uses the image of sin as sickness, with ailing persons desperate for healing, and states that unless "we are sensible of our disease, it admits no cure."[11]

John Wesley especially emphasized that in repentance the Christian believer must give particular attention to pride: "We may therefore set it down as an undoubted truth, that covetousness, together with pride, self-will, and anger, remain in the hearts even of them that are justified." He goes on to speak of

---

8. John Wesley, "The Repentance of Believers," sermon 14 in *First Series of Sermons*, vol. 5 of *The Works of John Wesley*, 3rd ed. (Grand Rapids: Baker Books, 1986), 156–70 (subsequent references are to the section and paragraph numbers of this sermon).

9. Ibid., intro., par. 1.

10. Ibid., sec. 1, pars. 10 and 11.

11. Ibid., intro., par. 1.

the ways in which pride infiltrates all our actions, and how fear or timidity leads us to sins of omission, the failure to do what we know we should do.[12]

For the Anabaptists, there are many sources to which we could turn, but one that is familiar to many Mennonites would be Menno Simons's exposition of Psalm 25, written in the form of a highly autobiographical penitential prayer. It is noteworthy that what motivates the penitent is not so much the terror of hell and death as the goodness of God. Simons, the penitent, deeply aware of his own failures, cries out to God, "Accept me in your grace and give me your mercy, blessing, and confidence, Lord, for the sake of your own goodness," and later, "I do come before your throne of mercy, for I know that you are gracious and good. You do not desire that sinners should die but that they repent and have life."[13] For Menno, the goodness and mercy of God summon forth a profound longing expressed through the imagery of sickness and healing. As in John Wesley's sermons, Christ is the healer. When Menno despairs before God of his wanton failures and error-prone life, he recognizes that "your word alone can heal all things. . . . I seek and desire this grace, for it alone is the medicament which can heal my sick soul."[14]

All three of these variations on the movement, then, are insistent on the vital place of the penitential in the Christian life. What catches one's attention is the motive for repentance: one's grief at having violated a relationship of love and, second, the desire for healing. At its best, the evangelical spiritual tradition affirmed that the Christian lives in humble awareness of the goodness of God, who unfailingly calls the believer from a disposition and pattern of behavior that is inconsistent with the Christian confession. A distinctive strength of the movement was its stress on the need for honest self-appraisal and understanding, and that the Christian has the capacity to take personal responsibility for one's life.

The Recovery of Confession

From both the biblical witness and the wisdom gleaned from the evangelical spiritual heritage, what strikes us is that although repentance is not synonymous with conversion, it is so integral that the Scriptures often speak of conversion through calling for repentance. Further, just as there is no conversion without repentance, even so repentance is vital to our spiritual growth. The Bible and

12. Ibid., sec 1, pars. 9 and 14.

13. Daniel Liechty, ed. and trans., *Early Anabaptist Spirituality: Selected Writings* (Mahwah, NJ: Paulist Press, 1994), 253; cf. Menno Simons, *The Complete Writings of Menno Simons*, ed. J. C. Wenger, trans. Leonard Verduin (Scottdale, PA: Herald Press, 1956), 63–86, here 70 (on Ps. 25:7–8).

14. Liechty, *Early Anabaptist Spirituality*, 257; cf. Menno, *Complete Writings*, 73 (on Ps. 25:11).

our spiritual heritage call us to an appreciation that the Christian life is one of continuous repentance and conversion.

Consider the following caveats and affirmations regarding the place of repentance in Christian experience:

1. *Confession arises from a deep appreciation and proclamation of the gospel.* The call to repentance is integral to the announcement that God loves the world and has offered life through his Son, Christ Jesus. The call to repentance is deeply distorted when it is not rooted in the context of the love and acceptance of God, when the call to repentance is divorced from our covenant relationship with God. Both the Scriptures and the evangelical heritage stress that what motivates our "turning" is the knowledge of God's covenantal love.

The evangelical tradition is at its best when the approach to confession highlights the wonder of the goodness and mercy of God. This is not an act of judgment; when we come to confession, we meet not our Judge but our Healer! In faith, knowing that we are loved and accepted, we turn from self-absorption, from self-preoccupation and pride, and from self-reliance. We joyfully receive the forgiveness of God, an act by which the Spirit empowers us to turn from sin and live in the light.

By anchoring confession in the gospel, we sustain a deep awareness that repentance is not about self-castigation but rather an act of intentionally receiving and embracing the gifts of God, most notably the gift of God's love that is offered to each one through Christ.

As we mature as Christians, confession becomes less and less a matter of identifying particular sins or thoughts and more and more a realization that we are "prone to wander," as the hymn writer has put it,[15] prone to become occupied with ourselves and being self-reliant rather than dependent on the grace of God. We need regular confession because our wandering happens so easily and invariably.

2. *Confession is a response to the divine healer.* Confession, as the expression of repentance, is a spiritual practice by which we bring integrity and consistency to our lives, and ultimately experience healing. The Christian seeks a realignment in thought, word, and deed around a personal awareness of God's call to be holy and the conviction thereof.

This continual realignment is an interactive process as we come to a deeper appreciation of the reign of Christ and its implications for what it means to be Christians in the world. The more we appreciate the full implications of the ascension, the more we seek to live consistently with this reality, the reality that Christ is on the throne of the universe. But more, the ascended one is our healer, who by grace makes us whole. We bring our sin-sick lives to Christ, and the Spirit provides us with the diagnosis. Hence, the act of repentance is supremely an act of hope. It is a declaration that evil does not have the last

15. From "Come, Thou Fount," by Robert Robinson (1758).

word, that there is healing for our sickness, and that the reign of Christ will ultimately find expression in every sphere and sector of society and in our own hearts. Through repentance we are declaring our confidence that one day the longing of our hearts will be fulfilled, when we pray, "Thy will be done on earth, as it is in heaven" (Matt. 6:10 KJV).

3. *Confession and repentance are at the heart of both conversion and spiritual growth*. Repentance is the pivot on which the whole spiritual life turns. No repentance, no conversion; but similarly, no repentance, no spiritual growth. The point at which we are learning to repent is precisely the point at which our lives are responding to the initiative of God's call and grace and the point at which we are turning and thus growing in faith, hope, and love.

But something critical is happening here: we are active, not passive. Repentance is human activity in response to divine initiative. Through repentance we take personal responsibility for our lives and for our response to the goodness and grace of God. We move from feeling victimized—we refuse to blame another, to plead extenuating circumstances. Our sinful predicament is always part of a broader human dilemma, indeed a cosmic dilemma! But through repentance we start with our own lives and insist that, starting with us, as we join hands with our brothers and sisters, we will live lives reflecting the reality that Christ is on the throne of the universe.

4. *Confession is one of the most crucial ways by which our lives are anchored in the joy and peace that is the gift of the Spirit*. It is not surprising that the hymns of Charles Wesley feature the place of both confession and joy in the Christian life; the two go together. The church embodies this vision, this practice, and this way of being. Thus the disposition of repentance and the practice of confession are a continual and abiding witness to what it means to become a Christian. We embody it, but we also teach what it means to come to faith and live in faith.

The call to repentance that we have in Acts 2:38 is therefore not an incidental call in the biblical witness. Any reader of the Gospels would not be the least surprised to find that the ministry of the apostles begins with a call to repentance, since repentance is likewise integral to the spiritual life of the covenant people of God in the Old Testament. Jesus came preaching the gospel of repentance; we only enter into the life of the kingdom (under the authority of the reign of Christ) when we enter through the spiritual act of repentance (Mark 1:14–15).

The call to repentance is a call to turn. There is the rejection of a former way of life (which the Bible understands to be the way of sin and death), coupled with the conscious and deliberate identification with a new way of life (which the Bible speaks of as the kingdom, or as life under the reign of Christ). What is so compelling about the biblical message is that this turning is "from the heart," meaning that it represents a radical reorientation of a person's life. What is equally compelling is that this is human activity. There is power in human agency. God through the Scriptures and through human conscience reveals both the deadly character of sin and the possibility of salvation (that is, of life). Repentance is the particular and biblical response to God's revelation to the heart and mind.

Therefore the church preaches repentance; for the church indeed preaches the gospel. In preaching repentance, we are declaring that there is hope; we are affirming the possibility of forgiveness and healing. To neglect the call to repentance on the fear that speaking of sin is awkward or off-putting is as absurd as a doctor not speaking of sickness when the possibility of healing and health is at hand.

8

The Sacramental Dimension
of Conversion

✣

We cannot speak of conversion, as we find it mentioned in the New Testament, without also speaking of baptism. The two are so closely linked that we cannot speak of the one without the other. We cannot speak of making disciples unless we appreciate that to be a disciple is to be baptized (Matt. 28:19–20).

Baptism gives structure and form to evangelism and to the initiation into Christian faith. It is the Christ-ordained means by which the faith of the church is *embodied* in the life of its members. Baptism sacramentalizes our conversion; it anchors our faith in our bodies and thus in our lives. Many evangelicals struggle to accept this, insisting that baptism does not "save" and that something so tangible and "human" cannot be required for a person to know the salvation of God. They resist the idea that baptism is a requirement to know the fullness of God's salvation.

But baptism is a commandment, and with good reason. We need such sacramental actions for the simple reason that we are embodied souls. The typical evangelical fear that this might create an artificial obstacle to knowing God's salvation need not enter the discussion at this point. We are simply asking the wrong question when we wonder if a person will know the salvation of God if they are not baptized. Rather, the point is this: in this life, if we want to know the transformation of God, we must affirm what it means to begin well, what it means to establish an authentic foundation for the Christian life. And for this, we must insist—yes, insist—on baptism as a requirement, as an integral dimension of the Christian understanding of conversion. Baptism does not cause or effect salvation, but that does not make baptism optional or secondary.

This being the case, it would be helpful to explore more fully the meaning of baptism. Since baptism is so integral to conversion, what does it mean? Baptism is a window in the meaning of conversion because it is the fundamental sign and symbol of initiation into the Christian life. So what implications does baptism have for the whole of the Christian life—such that the Christian life is marked, essentially, by a baptismal spirituality? We need to teach the meaning of baptism so that our faith is informed by and anchored in our baptismal identity.

Union with Christ

Baptism is a gift from Christ, an offering to the church, and it is ordained as the means by which we, in turn, are united with Christ. We begin and end here; baptism is fundamentally about our identity in Christ. It represents that we live our lives for Christ, with Christ, and in Christ. Galatians 3:26–27 speaks of being "clothed . . . with Christ." In Christ, through baptism, we find our identity: our hopes and dreams, our future and deepest aspirations—all are now deeply linked with Christ and thus with the reign of Christ.

Baptism speaks of both renunciation and anticipation. Looking back, it speaks of a radical break, an act of focused and intentional renunciation, of discontinuity with our life so far. We have lived a life alienated from Christ; now baptism speaks of our union with Christ and with the righteousness of Christ, with the person and the mission of Christ.

Baptism is the *via negativa* in that through it we experience a conscious and deliberate identification with the death of Christ Jesus: we walk the way of the cross, and through this identification with the cross of Christ, we establish a benchmark in our own life between our former way of life and the new life we will have in Christ. In this regard, it is critical to highlight the relationship between baptism and the cross. Baptism is an act of participation. Thus, as in Romans 6, baptism is not merely an act by which we *confess* the death of Christ, but one in which we actually enter into and thereby participate in this cross.

Romans 6 speaks of union with Christ in his death and resurrection, which gives content and focus to what we mean by "in Christ." We are not baptized into a Christ of our own invention, but only the Christ who is the crucified, risen, and ascended one. This point matters because it is so easy to reinvent Christ in our own image. Thus there must be a break, a conscious and deliberate break, from a life that is lived without reference to Christ. We die to this old life. We enter into Christ's death, and it becomes our death. In baptism we "take up" the cross and make it ours. Baptism demarcates this discontinuity as we embrace the way of the cross; the cross then marks our life, our work, and our relationships.

It is this close link with the cross (and the death of Christ) that led the ancient church to place baptism within the church calendar intimately close to the observance of the cross (i.e., holy Saturday). Baptism was linked to the

Easter vigil: after Good Friday, immediately before the celebration of the resurrection. This is a significant and appropriate way to highlight the meaning of baptism. Though we might not choose to restrict baptisms to one day a year, we certainly do need to sustain what is theologically depicted by this ancient practice. It *said* something. The form made clear the content (the substance of baptism) and reinforced that content.

Thus baptism is a moral act with moral consequences. Paul insists that because we are baptized, we turn from and reject the way of sin. We are no longer slaves to sin, but slaves to righteousness (Rom. 6:16–19). Baptism is a moral act, yet also a mystical act: an act of deliberate union with Christ in his death and life. In other words, in baptism the Christian renounces evil and the works of the evil one, but it is not merely an act of moral resolve, for this could happen without the water and the sacramental gestures of the church. Rather, while moral, it is specifically a mystical act wherein the Christian turns from the way of sin precisely because of the interplay of the Christian's life with that of Christ. John 15:4 speaks of abiding in Christ as Christ abides in the Christian; this is specifically what is being represented in this outpouring and immersion with water.

Yet we in baptism are also looking forward: our identification with Christ means that we identify with what the death and resurrection bring into being: a new dispensation, the kingdom of God at hand. The coming kingdom was foreshadowed in the baptism of John; then the baptism of Jesus explicitly marked the inauguration of his ministry of announcing the kingdom. Our baptisms are now an identification with this very reign of God. It is an act of identification with the Christ event and story wherein we intentionally and consciously declare that this event *defines* us and our future. What defines us now is the kingdom. The prayer "Thy will be done, on earth as it is in heaven" finds concrete, tangible expression in the life of the new Christian.

Dimensions of Meaning in Baptism

Recognizing the central and defining meaning of baptism, union with Christ, the church has always acknowledged that there are diverse meanings that flesh out the full significance of this rite. Different theological and church traditions tend to emphasize one dimension of meaning over another, perhaps, but as a rule the following are found within all Christian traditions:

- In baptism the Christian appropriates the *forgiveness of sins.*
- Baptism re-presents the *gift of the Spirit*: the promise of Christ that we would be baptized in the Spirit is profiled in our baptism.
- In baptism we are incorporated into the *Christian community.*

141

All three are found in the Acts 2:38 text. I will consider them in the order in which they emerge in the text: Luke speaks of the forgiveness of sins, the gift of the Spirit, and incorporation into congregational life. Their meaning is interrelated and overlapping. One dimension cannot be understood except in the light of the others, and all three are anchored in the experience of Christ and our union with Christ.

Cleansing and the Forgiveness of Sin

First, we can speak of baptism as representing the forgiveness of sins and the purification of conscience. It is a rite of purification and cleansing. Indeed, the actual language of baptism could be translated as a washing, through a plunging in the purifying water. Several New Testament texts carry this dimension of meaning, either directly or by allusion. For example, in Acts 2:38 Peter says, "Repent and be baptized . . . *for the forgiveness of your sins*" (TNIV, emphasis added).

Then Titus 3:5 makes a close link between cleansing and the Spirit, which will be considered more fully in the next point. We also have the explicit language of 1 Peter 3:21. Both the Titus reference and the reference in 1 Peter speak of baptism as an act of cleansing. Obviously, in this case one cannot avoid the wonder of water as not only being the very substance of life, but also having extraordinary power to clean. But the use of water is sacramental, speaking not of a literal cleansing of the body, but of the purification of conscience. Through our bathing in water, our interior lives are similarly bathed in the purifying grace of God. We are made clean; our guilt is absolved and eliminated. Although we are bathed in water, the fundamental meaning is what happens internally, not what happens externally; it is a *sacramental* cleansing. The apostle Paul's conversion is recounted again in Acts 22, where verse 16 refers to his baptism and clearly to cleansing. In his call to Paul, Ananias insists, "Get up, be baptized, and have your sins washed away, calling on his name."

From this perspective, we can only appreciate the meaning of baptism against the backdrop of the human predicament: because of sin, humanity is guilty and under condemnation. Baptism gets at the heart of the problem, the core of the human predicament, which is the problem of guilt. Thus it is important to stress that baptism represents the *forgiveness* of sin, not the removal of sin.

Yet this grace of forgiveness breaks the power of sin, the hold of sin over a person and over the church. The gospel appropriated through baptism is powerful. For the fourth-and-fifth-century church in the West, it was the common practice to have an exorcism as part of the baptismal rite. With an anointing of oil and appropriate prayers, the candidate for baptism was committed to Christ and to a holy life in Christ. On the one hand, forgiveness is received, in baptism; on the other, there is a turning, a repentance, a new direction toward the holiness of God. For the early church, it made sense to highlight this dimension of meaning in both word and symbolic action. Baptism embodied a deep hope that the power of sin was broken.

This surely assumes that the way into baptism is the penitential way. We come to faith in Christ while needing and seeking the forgiveness of God. We come fully conscious of our sin and our need for forgiveness and cleansing. Thus baptism without repentance makes no sense. It is an affront to the very meaning of this rite. Hence, for the ancient church, baptism was only administered after a period of sober reflection, fasting, and prayer: the penitential way. With baptisms at the Easter vigil, new Christians were invited to walk with Christ for forty days "in the desert" in anticipation of their baptism. Lent was originally designed for those coming to faith, but one does not enter into Lent or the penitential way with fear or any doubt about the mercy and compassion of God. Rather, one enters penitence while knowing that grace is freely given by the God of all mercy. Baptism represents the full circle of this journey through repentance to forgiveness. In baptism, the candidate confesses oneself to be a sinner, who along with others has found forgiveness in Christ Jesus. This point must be stressed. It is not merely forgiveness or cleansing of guilt that one experiences; it is also forgiveness *in Christ*. The baptized one, the new Christian, dies and is risen in Christ and thus knows the grace of forgiveness.

This is not a "cheap" forgiveness; it is forgiveness that accompanies the act of renunciation: in the baptismal rite of the ancient church, one is to "renounce the devil and all his works." We are forgiven that we might live in the light. Surely, then, this should be represented with as much water as is possible—if not an immersion, then a thorough pouring; the bathing of the body, perhaps a complete plunging of the body into the water, speaks of the thoroughness of God's forgiveness and cleansing.

This experience of forgiveness and empowerment is intimately linked with the second dimension of meaning, the grace of the Spirit.

Receiving the Gift of the Spirit

Christian initiation through baptism speaks of a new life, a new birth, that is effected in the life of the new believer by the Spirit. Three primary New Testament references speak of the close interplay between water baptism and the gift of the Spirit. Acts 2:38 makes an explicit link: "Repent, and be baptized . . . and you will receive the gift of the Spirit." Then there is Titus 3:5, as mentioned above, and John 3:5, where Jesus says to Nicodemus, "No one can enter the kingdom of God without being born of water and Spirit."

Many evangelical Christians are not convinced that John 3:5 speaks of baptism. Though not necessarily questioning the link of baptism with the Spirit, they do not see how this text informs our understanding of baptism, particularly in this regard. As a rule those who are nonsacramental insist that this cannot be a reference to water baptism, having a huge fear (and reaction to) any idea of baptismal regeneration (that we are born again by baptism). They insist that water in John 3:5 refers not to water baptism but to insemination, to the child in the "waters" of the mother's womb, or to childbirth.

But from other texts we know that there is an intimate connection between baptism and the gift of the Spirit, and further, that the Gospel of John speaks of the sacramental life not through direct reference, but through powerful allusions (e.g., John 6). Hence, I am inclined to take this as a reference to baptism when viewed alongside Titus 3:5–7. Both speak of the radical character of regeneration, and both link this with the experience of the Spirit with water. Indeed, in Titus 3:5 they are one and the same: the experience of forgiveness and the experience of the Spirit. Christian initiation is a new birth represented by baptism, a renewal of water and the Spirit. This renewal enables the new Christian to be united with Christ in his death and resurrection. This link to the Spirit in water baptism is not incidental or secondary; indeed, there is a marked contrast between the baptism of John the Baptist and that of Jesus precisely at this point. John baptized with water; Jesus's baptism was "with the Holy Spirit and with fire" (Matt. 3:11; Luke 3:16). Thus there is a water ritual, but it may be that the primary reference is not to the water per se, but rather to the grace of the Spirit.

Hence, it is imperative that in celebrating baptism we speak of the gift of the Spirit. Richard Longenecker makes the following point regarding Peter's response to what occurred when he spoke the gospel to Cornelius: "So, convinced by God and consistent with his conviction about the logical connection between Christian conversion, water baptism, and the baptism of the Spirit, . . . Peter calls for Gentiles who have received the baptism of the Spirit to be baptized in water."[1] Longenecker is particularly pointed in observing "the indissoluble connection between conversion, water baptism, and the baptism of the Holy Spirit."[2] In the book of Acts, the conversion narrative of Cornelius thus reinforces the significance of Acts 2:38 and the close interplay between repentance, baptism, and the gift of the Spirit.

Yet, even if someone does not accept that Titus 3 and John 3 refer to Spirit baptism, the fact remains that we cannot speak of conversion and of baptism as the rite of initiation into the Christian life and not insist that through baptism one is initiated into life in the Spirit. This needs to be made overt, obvious, and clear. One is initiated into life in the Spirit. If baptism does not mean this, what is the point? But more, one is initiated into a life that is impossible apart from the grace of the Spirit. Thus we must make this link and make it clearly. Gordon Fee puts it well:

1. Richard N. Longenecker, "The Acts of the Apostles," in *The Expositor's Bible Commentary*, ed. Frank E. Gaebelein (Grand Rapids: Zondervan, 1981), 9:395, referring to Acts 10:44–48.
2. Ibid., 284.

The general loss of the dynamic and experienced life of the Spirit *at the beginning of the Christian life* also accounts for the frequent malaise and unfortunately all to frequent anemia of the individual believer throughout much of the church's later history. This is obviously not true of everyone, of course. But it does in part account for the rise both of the monastic movement and of various Spirit movements throughout its history.[3]

Spirit baptism is not identical with nor does it replace water baptism. It is distinct, but inseparable. In what sense? What is the relationship between the two? This has been a point of considerable debate in the history of the church. Though there is a general consensus that water baptism signifies the gift of the Spirit, different traditions and denominations have quite different perspectives on how this finds expression. For some, it finds expression in a distinct experience *following* water baptism. Those within Holiness and Pentecostal traditions have assumed and taught that a "baptism of the Spirit" is experienced after one becomes a Christian, as something that happens after and distinct from the experience of water baptism. Water baptism sets the stage for the mystical or subjective experience that follows; the two are distinct and separable.

For the Roman Catholic Church, the baptism of infants is viewed as one thing; confirmation, the formal act of anointing for the gift of the Spirit, comes later, as the prerequisite for participation in the Eucharist. For many Protestant Christians, notably those within Baptist and Reformed traditions, it is generally assumed that the gift of the Spirit is the same as baptism. As a rule, nothing is said about receiving the Spirit, and it is assumed that nothing *needs* to be said at water baptism. If one has been baptized, then the Christian can live with the confidence that the gift of the Spirit has been received.

The early church assumed that the two, water baptism and Spirit baptism, were distinct but inseparable. That they are distinct is implied by the Acts 2:38 text; water baptism anticipates and speaks of the gift of the Spirit. For Karl Barth, it is important for us to keep them distinct primarily because one is a human action and the other an action of the Spirit; ultimately we do not become Christians through a human decision or action.[4]

We also insist that water baptism does not *cause* Spirit baptism. Alexander Schmemann maintains rather that water baptism enables us to receive the gift of the Spirit; we are baptized so that we might receive this gift.[5] This implies that the actual existential experience of the Spirit may come later, perhaps much

3. Gordon D. Fee, *God's Empowering Presence: The Holy Spirit in the Letters of Paul* (Peabody, MA: Hendrickson, 1994), 900.

4. Karl Barth, *The Christian Life, Church Dogmatics* 4/4, trans. G. W. Bromiley (Edinburgh: T&T Clark, 1960), 32–33.

5. Alexander Schmemann, *Of Water and Spirit: A Liturgical Study of Baptism* (Crestwood, NY: St. Vladimir's Seminary Press, 1974), 116–17.

later. Conversion itself is not a single event or moment, but a series of events, with both water baptism and Spirit baptism as indispensable parts. Since one is a human act and the other an act of God, they are distinct. Further, while distinct, the relationship between them is not causal.[6] The act of God is not confined to or even tied to the specifically human act: water baptism.

Though distinct, they are also inseparable because of the fundamental meaning of baptism and its relationship to the Spirit. Water baptism is precisely the act by which and through which we enter into the grace that is granted to us: Spirit baptism. In the end, water baptism without Spirit baptism misses the whole point. The promise given on the day of Pentecost was precisely that in being baptized they would receive the gift of the Spirit. This is the promise of God that they could embrace and appropriate. Karl Barth puts it this way: "[Water baptism] makes [baptism with the Spirit] possible and demands it. . . . Baptism with water is what it is only in relation to baptism with the Holy Spirit. Whether it looks back to this or forward to it, it pre-supposes it."[7]

First, water baptism and Spirit baptism are inseparable in that the gift of the Spirit is clearly and obviously the gift of Christ's Spirit. We anchor our experience of the Spirit in our union with Christ. There is only one Spirit, and it is the Spirit who is given to us in and through the crucified, risen, and ascended Christ. Our pneumatology is clearly and explicitly christological. Water baptism anchors our experience of the Spirit in Christ, the incarnate Christ, and it anchors it in our own embodiment. But also, as we will see, it anchors our personal faith and our personal experience of the Spirit in the group that is the body of Christ, the faith community. Thus the only Spirit baptism we know is that which unites us with Christ and incorporates us into the fellowship of the Spirit in the church.

The reverse is also true: our experience of Christ in baptism must find expression in the gift of the Spirit. We long not merely for a christological pneumatology but also a pneumatological Christology. Gregory Dix has observed that we must not think solely of the gift of the Spirit as the consequence of the experience of Christ's salvation simply because the Spirit is the one who actually graces the Christian with the salvation of God that is in Christ.[8] We cannot think of baptism and the grace that is known through baptism except with reference to the Spirit.

---

6. Ephesians 1:13 speaks of "the seal of the promised Holy Spirit"; and Andrew Lincoln observes that this seal is the baptism of the Spirit, the counterpart or, as Lincoln puts it, "the other side of the coin" from water baptism. Referencing Karl Barth and G. B. Caird, Lincoln maintains that we must not confuse the occasion with the event; we need to avoid a one-to-one correlation between water and Spirit baptism. They are linked, but they are not synonymous (Andrew T. Lincoln, *Ephesians*, Word Biblical Commentary 42 [Dallas: Word Books, 1990], 40).

7. Barth, *Christian Life*, 41.

8. Gregory Dix, *The Theology of Confirmation in Relation to Baptism* (London: Dacre, 1946), 36.

Baptism symbolizes the presence of the Spirit in our lives. At the baptism itself this needs to be articulated and clear. We need to celebrate and affirm the presence of the Spirit in the midst of God's people and in the person who is being baptized. The presence of the Spirit is both present and eschatological in that the Spirit's presence is something real and specific to our current circumstances, yet the gift of the Spirit is also a pledge or foretaste of our future resurrection life (Rom. 8:11; Eph. 1:13–14). We cannot live the Christian life without the Spirit, so it is a gift for now. It is not that one starts out on one's own and then, as one despairs of trying to live the Christian life, one then reaches out for the Spirit. One cannot live the Christian life without the Spirit. There is no other way. So we cannot and should not baptize anyone without making this abundantly clear. Through the Spirit we know the cleansing power of God's forgiveness. Through the Spirit we are united with Christ in his death and resurrection. Through the Spirit we are enabled to live the new life to which we are being called. It is the Spirit who will enable the newly baptized believer to live as a baptized person.

Surely this needs to be made explicit in the actual practice of baptism. At least we should *speak* of this. At the very least! As far *as minimal* practice, the one presiding should mention the wonder that this water baptism speaks to and that it is the act by which the one being baptized is opened up to the grace of the baptism and the outpouring or filling of the Spirit. Yet surely, following the more sacramental traditions, we should *re-present* this as well; it should be reflected not merely in our words but also in our actions: through the laying on of hands, the anointing of oil, and the prayer that indeed the baptized one would know the grace of the Spirit. The laying on of hands speaks of identification with the faith community (which I will speak to below). Oil is an essential religious symbol, calling forth our intimate awareness of the ministry of the Spirit. Oil is the symbol of the Holy Spirit; it signifies great joy, and surely the two (Spirit and joy) come together in baptism.

For some, water baptism is marked by a complementary rite of anointing, following the practice of the ancient church. In the early church it was common that oil for anointing was integral to the rite of baptism and initiation—at or near the water baptism itself, with the anointing sometimes before and sometimes after the water ritual. In the ancient Syriac rite, oil was poured into the actual baptismal waters. Either way, oil was used. Surely there is no reason to be hesitant or cautious. We need to find a way to highlight, as powerfully as possible, that water baptism points to and anticipates the fire of the Spirit that will overwhelm the Christian. Thus I wonder if I am much too hesitant in using but a little touch of oil, lest it feel awkward or lest I embarrass the newly baptized Christian. I wonder if we should not rather bathe the head of the baptized one in the oil of joy, the joy of the Spirit, so that they know the power of the grace described in Psalm 133: the anointing oil on Aaron's head, running down upon his beard and his robe "like the dew of Hermon, which falls on the mountains of Zion."[9]

Incorporation and Initiation into Christian Community, the Church

If we are baptized in Christ, we have a unique association with the people of God. If our sins are forgiven, we are united with Christ. As recipients of the gift of the Spirit, we are then part of God's people. We are joined with others who have found forgiveness in Christ. With them, we are drawn into the fellowship of the Spirit. Stanley Grenz suggests, "Above all, however, baptism is oriented toward our participation in community."[10] Contra Grenz, I argue that baptism is "above all" oriented toward our participation in Christ, of which our participation in community is derivative. And yet Grenz is right in this: we cannot speak of baptism without speaking of the community. Through baptism we formally signal that in coming to faith in Christ, we become participants in the life of the faith community, the others who have chosen to be baptized in Christ. There is a deep and profound change in our social identity. Because we are now baptized in Christ, our primary social identity has been altered. Our sense of family and kinship is now oriented around the identity of those who by faith are children of Abraham and Sarah, and thus in a new family.

Baptism is about our union with Christ. Yet we must do all we can to avoid any suggestion that we can be united with Christ and not be in dynamic fellowship with the faith community. Conversion is not merely a conversion to Christ; it is also an act of initiation into Christian community. Christian faith is distinctly *social*. A baptized person is necessarily a member and participant in the people of God. Baptism is not merely a matter of appropriating the forgiveness of God while we celebrate the gift of the Spirit. It is a conscious and deliberate act by which the Christian is incorporated into the faith community. Thus baptism is related to community—both the witnessing community that was there as one came to conversion, and the receiving community that accepts the convert. As often as not they are one and the same.

Therefore, even as the link with Spirit baptism needs to be made explicit in word and ritual action, even so this dimension of meaning also needs to be clearly made in the act of baptism. We need to speak of the one being baptized as being incorporated into the faith community. In how we speak of baptism, we make abundantly clear that in this act of being united with Christ, the new Christian does not now walk alone but enters into a journey arm in arm with

9. In traditions that practice confirmation with oil, this suggests that while water speaks of identification with Christ and oil of identification with the Spirit, these two realities, though distinct, are ultimately inseparable, and so they must be linked (and practiced) in one rite or, at least, in one rite with two parts.

10. Stanley J. Grenz, *Theology for the Community of God* (Grand Rapids: Eerdmans, 2000), 523.

fellow Christians. But we also re-present this; anyone who observes a Christian baptism should be able to clearly appreciate this dimension of meaning.

For starters, at its most basic, this means there are no private baptisms: a "private baptism" is an oxymoron. The baptismal service is not a private ceremony for family or personal friends; it is not merely a matter of getting this "done." When someone, recognizing the need for baptism, asks a friend to join him at the seaside to baptize him, this can hardly be called a Christian baptism.

Then also, we need to make it as clear as possible that not only is baptism mediated to the new believer by the church; baptism is also the act by which the new believer is incorporated into the church. Thus it is appropriate to link baptism to church membership; now, through baptism, we enter into a common identity through an active participation in congregational life. Baptism is then the sacrament of the unity of the church (every bit as much as the Lord's Supper). As Timothy Gorringe puts it, "Baptism is then an 'ecumenical' sign, a sign for the whole inhabited earth of the overcoming of all divisions—not only of Jew and Greek, but [also] of slave and free and even of male and female."[11]

We embrace Christ as the head of the new humanity, and in so doing we are joined together with the body of Christ, the faith community, with whom we live in mutual submission as the fellowship of the Spirit. This union is not merely with those present—the faith community or congregation where we worship and are baptized; it is an act of identification with all Christian believers everywhere. Indeed, this affiliation within and with the church community now becomes our primary kinship and affiliation, trumping family, tribe, and nation.

Furthermore, this means that it is appropriate if not essential that the one who baptizes us be the one ordained by the church to represent the faith community. This is not because we discount the significance of the layperson within the Christian community. It is, rather, that it is the church that baptizes, and thus the one who baptizes has been set apart, ordained, to represent the church to the baptized one and to act on behalf of the church in the baptism.

Surely the one baptizing should not be a family member. If one's parent is the pastor of the church, the familial connection muddies the water. Baptism is not about blood ties or affiliations; rather, in this act of baptism one is being incorporated into the faith community. One actually now turns from primary identification with the family of biological origin and is initiated into a new primary social identity: the family of God. Thus what is needed is that the baptizing be done on behalf of the church, to stress that now this person's primary social identity is no longer family or tribe or nation but our common identity in Christ.

11. Timothy Gorringe, *Redeeming Time: Atonement through Education* (London: Darton, Longman & Todd, 1986), 211–12; referring to Gal. 3:27–28.

Finally, this connection between baptism and the church reminds us that our faith is not ultimately merely "our" faith; it is the faith of the church. Schmemann makes an interesting observation at this point. Part of his argument for infant baptism rests on the question of faith. For the Eastern church, infant baptism rests not on the faith of the parents per se, but on Christ's faith, which in turn is owned and embraced by the church. Baptism, he states, depends on Christ's faith, even though we baptize as an expression of our own faith.[12] There is every reason for those who affirm the baptism of adults to also insist that in our own baptism the faith of the baptized one is sustained and strengthened by the faith of Christ, which is embodied in the life of the church. We represent this by inviting participation from the congregation in the process. Many traditions follow the ancient practice mentioned in the *Apostolic Tradition*, by Hippolytus of Rome, and thus have a sponsor or guarantor, who is friend and companion through the process of preparation for baptism and who stands with the one to be baptized, perhaps bringing words of encouragement, sometimes publicly given, on the occasion of the baptism.[13]

As with the previous dimension of meaning, the gift of the Spirit, here too we must insist that this community dimension of meaning cannot be understood or appreciated except in light of the fundamental meaning of baptism: union with Christ. Only by sustaining this prior and crucial orientation can we avoid the propensity to think of baptism as something that is owned by the church or that by baptism we are joining some kind of religious club. Though we cannot speak of union with Christ except by also speaking of fellowship in community, we must not confuse them. The church is not one and the same as Christ; by our baptism we are entering into union with the risen and ascended Christ, an identity that is not in the end confined to or limited by the life of the church. It is not the church that ultimately gives meaning to baptism, but Christ.

It is vital that we sustain a broad vision of the meaning of baptism; it speaks of forgiveness, the gift of the Spirit, and incorporation into Christian community. Each of these dimensions of meaning is sustained and renewed by the Lord's Supper. Through this holy meal, we enter into communion with Christ, we celebrate the grace of divine mercy and forgiveness, we reappropriate the gift of the Spirit, we reaffirm our life together in community—so that through the Lord's Supper we are reawakened and renewed in our baptismal identity and life.

This reminds us that there is an intimate connection between the meaning of baptism and the meaning of conversion; my point here is that the New

12. Schmemann, *Of Water and Spirit*, 69.

13. See Kevin P. Edgecomb, trans., *The Apostolic Tradition of Hippolytus of Rome* 15.2; 20.2, http://www.bombaxo.com/hippolytus.html.

Testament links these two such that we cannot speak of conversion without speaking of baptism, and further, that the very meaning of baptism is, precisely, the meaning of conversion. The wonder of the baptismal act is that its meaning is so richly nuanced and complex. Surely, as I have been implying all along the way, it makes full sense that we would represent *each* dimension of meaning in our practice of baptism.

When it comes to baptism, the usual debate (aside from the question of mode) is whether baptism is the work of God or a human testimony to the work of God. I appeal for the sacramental vision, which affirms that this is indeed the work of God—but not in a manner that discounts our response to and participation in this work. It is a sign of identification with the faith of the church, mediated to us by the church, but only insofar as it is an act of faith in God's grace to make us new. Thus it is an act of response to God's faithfulness, whereby we choose, with others, to participate in the death and life of Christ Jesus and to make his reign (the narrative of God) our story. Therefore, baptism speaks of both the salvation of God *and* the response, the conversion, of the new believer.

The oldest building in the central square of Florence, Italy, is the Baptistery of San Giovanni (St. John). It truly is a magnificent space and an extraordinary testimony to the meaning of baptism. The baptismal pool is marked into the floor as an octagon, representing the eighth day, the day of the risen Christ, the completion of the seven-day cycle of the week. Such symbolism is pertinent—relevant to the meaning of baptism—since through this sacrament Christians were initiated into Christian faith and thus into life in Christ, which is eternal, life without end. The octagon expresses the Christian hope in resurrection, specifically a resurrection *in Christ*.

The Indispensability of Baptism

This brings us back to the question already raised: Is baptism indispensable to Christian conversion? Can we even speak of conversion without speaking of baptism? What all of this suggests is that baptism is actually the nodal point of a Christian conversion. There is certainly more to conversion than the experience of water baptism, and we must not confuse baptism with salvation, as though the redemptive purposes of God are limited to the human experience of baptism. Rather, what we must affirm is that the clear guidelines and intent of the New Testament are that baptism is integral to the experience of conversion and that anything else is anomalous.

Baptism and conversion are linked, and the church is most effective in its witness to the meaning of baptism and the power of conversion when baptism is very intentionally spoken of as integral to rather than subsequent to conversion.

As recognized in chapter 4, the greatest challenge in this regard is for those faith communities in contexts where baptism creates a massive break from one's social context, as illustrated in the experience of Bilquis Sheikh (in her conversion from Islam). This has led some to conclude that baptism is optional and an unnecessary obstacle to Christian conversion. They argue that baptism breaks social and familial bonds vital to the social health of new Christians and vital for the future witness of those new Christians to their own community.

This is a challenge for conversions from both Muslim and Jewish backgrounds, but it also is a major issue in discussion about the church's mission in India. Here too some argue that baptism only adds divisions and creates hostility from the Hindu community. They claim that it is far better to emphasize the personal and interior relationship with God, without the undue complications of institutional rites and rituals. Thus runs the argument for what some have called "mission without baptism."

Is it possible to be a disciple of Christ Jesus without baptism and church affiliation? Would it not be better to remain unbaptized, but a Christian in one's heart and, in the meantime, continue to be an active member of one's original social community? Can one be a Muslim Christian or a Hindu Christian? This is a complex question. Excellent minds and sincere leaders of the church are giving it considerable attention, for the sake of the church and for those who are coming to faith in Christ.

Yet surely there is no avoiding the expectation of baptism in the New Testament; it is deeply integral to Christian identity. Perhaps there is a place for secret baptism, in the quiet company of a small faith community that will have a continuing role in the life of the new Christian. Or perhaps baptism is delayed provisionally, but only provisionally and for a time, while a believer for a season sustains the connection to one's original community. But it can only be for a season, as part of a continuing process, until the one who is coming to faith feels that baptism simply cannot be postponed any longer. As Andrew Wingate reports, in his exhaustive study of conversions in southern India, even when church leaders discourage baptism in Hindu contexts, for the reasons mentioned above, it is often the new Christian who comes to a recognition of the clear and unambiguous teaching of the Bible and who then insists on receiving the gift of baptism.[14]

A Baptismal Spirituality

In recovering the close link between conversion and baptism, we can speak of a *baptismal spirituality*. Baptism informs and shapes the conversion experi-

14. Andrew Wingate, *The Church and Conversion: A Study of Recent Conversions to and from Christianity in the Tamil Area of South India* (Delhi: ISPCK, 1997), 202–3.

ence. In similar fashion we speak of the baptismal character of the Christian life, the whole of the spiritual life. F. W. Dillistone is famous for the line, in his *Christianity and Symbolism*, that "to find a way of allowing baptism to exercise its power within the Christian community at the deepest level of the human psyche is one of the most urgent tasks of our day."[15] He spoke of this as an urgent concern in 1955, but it could fairly be said that we are nowhere near knowing what it would mean if baptism were deeply to shape the experience of the average contemporary Christian. Alexander Schmemann puts it this way: "The whole of the life of the Church is, in a way, the explication and the manifestation of baptism. . . . Baptism forms the real content, the 'existential' root of what we now call 'religious education.'"[16]

If and when we are able to allow baptism to exercise this power and form within us a distinctly baptismal spirituality, this way of being, in Christ, will have some distinct marks or features:

1. Our baptism will be the central and critical benchmark of our lives; indeed, the anniversary of our baptism may well be of more significance to us than our biological birthday. Without oversentimentalizing this anniversary, we will be conscious of the discontinuity that this moment in our life represents, for it speaks of our primary allegiance (to Christ), our experience of the forgiveness of God, the indwelling of the Spirit, and our participation in the church.

2. Our baptism will consistently call us back to our identity as a forgiven people. As such we will refuse to live under a cloud of guilt but will rather know that in Christ, as a baptized people, we are forgiven and thus live under and in the mercy of God.

3. Our baptism profiles our commitment to live in righteousness—in truth, justice, and peace. This is the primary point that the apostle Paul emphasizes in Romans 6: by virtue of our baptism, sin is now something that is deeply inconsistent with our baptismal identity. For the Christian, indeed, confession and repentance are precisely the acknowledgment that in thought, word, and deed, we have acted in a manner that is inconsistent with our baptismal identity.

4. Baptism itself is a political act as much as it is a moral act. Through baptism we declare that our ultimate allegiance is not to family of origin, tribe, or nation, but to Christ; indeed, baptism is an act of defiance against any human authority—family or culture or nation—that would in any way, shape, or form compete with or undermine our loyalty to Christ. We now stake our lives not with the principalities and powers of this world (Col. 1:15–17), but with the reign of Christ.

15. F. W. Dillistone, *Christianity and Symbolism* (Collins: London, 1955), 187.
16. Alexander Schmemann, *For the Life of the World: Sacraments and Orthodoxy* (Crestwood, NY: St. Vladimir's Seminary Press, 1998), 69.

5. Further, our baptism marks us as part of the faith community, where race, gender, or economic rank is secondary and incidental; for there is one baptism, and in and through that baptism, we are marked as one people. It is baptism that makes the church catholic. In celebrating our baptism, we celebrate this common identity. Baptism leads to an intentional ecumenicity, for there is "one baptism" (Eph. 4:5); a baptized person is committed to the unity of the church and to actively maintaining that unity. We are not baptized Methodist, Catholic, or Lutheran; we are baptized in Christ. This means that we affirm and honor the baptism of our sisters and brothers in other theological and denominational traditions.

6. Finally, our baptism marks us vocationally: now our work, our engagement in the world, is that of those who have been immersed in the waters of baptism. Now, everything we do—from the raising of our children to the work in our garden; from our buying and selling in the marketplace to our active pursuit of justice and peace both locally and internationally; from our work in the library as scholars or the studio as artists to the apostolic work of the pioneer missionary—all of this work, this engagement in the world, is that of those who live and work in response to the ascended Christ, into whom we have been baptized.

With a baptismal spirituality shaping and informing the life of the church, we will also find that our central activities have a baptismal orientation: I speak of two in particular, and I will add a third as something to consider.

First, preaching will be, specifically, preaching to the baptized. The seeker can certainly listen in and listen with profit. But the focus, the intention, of the preacher is to proclaim the Scriptures to the baptized and through the sermon equip the baptized to live in a way that is consistent with their baptismal identity. Their baptism gives them a way of seeing and thus of reading and responding to the Scriptures.

Second, the Lord's Supper then certainly becomes the renewal of one's baptismal identity and vows, as noted above.

Third, I suggest, there is a sense in which water is always for the Christian something that they value, cherish, and appreciate as a sign of their baptismal identity. Every rain shower, every walk along the seaside, is a reminder of the wonder of water as the sacramental element in which they were initiated into their Christian faith and identity. Just as a ring for a married person is a continual reminder of their covenant identity, commitments, and the joy of married love, so also for the Christian, water becomes a reminder of the wonder of their union with Christ.

As an evangelical, I have come to a renewed appreciation of the place of holy water typically found at the entrance to a Roman Catholic Church building. Why not have a way to tangibly remind myself of my baptismal identity, even as I come into the church building that represents both my relationship with God and with the church community? Baptism symbolizes our entrance into the faith community. Then each time we gather, we might rightly seek some way to be reminded of what it means to be a baptized people—not as a merely intellectual reminder, but as a reminder tangible in much the same way that baptism is so very tangible.

In this regard, each baptismal service is an opportunity for the church community to renew its baptismal vows and affirm afresh its baptismal identity. Just as a wedding is an opportunity for all present to affirm their commitment to marriage as a sacred space and sacred relationship, even so each baptism is an opportunity for all present, if they are baptized, to reaffirm what it means to be a baptized people. Thus it makes sense that those who preside at a baptism also use the opportunity to speak not only to the baptismal candidates but to all present and call them to renew the vows they made at their baptism.

In marriage, the wonder and meaning of one's wedding grows in meaning and significance. Likewise, though at our baptism we might well have had a significant appreciation of the meaning of baptism and of what it means to be baptized, this can only grow as we deepen our gratitude for the things to which baptism points.

Concluding Comments and Observations

In conclusion to this overview of the meaning of baptism and its place in the experience of conversion, two additional comments may be appropriate.

First, evangelical Christians (and others) often are quite concerned about this emphasis on baptism out of a deep conviction that baptism itself cannot be a "condition" for the experience of God's salvation. Baptism itself does not "save," and they further insist that it cannot be a condition for knowing salvation. Our response is simple. We have the clear teaching of the New Testament: "Repent, and be baptized" (Acts 2:38). Yet one can and must also examine the theological assumption lying behind such a protest. It is more helpful to appreciate that God alone is the Savior; God alone saves. All we are speaking of here are the God-ordained acts and means of response to the salvation of God. This gift of salvation is freely given, in compassion, mercy, and grace. And repentance and baptism together are an act of faith in this salvation of God.

What happens if a person is not baptized? Surely we can and must teach that if a person dies while seeking the grace of God, they die in grace. Their intentions and longing for God's grace are clear in the eyes of God, but we do not thus institutionalize this anomaly and make baptism optional or incidental to the Christian life.

Second, I have intentionally avoided reference or comment regarding the merits of either infant baptism or believer's baptism. But the more I have given concentrated and critical thought to the relationship between baptism and conversion, the more I have had to conclude that baptism properly belongs with repentance. It rightly comes as the nodal point in the adult experience of coming to faith in Christ. Whether by immersion or by pouring or sprinkling, baptism is properly an adult act that accompanies repentance.

This is offered as one who has a deep appreciation of pedobaptist traditions. Over many years I have urged students in multidenominational seminaries to appreciate that there are good reasons to argue for either infant baptism or believer's baptism. Those who practice infant baptism have a much more intentional and well-developed theology of the child as a member and participant in the covenant community. Within my own denomination I have protested the practice of requiring those who come from Anglican and other backgrounds, who choose to join our community, to be rebaptized. This makes no sense.

And yet one wonders if infant baptism was perhaps appropriate in an age or era when Christianity was institutionalized within the culture or nation. Is it not a feature of Christendom, where one could understandably assume that if you were born into a Christian country and family, you would be a Christian?

Now in a post-Christian secular society, what is the best way to foster authentic conversion and faith? I am inclined to think that there is no substitute for the powerful act in which a person declares that they believe in Christ, renounce the forces of evil, receive the gift of the Spirit, and join themselves to the faith community; indeed, no one can do this for them. The irony for me is that nothing has so persuaded me of this as observing the rite of adult baptism in a Roman Catholic parish, at the Easter vigil, as I came away thinking that this was the way it should and needed to be done; this is how a person should be incorporated into Christian community. An adult, on the basis of their own confession, stands in a pool of water, and three times a full pitcher of water is poured over their head: once in the name of Father, once in the name of the Son, once in the name of the Spirit. This act of grace, offered by the church to adult converts, is precisely the act of grace that should be offered to all who come to faith.

Most of all, the point to be made is that the church needs to find ways to reestablish the vital place of baptism as the defining practice and event of a Christian conversion. It should be the point of departure for the Christian life, the event that shapes and informs the whole of the Christian life.

9

Spiritual Autobiography
and Conversion Narrative

✚

One of the traits of the evangelical spiritual and theological tradition is the recognition of the value of spiritual autobiography. In his defining study of the emergence of the genre, Bruce Hindmarsh has demonstrated how the conversion narrative was integral to the rise of evangelicalism and how the phenomena of narrative fueled and sustained the movement.[1] Hindmarsh observes that conversion narratives did not merely reflect experience; they also defined it and thereby strengthened it—giving meaning and clarity, confirming the contours and elements of an experience, establishing identity.[2]

Many contemporary evangelicals have abandoned the conversion narrative because it seems contrived to them. They could not make a personal connection to the conversion narratives they were hearing in congregations since the dominant themes came from revivalism. More recently, evangelicals and others have come to a greater appreciation of this side of their spiritual heritage and recognize the value of the conversion narrative and spiritual autobiography as a means of critical reflection on the nature and character of the conversion experience.

The renewal of evangelicalism in our day may well come, in part, by a recovery of the power of the conversion narrative to shape and define and give meaning to the experience of God's salvation. Hindmarsh observes that the demise of Christendom and the emergence of modernity provided a unique confluence, a social and intellectual climate in which the evangelical conversion narrative could emerge. I wonder whether the post-Christian West of the

---

1. D. Bruce Hindmarsh, *The Evangelical Conversion Narrative: Spiritual Autobiography in Early Modern England* (Oxford: Oxford University Press, 2005).
2. Ibid., 325–26.

twenty-first century, experiencing the demise of modernism, might not offer a comparable time of change. The shifting foundations may once more open the way for the conversion narrative to be a means of grace, a way of giving definition to experience, establishing identity, and clarifying the elements of a life that is lived in response to the initiative of God.

To recover the conversion narrative will require two things. First, evangelicals will have to move some distance from their revivalist heritage that I described in chapter 1. They need to dispense with some of the deep assumptions of that heritage, especially that conversion is punctiliar. It will mean seeing that conversion is a journey, a pilgrimage, something that is narratable—a story that can be told. Second, evangelicals must rediscover a theological vision or basis for interpreting their experience. As suggested, this theological vision will need to draw on both the full scope of the evangelical heritage (Reformed, Anabaptist, and Wesleyan) and the whole church's witness to the experience of coming to faith in Christ. It will be a theological vision that is thoroughly biblical and takes account of the comprehensive vision of God's salvation (such as that, for example, which is articulated in the Epistle to the Ephesians).

In other words, it will be an exercise in which we do both constructive theology and critical reflection on experience. It will mean taking *experience* seriously. Throughout this study I have consistently illustrated and set up some of the critical theological reflections by providing examples of conversion narratives. This is done in part out of the assumption that all theology is autobiography, or at least is deeply influenced by autobiography. Thus the key to theological analysis and reflection on the nature of conversion and its implications for the church is precisely the interplay between autobiography—the church reflecting on its experience—and critical theological reflection that arises from the study of Scripture.

It is not that both are equally authoritative; we recognize the primacy of the Scriptures for theological reflection. But we cannot make this assertion in a way that discounts the power and significance of observations about the nature of authentic experience. Part of the genius of John Wesley, for example, was his extraordinary capacity to do critical reflection on his own conversion experience, and part of the genius of Jonathan Edwards was his capacity to provide critical reflection on not merely his own conversion, but also the conversion experience of others.

Another way to speak of this interplay is to acknowledge that both the Scriptures and experience provide an authority for theology, but in different ways. The Scriptures are the bass line of the music; the Scriptures provide the contours and parameters, the boundaries and markers, for authentic religious experience. But it is experience that actually fills out these contours, which remain empty and lifeless apart from the learning that arises from experience.

Yes, the church has certainly often strayed in this regard. I am consistently struck by how the nineteenth-century holiness teachers superimposed their own experience on the Scriptures and thereby created a grid by which they did their exegesis. Because of their experience, they "found" things in Scripture that any contemporary exegete would simply say are not there. Yet they sought these things in Scripture to validate their experience precisely because they affirmed the authority of the Scriptures and also because they knew that their own experience was, in some significant way, authentic. They may not have negotiated the interplay between experience and Scripture effectively, but they were right in their attempt to do so, in their attempt to make sense of and take seriously their own experience. In other words, they were doing what needed to be done, even if they confused the categories and unnecessarily stretched the meaning of the Scriptures to fit into the grid created by their experience.

The solution is not to discount experience. This is simply not possible. Everyone, in all times and places, inevitably reads the objective authority (Scripture) through a subjective lens. There is no other way to engage the text. Our reading of grace, love, and mercy in Scripture is fundamentally altered by our own experience of grace, love, and mercy. Thus the call to the church is to allow for the powerful and necessary iterative interplay between Scripture and experience—always ultimately subject to the grand narrative and contours provided by the Scriptures, but appreciating and entering into this narrative through the lens of our own experience. Experience often forces us to rethink our reading of the ancient text. Indeed, many who did not experience a classic revivalist punctiliar conversion were driven to reread the Scriptures and, I am suggesting, to read them more truly. It was an experience that called forth the more consistent and biblically appropriate reading.

Specifically, we seek an honest and theologically informed reflection on experience of conversion. We can only wade into the study of religious experience with some kind of interpretive grid, some way of making sense of what has happened, and that interpretive grid surely comes from the Scriptures. Thus the theology of religious experience, of conversion and transformation, arises from the intentional and critical interplay between the critical study of the Scriptures and, similarly, the critical study of religious experience—in this case, the experience of conversion.

In the consideration of conversion narratives, it is valuable for each person to consider their own story. We cannot give critical attention to the matter of conversion as "objective" bystanders. We only come to this through our own experience of grace, and in so doing, we grow in self-knowledge, as we see more clearly the character of our own experience and thus of our own identity. The practice of preparing a conversion narrative also heightens our appreciation of God's work in our lives and thus the presence of God in our lives. This in turn fosters our capacity to be alert to the presence and initiative of God in the rest of our Christian journey.

There is also great value in reading and considering other conversion narratives. It expands our horizons as we see that no two conversions are alike; indeed, we can speak only of conversion as the work of the Spirit and acknowledge that there is no one form or approach or way in which the Spirit brings people to faith in Christ. We must consider other conversion experiences lest we institutionalize our own and wittingly or unwittingly assume that our conversion experience establishes a normative pattern. This has significant implications for the way in which we think about the ministry of evangelism.

"Waiting for God": Four Examples of the Experience of Conversion

This study of conversion has explored many conversions and conversion narratives—in the book of Acts, in the early church (Anthony of Egypt, Augustine of Hippo), and then later in the history of the church, all the way up to a sample of a contemporary Muslim converting to the Christian faith. In this chapter, I am going to consider four more—Blaise Pascal, Simone Weil, George Grant, and Paul Williams. Then, working with these as an immediate backdrop and the other narratives thus far considered as a backdrop one step removed, I will provide some suggestions and guidelines for writing a conversion narrative. I will do this specifically so that such a narrative can be a source of good theological reflection on the nature of religious experience, showing how our own experience of conversion can inform our understanding of conversion.

1. Blaise Pascal (1623–62)

Blaise Pascal, the seventeenth-century French mathematician and philosopher, was born in 1623 (June 19) and grew up in the France of Cardinal Richelieu, who epitomized the merger of ecclesiastical and civil power. Pascal died August 19, 1662, at a mere thirty-nine years of age, but during his few years he was recognized as a leading mathematician of his day and a brilliant philosopher.

He never attended any school or university but was taught by his father, Étienne Pascal. While Blaise was very young, his father moved with his family to Paris (1631), where his father was a civil servant. Their religious life was conventional seventeenth-century Roman Catholicism. When he was seventeen, his family moved again, this time to Rouen, where his father continued as a civil servant. While there, he came under the influence of a priest, Jean Guillebert, who preached the gospel in a way that challenged the Roman Church of the day.

As a noteworthy aside, this priest was a Jansenist, a member of a school of thought that was quite antischolastic and was seeking to reform the church through a revival of the teachings of Augustine of Hippo. Many have compared

Jansenism to Calvinism in this regard, except that the Jansenist affirmed a sacramental piety, the contemplative or mystical vocation of prayer, and the call to the priesthood. But most of all, what was central to Jansenism was what was so ably captured by Augustine: the idea of the "restless" heart that "can find peace" only in God (*Confessions* 1.1).

Though this movement stressed this heartfelt longing for God, it also did not tolerate moral laxity in the spiritual life. Through the influence of Jean Guillebert, Pascal was introduced to the vision of the spiritual life of Jansenism, and this persuaded him to move beyond the formal, conventional brand of Roman Catholicism with which he had been familiar thus far and to embrace the good news of the gospel. This did not mean that he denied his Roman Catholic heritage; to the contrary, he embraced it while fully appreciating the depth of his sin and his need for God's grace.

The primary testimony to this transition, this conversion, is not from Pascal himself, but rather from his sister Gilberte Pascal: "The Providence of God having provided an occasion for my brother to read certain books of piety, God so enlightened him through this kind of study that he came to understand perfectly that the Christian religion obliges us to live only for God and to have no other objective in life but to serve him."[3]

The overall religious context in which this is described perhaps comes out best by contrast with the spiritual orientation of his father, Étienne. Years later, Gilberte's daughter would describe her grandfather as a "pious enough man, but he had not yet received the gift of illumination," and then add: "He thought he could combine the values of secular success with the practice of the gospel."[4]

Not so, Blaise Pascal. However, while this was a defining and definite turning point for Pascal, it was not something that brought depth of joy or peace to him. In time he was heavily involved in the debates between the Jansenists and the Jesuits, and he was the person to coin the term "jesuitical" as part of his own diatribe against what he and his fellow Jansenists viewed to be laxity about who could participate in Holy Communion. Further, he was a good man, moral, not subject to what his sister called "ordinary vices." Yet despite his involvement in these theological debates and despite the moral pattern of behavior, he was not a happy man. He was frequently lonely, depressed, and in financial straits. As many have noted about his experience, and Pascal himself said and wrote plenty that would suggest as much, he had in effect accepted God and the reality of God's claim on his life, but this acceptance was largely cerebral and intellectual; it had not captured his heart. In what his biographer calls his "winter of discontent,"[5] he wrote a little tract titled

---

3. Quoted by Marvin R. O'Connell, *Blaise Pascal: Reasons of the Heart* (Grand Rapids: Eerdmans, 1997), 51.

4. Ibid.

5. Ibid., 91.

"On the Conversion of the Sinner," in which he sought to describe the predicament of his heart and to try to find the source of his unhappiness and discouragement.

While intellectually accepting the gospel, he was heavyhearted and listless and powerless against all that which is vain and empty, as he put it. He came to a deep yearning for a conversion that would be deeper, more pervasive. Pascal himself observed that what little bit of grace he had only left him all the more conscious of how much he was missing. In 1651 his father died. A year later his sister Jacqueline (five years younger than his sister Gilberte and nearly two years younger than Blaise) became a nun despite his strenuous objections. For a time they were not speaking to each other; their relationship was further stressed over their inheritance: she wanted to give her portion to the convent. Yet this tension between them was only for a season. By 1654 Pascal was reconciled with his sister and indeed often visited the convent as a place of spiritual retreat and renewal.

Then on Monday, November 23, 1654, we have the event for which Pascal is most known, the event often called "the night of fire" (*la nuit de feu*). He solved the dilemma, the problem that had been hounding him since the death of his father.[6] Only after his death, nine years later, did the full extent of his experience on this night come to light. A servant noticed what appeared to be some extra padding in his vest (a doublet). What they found sewn in the lining was a piece of paper or parchment on which Pascal described what he had experienced on that night. It was a powerful event, but one about which he chose to remain silent—to keep the particulars of the experience between himself and God.

At half past ten in the evening, for the next two hours he had an encounter with fire, with the one he knew to be the God of Abraham, Isaac, and Jacob, the God and Father of Jesus Christ, a God who granted him in this hour a deep serenity, joy, and peace. Indeed, he speaks of tears of joy and describes the experience as a "renunciation total and sweet."[7] It was a deeply mystical experience in which Pascal found joy and peace. Yet more, he found that all he needed and longed for was found in God and in God alone. It was an affective knowledge of Christ, an encounter of persons—not merely an encounter with truth, or an idea, but with God's very self. It would prove to be the most defining moment of his life, the fruit of all that he had longed for. He was a philosopher and a mathematician who longed to know God and to know truth, and he found that his pursuit of understanding left him empty and cold, listless and lonely, and that his only hope for joy came through an affective encounter with Christ: a meeting with God that did not bypass but certainly transcended his rational capacities.

6. Ibid., 95.
7. Ibid., 96.

Pascal continued to live outwardly much as he had before. But, as his sister put it, he was now recognized to be a "jolly penitent."[8] Further, starting in January of 1655, Pascal was meeting regularly with a spiritual director, Father LeMaître de Saci, a prudent and wise man. Pascal never truly turned against philosophy and mathematics. Though it had not satisfied the deepest longings of his heart, he did not then pour disdain on his own work as a scholar or discount the life of the mind.

What he learned was that the God of Abraham, Isaac, and of Jesus Christ was not the God of the philosophers, but the God who is known through prayer and experience.[9] This in turn informed his apologetic for the Christian faith, particularly the tradition of Jansenism, within which he stood. He was convinced that the gospel reveals both the glory and the wretchedness of the human person; his apologetic was intended to affirm the analytical and mathematical as well as the intuitive and affective. This work was never finished, due to his premature death at age thirty-nine. But before his death he was taking scores of notes, and we have these, published as his *Pensées*.

2. Simone Weil (1909–43)

Simone Weil, born in 1909, was a remarkable woman and insightful thinker whose intellectual capacities were matched by her extraordinary Christian devotion.[10] Yet we cannot deny that it was her troubled and tortured life that eventually led to her early death. She was raised in an affluent, secular Jewish family in Paris, and even as a child, Simone was recognized to have unique intelligence. Very early she pursued studies in philosophy and science and eventually taught philosophy in the public school system of France.

However, what stands out even more, especially in her early years, is her obvious concern for those in need, especially the poor. This led her to associate with the rising leftist movement in France and to identify with the laborer as her cause célèbre. Without needing the income, she chose to take a job in an auto factory to experience for herself what it was like to be a laborer (1934–35). Then in 1936 she went to Spain and served as a cook for soldiers fighting for the leftists (Popular Front) against Franco.

With regard to her Christian faith, she spoke of her early life as characterized by Christian sensibilities. Even though she was raised in a secular Jewish home, she grew up within a "Christian inspiration," as she put it. Her actual coming to faith was marked by three notable and pivotal experiences.

8. Ibid., 105.
9. Ibid., 129.
10. For the basic outline of Weil's life, I am dependent on Francine Du Plessix Gray, *Simone Weil* (New York: Penguin, 2001).

THREE NOTABLE EXPERIENCES

In 1937 she was in Portugal, spending time with her parents. She was there to recover from burns she had received from boiling oil (while on the kitchen staff in Spain). They stayed in a small fishing village. In her autobiography, *Waiting for God*, she writes:

> In this state of mind then, and in a wretched condition physically, I entered the little Portuguese village, which, alas, was very wretched too, on the very day of its patronal festival. I was alone. It was the evening and there was a full moon. It was by the sea. The wives of the fishermen were going in procession to make a tour of all the ships, carrying candles and singing what must surely be very ancient hymns of heart-rending sadness. Nothing can give any idea of it. I have never heard anything so poignant. . . . There the conviction was suddenly borne in upon me that Christianity was pre-eminently the religion of slaves, that slaves cannot help belonging to it, and I among others.[11]

At the time, she spoke to no one about this experience.

Later that same year she visited Switzerland and Italy. She suffered terribly from migraine headaches and went to Switzerland for treatment. While there she developed a friendship with Jean Pasternak, also there for medical treatment, and they entered into a regular correspondence that continued after she left for Italy.

. In Italy, Weil was particularly taken by the religious art of Milan and Florence; then in Rome she was quite overcome by the beauty of the Catholic liturgy, especially her experience of the Pentecost Mass in Saint Peter's in Rome. She wrote her friend that "nothing is more beautiful than the texts of the Catholic liturgy." Then on to Assisi, sharing in her letters, "At Assisi I forgot all about Milan, Florence, Rome, and the rest." In *Waiting for God*, we read: "There, alone in the little twelfth-century Romanesque chapel of Santa Maria degli Angeli, an incomparable marvel of purity where Saint Francis often used to pray, something stronger than I was compelled me for the first time in my life to go down on my knees."[12]

Yet back in Paris, teaching at a school for girls, Weil was increasingly disillusioned, her passion for leftist causes shaken by the movement toward the right and the ultimate victory of Franco in Spain. This disillusionment, though, drove her further on her spiritual pilgrimage. She speaks of a persistent reading of the Bible, especially the Gospels. She was also reading Pascal. In the following year, 1938, she spent ten days, including Holy Week, in Solesmes (a Benedictine abbey in northeastern France). While still suffering from headaches and experiencing no relief from the pain, she nevertheless found deep

---

11. Simone Weil, *Waiting for God*, trans. Emma Craufurd (New York: Putman's Sons, 1951; reprint, New York: HarperCollins, 2001), 26.

12. Ibid.

consolation in the beauty of the liturgy, especially the chanting. She speaks of this experience as enabling her to "understand the possibility of divine love in the midst of affliction."[13] Most of all, she had what she spoke of as an encounter with Christ's passion, of which she wrote: "Christ himself came down and took possession of me."[14]

Weil was deeply attracted to the Eucharist and was reading also the poetry of George Herbert, to whom she was introduced in Solesmes. She mentions in particular his poem "Love Bade Me Welcome," of which she was later to say that it brought her "into Christ's presence."[15] Weil came to the conclusion that "the name of God and the name of Christ have been more and more irresistibly mingled in my thoughts."

COMMITMENT TO CHRISTIAN FAITH

The persecution of the Jews in the late 1930s forced Weil to leave France with her family, but before their departure, in Marseilles, she met a Dominican priest, Father J. M. Perrin, to whom she would eventually dedicate her little book *Waiting for God*, written in 1942. She was trying to decide whether to become Roman Catholic, and through her conversations with Father Perrin, she came to, as she put it, accept the central mysteries of the faith: the Trinity, the incarnation, the cross, and the resurrection.

It was not long, though, before she and her family made their way to the United States. She was there for a while, and eventually she made her way to England, where she died, only thirty-four years old. Despite her positive affiliation with the Christian faith, she remained deeply antagonistic to her own Jewish heritage, and actually to anything Jewish in Christianity (refusing, for example, to believe that God spoke through the Old Testament prophets). And despite her positive experiences in Rome, Assisi, and Solesmes, she was never able to reconcile herself to the church hierarchy: she refused to be baptized. One can only speculate what might have been if Weil had not met a premature death. I would like to think that in time she would have been reconciled to her heritage. Perhaps. And further, that in time she would have been able to come to terms with the phenomena of the institutional church. We don't know; yet it is noteworthy that all through her time in New York City, she went to Mass daily, and we know that she urged her brother to have his children baptized.

13. Ibid.
14. Ibid., 27.
15. Herbert was also a significant influence on C. S. Lewis. In his own conversion narrative, Lewis speaks of Herbert as one who excelled all other authors he had ever read in "conveying the very quality of life as we actually live it from moment to moment" (*Surprised by Joy: The Shape of My Early Life* [London: Collins, 1955], 171); cf. http://www.geocities.com/suonnoch/Anthology/love_bade_me.htm.

3. *George Grant (1918–88)*

George Grant may well be the most significant Canadian philosopher before Charles Taylor, especially when it comes to an articulation of the primacy of experience for theology.[16] He argued that experience rightly understood moves us into thought that is rightly expressed.

He was born, baptized, and raised within an Anglican family. This seems to have provided him a context, language, or significant reference for his religious experience. Most notable, though, is that Grant's coming to faith cannot be appreciated except against the backdrop of the twentieth-century wars. As a young man he felt compelled to participate in the Second World War but insisted that it had to be in a nonviolent way. So he went to London and served as an Air Raids Precautions Warden, managing curfews and blackouts, investigating unexploded bombs, providing first aid, and the most difficult task of all, informing the families of those who had been killed. It was this exposure to suffering that left Grant in deep emotional and spiritual upheaval. His inner life could not contend with the circumstances of suffering in which he lived and worked.

His later work would always accept this dilemma—that he could not provide answers and that indeed perhaps the primary work of a philosopher is to pose questions. Grant is known for his huge distaste for clichés, particularly religious or theological clichés. Thus he was not looking for simple answers as he sought to make sense of the chaos around him.

He tells how, in the midst of this turmoil, he had a unique experience. He was making a delivery to a farm just outside of London. As he dismounted from his bicycle to open and pass through the gate into the front yard, it suddenly came to him that "God is."[17] In his own commentary on this experience, Grant speaks of a deep confidence that he knew that in the end "all is finally well": there is order behind the chaos, and this destruction does not have the last word. But in this moment he also realized that he was not his own: he belonged to another; indeed, he had been taken up into something mysterious and tremendous, and he was overwhelmed by the sense of love flowing through him.

In an insightful study of Grant's thought, Harris Athanasiadis makes some noteworthy observations about the intersection of this man's thought and his experience of both suffering and grace. He observes that Grant realized there is "no rational or causal connection between the experience of suffering and the experience of God."[18] Indeed, the experience of suffering is essential

---

16. For a very fine biography of George Grant, consider William Christian, *George Grant: A Biography* (Toronto: University of Toronto Press, 1993).

17. George Grant, "The Owl and the Dynamic: The Vision of George Grant," interview on *Arts, Music and Science*, CBC-TV, February 13, 1980.

18. Harris Athanasiadis, "George Grant and the Challenge of Theology as Public Discourse in a Post-Christian, Post-Modern World" (paper delivered at the meeting of the Canadian Theological Society, May 2003), 5.

if we are to know God, Grant decided. For, as Athanasiadis puts it, "without entering into the experiential truth of suffering, . . . the experience of God cannot be trusted as real in contrast to . . . subjective . . . escapism, . . . so that the experience of the cross without the resurrection leads to despair, and the experience of the resurrection without the cross cannot but lead to false, triumphalistic and escapist hope."[19]

What Grant experienced as he opened that gate became a major theme in his writing: the experience of divine grace is found amid the reality of suffering and tragedy in a deeply fragmented world. And the intersection between the two is surely found in the cross of Christ.

Much more could be said about Grant, but now consider the experience of one of our contemporaries, Paul Williams.

4. Paul Williams (1950–)

Paul Williams is professor of philosophy at the University of Bristol. He was raised by what he describes as a not particularly religious family; yet he was baptized an Anglican and as a young boy sang in an Anglican church choir.

As a young man, he did not pursue the Christian option. Rather, he lost contact with the church. When he went to the university, he chose to study philosophy and in the course of his studies developed an interest in Indian philosophy and thought, eventually completing his doctorate at Oxford, with a growing interest in Buddhism. It was not merely an academic interest. By 1973 he had come to the conclusion that he was a Buddhist; Williams formally became a Buddhist when he "took refuge," to use the language of the Tibetan tradition's stream of Buddhism. In time, he had a rather prominent role within British Buddhist circles, not only teaching at the university but also doing radio programs and public interfaith dialogues.

Yet now he is a Christian, and in his autobiographical reflections, *The Unexpected Way*, he describes the various factors that led to his conversion.[20] He describes how he was not able to shake his early Christian roots and the fact that he was baptized a Christian, and how when he visited Christian churches, he felt like he wanted to be part of what happened in these churches. He began to wonder if he had really given Christianity a chance, so to speak. Williams began to ask himself if he had really considered the claims of the Christian faith.[21]

He also speaks of a dilemma he felt: a discomfort or unhappiness when chanting Tibetan, particularly a phrase in Tibetan that sounds like the word "Jesus." But beyond this, he was increasingly feeling an unease with dimen-

19. Ibid., 5–6.
20. Paul Williams, *The Unexpected Way: On Converting from Buddhism to Catholicism* (Edinburgh: T&T Clark, 2002).
21. Ibid., 4–6.

sions of Buddhist practice and thought. In terms of thought, he was struck by the emphasis in Buddhism on "positive experiences," on the positive benefits of meditation and the need to avoid suffering: essentially a religion of self-empowerment, of pleasant feelings and calm.[22] Though all of this sounded good, Williams came to wonder whether it was truly a basis for being a Buddhist.

Over time, his convictions about Buddhism began to weaken. For example, he began to wonder about the Buddhist emphasis on self-development: that one achieves perfection through self-power, through one's own efforts. But the most crucial thing for him was the conclusion that Buddhism lacked hope: as far as Buddhism is concerned, there is no real significance to the human person, since the human person, in the end, converges on nothing.[23] Williams came to an extraordinary conclusion: "If Buddhism is correct, then this life will be the end for me and for all my loved ones. If Buddhism is right, then finally, for almost all of us, our little lives count for virtually nothing."[24] In contrast, he came to see that "if Christianity is right, on the other hand, our lives—as the lives of the individual persons we are—are infinitely valuable, and we all have the possibility, as the persons we are, of unimaginable perfection."[25]

Williams also speaks of something that is seemingly insignificant, but likely noteworthy: he *liked* Catholic Christians! He liked them! Both the living, meaning his friends, and the dead: his particular influences (in his reading) include Thomas Aquinas and G. K. Chesterton. Williams read both of them extensively: Aquinas, on God, creation, and knowledge; Chesterton, on contemporary culture and religion (being particularly struck by Chesterton's comments on what draws Westerners to Eastern religions).

In retrospect, he was moved—as many others before him—by Francis Thompson's poem "The Hound of Heaven":

> I fled Him, down the nights and down the days;
> I fled Him, down the arches of the years;
> I fled Him, down the labyrinthine ways
> Of my own mind; and in the midst of tears
> hid from Him, and under running laughter.
> Up vistaed hopes I sped;
> And shot, precipitated
> Adown Titanic glooms of chasmèd fears,
> From those strong Feet that followed, followed after.

22. Ibid., 8.
23. Ibid., 15.
24. Ibid., 19.
25. Ibid.

> But with unhurrying chase,
>   And unperturbèd pace,
> Deliberate speed, majestic instancy,
>   They beat—and a Voice beat
>   More instant than the Feet—
> "All things betray thee, who betrayest Me."
> . . . .
>   Halts by me that footfall:
>   Is my gloom, after all,
> Shade of His hand, outstretched caressingly?
>   "Ah, fondest, blindest, weakest,
>   I am He Whom thou seekest!
> Thou dravest love from thee, who dravest Me."[26]

Williams concluded that God was chasing him and would not let him go.[27] He wondered if his baptism (as an infant) was a kind of tattoo, declaring that he belonged to God, that "God seeks those with His tattoo." After a time, he made a shift. An interesting one. He decided, in his words, to "switch my perspective, to see what things would look like if I saw them as if I thought Christianity were true. In that switch of perspective I now think I invited Christ to return. He came."[28]

He concluded that God is the creator of all things, a particularly Thomistic vision of creation, and that Christ Jesus had risen from the dead, and that there was no other possible explanation but that what had happened was a physical, bodily resurrection. Williams fully acknowledges that he *chose* to believe. His faith was an act of the will, affirming, in the words of Saint Augustine, that "to believe is nothing other than to think with assent."[29]

He became a Roman Catholic Christian in part because he recognized the legitimacy of the pre-Reformation vision of the Christian faith, which affirmed that Christianity is a public act of "communal inclusion."[30] He puts it this way: "One cannot be a Christian and not in some way be a member of the Church."[31] He was received into the Roman Catholic Church in November 1999. Of this, Williams writes: "At the moment all I can say is that I am very, very happy. For me, like so many others, it really does feel like coming home."[32]

---

26. Francis Thompson (1857–1907), "The Hound of Heaven" (1893), http://www.cs.drexel .edu/~gbrandal/Illum_html/hound.html.
27. Williams, *Unexpected Way*, 12.
28. Ibid., 15.
29. Ibid., 21.
30. Ibid., 22.
31. Ibid., 25.
32. Ibid., 24.

Reflections on the Character of Conversion

This sampler of conversion narratives is no more than that—a sampler. But the accounts are not really unique. Well, they are unique. No two conversion experiences are the same. Yet we can also see that there are some deep commonalities. What strikes me is that the experiences recounted here are representative of the experience of those who, on the one hand, take the world of ideas seriously and, on the other, are drawn to Christian faith through the grace-filled ministry of the Holy Spirit.

Much could be said about the conversion experiences of these thinkers, but I wish to make three observations on aspects of their common experience that seem to have tremendous significance for how we speak about the faith and how we think about those who are coming to faith in Christ.

Intellectual Honesty

First, we need to speak about the need for intellectual honesty, on two fronts, for those who come to faith and for those in the church, who witness to that faith. For those coming to faith, it is clear that the Spirit's compelling witness to Christ and the cross will only be experienced if there is an intellectual honesty about the plausibility of God—particularly an openness to the possibility that Jesus is who he says he is, the Son of the living God. This is a huge barrier for so many. They may claim to be open-minded, but in reality they have made an a priori decision that discounts the transcendent or the spiritual. Or, even if they acknowledge that matter is not all that there is, they have closed out the possibility that Jesus might be the Son of God, risen from the dead and Lord. All that is needed is to be open to the possibility that this might be true—to give it intellectual space, to not assume that it cannot be true. There must be a willingness to believe.

This intellectual honesty on behalf of a potential convert is perhaps nowhere so powerfully evident as in C. S. Lewis's account of his own coming to faith. At a key point in his narrative, he speaks of his reading: "In reading [G. K.] Chesterton and [George] McDonald, I did not know what I was letting myself in for. A young man who wishes to remain a strong Atheist cannot be too careful of his reading. There are traps everywhere—'Bibles laid open, millions of surprises,' as Herbert says, 'fine nets and stratagems.' God is, if I may say it, very unscrupulous."[33] We might chuckle at this, but we only do so because we appreciate that what strikes us in this comment is Lewis's powerful honesty about the truth and about his openness to truth; he exhibits a fundamental willingness to believe.

---

33. Lewis, *Surprised by Joy*, 154. Lewis would later speak of reading G. K. Chesterton's *Everlasting Man* and observing that he had come to appreciate him as the most "sensible man alive," with the added aside "apart from his Christianity" (ibid., 171, 178), which he eventually came to see as the very heart of Chesterton's sensibleness.

But there is more. Intellectual honesty is required of the potential convert, but it is equally required of those who witness to the Christian faith, particularly when it comes to the question of pain. In our witness to the Christian faith, the church must also embrace an intellectual honesty about the presence and power of evil, the fragmentation of our world, the seeming absence of God, and the inexplicability of all that is so wrong. In the end there are no facile answers for the phenomena of tsunamis, drowned-out cities at the mouth of the Mississippi, or earthquakes that pummel northern Pakistan. We need to speak honestly about the reality of pain and suffering that makes no sense.

A recent publication by Frederick Buechner brilliantly and cogently captures what I am seeking to say, and he does it with such eloquence, in *Speak What We Feel (Not What We Ought to Say): Reflections on Literature and Faith*.[34] What strikes us in this book is the power of intellectual honesty. His main point is that the genius of Gerard Manley Hopkins, Mark Twain, G. K. Chesterton, and William Shakespeare resides precisely in this kind of honesty: the refusal to sentimentalize the pain of the world and the intention to speak (or in their cases, write) out of that pain, but to do so without sentimentality or self-indulgence.

What he says has enormous implications for how we speak about the faith with those who might be searching for home, to use the language of Paul Williams, or who might be "waiting for God," as Simone Weil speaks of it in the title of her reflections on her own spiritual journey. A side of us assumes that when we speak the gospel, we need to answer questions, providing an apologetic that is convincing and airtight. For so many Christians, there is a huge assumption that we need to be able to answer questions, explain everything, and particularly explain God and the presence of evil. The danger is that we would turn from intellectual honesty and sentimentalize the Christian faith.

I am struck by the intellectual honesty that is integral to the theological vision of Jeremiah and Habakkuk, whose prophetic calling was one in which they were not merely freed to but also compelled to speak the truth. So they spoke what they felt and saw, without the need to have it fit comfortable categories. They lived with the discomfort—not just physical discomfort, but specifically *intellectual* discomfort, and they did so out of the conviction that, in the words of Habakkuk (2:4), "the righteous live by their faith."

This intellectual honesty is not about embracing either skepticism or cynicism. We are not choosing the way of either objective neutrality or hopelessness. Rather, we accept that understanding comes from the willingness to believe. We accept that this willingness to believe is often, so often, found in the midst of suffering and pain that cannot be explained away. This willingness is the fruit of the Spirit, and so is the capacity to see God in the fragmentation of our work.

34. Frederick Buechner, *Speak What We Feel (Not What We Ought to Say): Reflections on Literature and Faith* (San Francisco: HarperSanFrancisco, 2001).

The Person and Ministry of the Spirit

Second, we need a language of conversion that both assumes the person and ministry of the Spirit and is saturated by references thereto. This third member of the Trinity does the work of God in God's time. Nothing in what I am about to say is meant to discount the significance of human agency. It is merely to show an urgent need to recover a deeper appreciation of the work of the Spirit in conversion.

The Spirit and *the Spirit alone* is the evangelist. Any participation on our part is not incidental but is surely secondary and auxiliary to the Spirit's work. The Spirit does the Spirit's work in the Spirit's time, and as often as not, the work of the Spirit happens slowly and incrementally. Though the experience of conversion will often include a crisis or significant punctiliar event, the drama of the Spirit in a person's life plays itself out over what is often a remarkably long period of time. One gathers the feeling that the Spirit is in no hurry— rather than a sense of urgency or panic. Instead, each conversion narrative is a witness to One who works surely but patiently to bring women and men to an intimate encounter with God.

Further, the work of the Spirit *cannot be programmed* or manipulated. It is choreographed by the Spirit alone, and all we do is witness to the work of the Spirit in the life of the other: some plant, others water, and yet others may harvest, but in the end, what impresses us is that this is the work of God, who by his Spirit draws people to the risen Christ. Consequently, we might be well advised to foster the kinds of capacities that enable us to walk alongside another, not so much to be telling another what they need to know or do, but rather speaking only after we have listened, and then speaking in a manner that as much as anything enables another to make sense of the work of God in their lives. In this regard I am particularly struck by the Puritan view of conversion as an act of discernment, an intentional response to the saving initiative of God. I would add that this divine initiative is always particular, and thus our answers can never be formulaic. We must learn to listen well, and in particular to listen to those whose coming to faith happens within the context of pain and suffering.

Additionally, this encounter with God, effected in our hearts by the Spirit, will always have an *affective quality* to it, something about which there is no other word but *joy*. Nothing about the conversion experience of those called into an intellectual vocation would lead one to think that conversion, for them or anyone, is fundamentally or even primarily an intellectual question. Intellectual honesty provides the setting in which the Spirit does the Spirit's work of enabling someone to find the joy of God.

Encounter with the Ascended Christ

Third, there is an urgent need to appreciate that conversion is the fruit of an encounter with the ascended Christ. Conversion comes not in response to an idea or a principle, but rather conversion is a transforming encounter precisely because it is an encounter with the transforming One. Though this may or may not involve something as dramatic and powerful as Pascal's "night of fire," it will always nevertheless be an encounter with the crucified, risen, and ascended Christ.

This is a *real-time* encounter. In the end, it is not a matter of coming to terms with certain laws or principles, or having the right answers to the right questions, or even praying the right prayer. It is a matter of encounter: meeting Christ. This encounter cannot be choreographed or programmed, no more than it was in the case of Christ's appearance to Saul, on the road to Damascus.

This means that the power of worship as an evangelistic event is not that the church is focused on the seeker or the inquirer, but rather that the church is in a real-time encounter with the risen Christ. To "dumb down" the worship for the sake of the seeker is counterproductive, in the end. Yes, we are certainly sensitive to the ways in which newcomers try to make sense of a worship event, but they are observers, who gradually become participants as they too come to know what it means to meet Christ.

As a side note: this is, in part, why it is so vital that we recover a sense of the Lord's Supper as a real-time encounter with Christ, the Lord of the Feast, who hosts a meal for the people of God. The Table then becomes a transforming event, so much more so than it could possibly be if all we are doing is being urged to remember a long-ago event. We are remembering! Certainly; but we are also in a real-time encounter with the crucified, risen, and ascended Lord.

Further, this means that the power of our personal witness resides precisely in the reality that we live in a real-time relationship with Christ—a relationship sustained by prayer, yet particularly evident in the formation of character and in our persistent joy amid a fragmented world. When this occurs, as it does again and again, we are witness to something of extraordinary beauty: the regeneration and transformation of the human soul, with intellectual honesty, being open to God. As the Spirit works in the timing of the Spirit, women and men meet Jesus. And when they do, they are no longer the same.

Spiritual Autobiography: Learning to Be Attentive

The practice of spiritual autobiography allows us to highlight how the Spirit has enabled us to come to faith in Christ. As mentioned, no two experiences of conversion are the same; each is unique. And the diversity of experiences is not merely a matter of social or psychological curiosity. The distinctiveness of each is significant because one's conversion becomes part of the fabric of a person's life. Psychologists and counselors want to know about a person's

173

family of origin; for a spiritual director, a key reference for good conversation is a spiritual autobiography: Who are you? What is the history of your experience with the Spirit of God? A counselor observes how patterns emerge and vocational and relational challenges arise due in large measure to the unique family-of-origin dynamics. Similarly, spiritual autobiography, if it is done well, can help one discern patterns, strengths, and gaps in the genesis of a spiritual journey, features that have significance far beyond the time when a person actually came to faith.

Spiritual autobiography requires that we learn to practice the "spiritual discipline of noticing," as Richard Peace puts it.[35] But to be able to notice— to see and make sense of what we have experienced—we need a language of conversion, a way of thinking about our religious experience that makes possible an authentic account of that experience. Here is where evangelicalism has so frequently failed its constituency. For many evangelicals, there is a language of conversion in the preaching, hymnody, and daily speech of their church that is completely foreign to their actual experience. They may hear the language and may sing the hymns, but what they sing is not congruent with what has happened to them. They are alienated from their own experience, largely because of a language that assumes a punctiliar conversion experience. Thus they frequently become caught up in using religious clichés to describe their experience as a way to make the best possible sense of what has happened. But thereby they are not served well, and they cannot, in turn, truly appreciate the power of a conversion experience to shape and inform the whole journey of faith.

So we need to let folks tell us their story, insisting that they just describe what they have experienced (without interpreting it, necessarily, through some preconceived notion of what it was supposed to be like). Let them describe what has happened and describe how they have responded. Rather than saying that as a child they "received Jesus into their hearts"—a phrase that, in the end, really tells us very little—describe what has *actually* happened. Perhaps a parent or Sunday-school teacher urged a particular response, and perhaps as a child it was meaningful to say the words or pray the "sinner's prayer." But how? How was it meaningful? Let them say no more, no less. One can learn the art of the journalist, who knows that nothing is gained by overstating or by hyperbole. A believer can describe, without melodrama or interpretation, the years of being a teenager and of coming to an adult faith amid the challenge of finding differentiation from one's parents. Those with a non-Christian background can describe the experience—of being a Buddhist or a Communist or whatever—and recognize that (as it was for Augustine and his Manichaean and Neoplatonist years, or for Dorothy Day and her Communist years) these

35. Richard Peace, *Spiritual Autobiography: Discovering and Sharing Your Spiritual Story* (Colorado Springs: NAVPress, 1998), 89.

early religious and ideological affiliations may well have been the stepping-stones that enabled one to come to faith.

In a spiritual autobiography, we can identify the people who played a formative role in one's coming to faith. Some may speak of a childhood experience as spiritually significant even though the adult involved had no particular agenda in mind. Others may speak of incidental conversations along the way, or the formative influence of a preacher or teacher who week in and week out provided a faithful and convincing articulation of the Christian faith. But in attending to the role of individuals, it is important to see that usually, if not always, the experience of conversion was occasioned by the influence of many people.

A spiritual autobiography can also reveal gaps in one's spiritual experience. Sometimes one hears the account of a person's coming to faith and realizes that something is missing. They lack, perhaps, a strong and definitive penitential element to their experience, or perhaps one realizes that the need for thorough engagement with the community of faith was somehow aborted or never fully realized. The first may happen through simple neglect; much contemporary evangelical evangelism downplays the need for repentance. The second could come about simply because the person's coming to faith happened to occur when they were in a time of transition—off to college or changing jobs—changes that may have been for the good, in opening a person up to the possibility of faith, but changes nevertheless meaning that the outcome was a highly individual faith and lacked true communal integration. The account of the coming to faith can, then, guide both the subject and a spiritual friend, pastor, or director in suggesting a course of action in response to these "gaps."

Each conversion narrative has a distinct energy to it: a focus, a movement, an emotional longing that is fulfilled, or a sense of purpose or destiny that moves the experience and thrusts the narrative forward. An honest and authentic spiritual autobiography has the potential to provide the subject with a sense of his or her own vocation and destiny. It helps one answer the question who am I? but it also gives clarity to the question what is my calling? Just as the conversion experience of the first disciples (see Luke 5) and for Paul was, essentially, both a conversion and a calling, in similar fashion many will find that their conversion experience has within it the seeds of their vocation. Reflection on their experience can give them clarity about how they are being called to engage the world. This is not to suggest that in reflection upon their experience, they will find actual words calling them to be a plumber or a pastor. It is rather that the character of the experience establishes contours, fulfills emotional longings, and reflects some sense of meaning and purpose to this particular individual. As such, a spiritual autobiography helps a person come to terms with what matters most to them, what they want most—their deepest, most powerful, inner desires.

All of this suggests that we cannot foist a single model or pattern of conversion on one another. We need to allow—indeed encourage and enable—each one to tell their own story of grace. This is not an act of narcissistic self-preoccupation. It is but the recognition that we only have one lens through which to make sense of the gospel revealed through holy Scripture, the lens of our own experience. We know the power and depth of God's mercy because we know it personally—not abstractly or theoretically, but personally and individually in *our* experience. The practice of spiritual autobiography is a means by which we access this experience, make some sense of it, and allow it to shape and inform our journey of faith.

It is also vitally important that we affirm that the Spirit often works in quiet and incremental ways. Be careful not to search solely for the dramatic or emotionally weighted moments and miss the equally significant moments in our lives that do not shout at us. Elijah learned that God's presence was not so much in the earthquake, wind, and fire as in the "sound of sheer silence" (1 Kings 19:12). Jesus urged his disciples to appreciate the kingdom significance of the woman with two small coins. This requires that we notice and listen and appreciate the power of the incremental and the seemingly insignificant, where the full significance is only appreciated in retrospect.

In putting together a conversion narrative, identify the people who played a formative role in your coming to faith. Not all of these encounters will be with Christian believers. God often uses non-Christians to play a significant role in a person's coming to faith. Further, a person's writing or poetry or art may have an impact on another; it is not merely face-to-face witnessing that we need to attend to.

So then, what should be included in a conversion narrative? When we are attentive, what do we seek to notice?

Guidance for Writing a Conversion Narrative

Tell the story, attentive to the following:

1. Notice the social and religious context. The work of the Spirit never happens in a historical or social or religious vacuum. We appreciate the Spirit's work when we are attentive to the setting in which the Spirit is at work. In particular, we note a person's religious heritage and their experience (positive or negative experiences of this heritage—i.e., the Muslim who lacks a heartfelt experience of God but also deeply appreciated the sense of reverence that he associates with Islam).

2. Watch for the influence of persons, beginning with family systems and communities, and then other influences along the way. Be careful of overstating the influence of one person. Be attentive to the influence of those whose impact may have seemed incidental at the time (but later recognized as forma-

tive). Some plant, some water ("I planted, Apollos watered, but God gave the growth"; 1 Cor. 3:6). The influence of a variety of persons typically helps us to see that only God can choreograph a conversion experience.

3. Consider the role of the Scriptures. Rare is the conversion where the Scriptures do not play a distinctive role (through either personal reading or the Scriptures preached).

4. Observe the significance of crises or turning points (death or divorce in the family, national crises, or issues of work and career). Yet it is essential, as noted above, that we not overstate the significance of an event. Just describe what happened before moving to the theological interpretation of what occurred. If we overstate the significance of one experience in our lives, we are inclined to discount another experience because it does not fit into our categories or into the categories of revivalist Christianity. We may be inclined to see significance to "I asked Jesus into my heart" and then miss something else that may have had more lasting spiritual significance in our lives. We tend to affirm certain things and discount others because those other events or experiences are less affirmed or legitimized by our religious community.

5. Recognize the impact of the church, our faith communities (positively and negatively). Also, speak here or elsewhere of the experience of baptism and what this meant at the time.

6. Remember experiences of the ineffable. Many conversion experiences include a moment or moments or event in which someone has an encounter with the Other, perhaps through the created/natural order or through liturgy/worship, that cannot be explained (and certainly is not choreographed by the church or its leadership) as other than an intervention of the Spirit of God. Often it is through the witness of the church afterward, and indeed sometimes long after the event, that a person is able to put a name—perhaps Jesus—to this experience. Sometimes this might be an experience that one has as a child (such as C. S. Lewis and his brother's toy garden).

As we listen to another's conversion narrative or make sense of our own experience, certain theological reference points must guide our thinking, for indeed it is not just any experience that counts as a *Christian* conversion. These at least are the following: (1) It is an experience of Christ, an encounter with Christ himself and not merely the idea of Christ or the doctrine of Christ; it is an encounter with the Christ to whom the Gospels witness and to whom the creedal tradition of the church attests. (2) It is initiated and choreographed by the Spirit. Such a conversion narrative is in many respects the account of the Spirit's gracious work in the life of a person or a community. The Spirit's work of bringing a person to Christ is typically a journey that in some cases might take several years.

10

What Then Does It Mean to Be a Congregation?

✢

Now we come to the bottom line: what does it mean to be the church? More specifically, what does it mean to be a congregation, a community of believers who together respond to the call of God to be God's people in a particular time and place?

As was evident in the overview of Ephesians (chap. 2 above), our study of conversion must take the church seriously. This was further evident in the overview of the history of the idea of conversion: we cannot speak of the relationship between conversion and discipleship without also speaking of the relationship between the church and the experience of conversion. This leads us to speak to two dimensions of conversion at one and the same time: conversion is initiation into congregational life, and conversion is also mediated to the new believer by the life and witness of a congregation. It is both.

In these comments I am intentionally building on the conviction of Lesslie Newbigin that the mission of God in the world is fundamentally ecclesial: in continuity with Israel and the prophets, Christ commissioned his disciples to be his witnesses to the world. Through them the church would be established. Between Pentecost and the return of Christ, the church would be empowered by the Spirit to call women and men to believe in the gospel, repent, and live under the reign of God.[1] What does it mean to be the church? What are the marks or features of the church, particularly when considered against the backdrop of this discussion regarding conversion?

1. Lesslie Newbigin, *The Household of God* (New York: Friendship, 1954). In this work his thesis is that the church needs to be understood as fundamentally a missional entity.

Two Constituencies

When we speak of conversion, there are two constituencies that matter deeply to the church. First, the children of the church, the sons and daughters of Christian believers. And second, those outside the church community who are on the way, who have some interest in the Christian faith.

For both groups, our children and the seeker or inquirer, the way of being the church is fundamentally the same. And yet, the particular sensibilities and needs of each constituency are different and distinct.

The Children of the Church

When it comes to faith transmission, the first call of the church is surely to its children, those born and raised within the Christian community, typically the children of members of a Christian congregation. This has always been one of the most dynamic challenges and concerns of the church: how to sustain the faith from one generation to the next. Rare is the parent for whom this is not a major burden, with the desire to see a child come to an adult faith in Christ.

One thing is clear: there are no guarantees. There is no method for assuring that our children come to an active faith in Christ. They have minds and wills of their own. If and when they come to faith, it will be in the timing that is the unique confluence of the work of the Spirit and their own readiness. It cannot be forced, and it cannot be presumed; indeed, it may well be that the harder we try or the more pressure we exert, the more inclined our children will be to resist the overtures of the Spirit.

Our approach to nurturing the faith of our children needs to be informed by the interface between theological reflections on the child, including the place of the child in the church, and the wisdom that has emerged in recent decades on the character of faith development. I am thinking here of the insights of adult psychological theorists and their perspective on adolescence as a critical transition from childhood to adulthood, particularly in the work of Robert Coles[2] and James Fowler.

A theological vision for the children of the church affirms that they are very much part of the faith community, the covenant people of God. Indeed, our children are raised *within* the faith: they are nurtured, taught, encouraged, and supported as they come into adulthood. They do not need to be "evangelized" per se. Though at some point they must make their own decision and come to a personal faith in Christ, there is no urgency to pressure them into

---

2. Robert Coles is a prolific author on the spiritual and moral life of children and adolescents, but in particular consider *The Moral Intelligence of Children* (New York: Random House, 1997).

this move earlier rather than later. There is no need to press children to make a commitment as children when they are not yet capable of an adult faith in Christ. That time will come, and it will come, ideally, when they move from being a child to being an adult.

We also reckon with the challenge of adolescence, a period that psychologists and sociologists increasingly recognize to be an extended period, lasting perhaps as long as twenty years! Girls are moving into adolescence so early—too early, many would say—and boys are as often still in psychological and social adolescence well into their late twenties. This is a liminal period, a time of rebirth, of coming into one's own life; it is a season of differentiation, when one recognizes that one is not merely the child of one's parents but now also a person in one's own right. It is a vulnerable and potentially difficult season of life: separation from parents, differentiation, is never easy—either for the child or for the parent. Yet however difficult, it is crucial. The marks of this transition need to be clear for the Christian community.

First, it means that young people find their primary identity in Christ, as members of the faith community. The church now becomes their primary "family" identity, and their identity is that of a child of God. Second, it means that their primary confidence or trust is in God as their provider. They move from dependency on parents as their surrogate "god" to a dependency on God and responsibility before God for their own lives. Third and perhaps most crucial, their loyalty and obedience are now due to their Lord and Christ. All of this is represented by baptism or, for those who baptize infants, in a late adolescent rite of passage.

This move to baptism or an adolescent rite of passage requires two crucial acts of the church that I will speak to below: hospitality, a radical welcome to the child and the teen, an eager embrace of our children; and, teaching and spiritual nurture that is age appropriate. Yet it may be that the most crucial piece is the quality of relationships that our children have with other adults in the faith community. Perhaps the most critical factor in a child's coming to faith is not so much their parents or their peer group, however powerful these may be, but the connection our children have with the peers of their parents.

If a child is going to appropriate an adult faith, the most vital need is older women and men who are present to that young person, demonstrating generosity and hope through blessing and encouragement. It is a nonjudgmental presence that is thoroughly present without being an unwelcome burden, a presence that allows God to do God's work in God's time in the life of the child and the young person. This means patience, the greatest gift we give our children: patient men and women (as a rule it would be gender specific, older men with boys and older women with girls) who are a grace-filled, wise presence in the lives of our children, who are moral companions and guides, yet certainly who are first and foremost older friends along the way.

181

This suggests that churches need to avoid the propensity to "stratify," to make the life and ministry of the church so age specific that young people and those in midlife are separated for worship, learning, service, and play on the assumption that each age group wants to be with their own group. Segregation may be quite counterproductive. Though there is certainly a place for age-specific activities, surely one of the greatest needs of the church is for old and young to explore what it means to worship together, learn together, serve together, and play together. Together the activities of worship, learning, service, and play become the moral and spiritual landscape for the formation of our children—all within the context of a faith community and given energy by the quality of relationships between old and young.

The Inquirers—Those Who Are Seekers after God

The second vital constituency is the women and men who come to faith as adults, from either a secular or another religious background. This experience of coming to faith will surely be an extended time, a journey of learning the meaning of the faith and then adopting that faith as one's own. They come with some kind of spiritual longing in their hearts, with a desire to make sense of their lives or to find fulfillment to the yearning of their souls.

It is fruitful to consider what deep yearning of our culture and society is ultimately fulfilled only by the gospel. What is the yearning of the hearts of our neighbors that perhaps leads them to explore what it might mean to become a Christian? What is the inquirer seeking? Though they may not be able to name this and define it—it may feel ineffable to them—as often as not this is the work of God in their lives. Something in their hearts seeks the good, the noble, the excellent, what is "worthy of praise" (Phil. 4:8). N. T. Wright, for example, suggests that within the human heart is a longing for justice, the quest for spirituality, a hunger for relationships, and a delight in beauty.[3] Any or all of these might lead a person to darken the door of the church, or more likely, enter into a conversation with a Christian believer about what marks the life of the believer and the life of a Christian community.

This yearning may be occasioned by a crisis in their lives, perhaps a divorce or a death or a job loss, or perhaps they seek to explain and interpret a spiritual experience and wonder if the church might give them language to make sense of that experience. Whatever the case, women and men do affiliate with the church community; they come as seekers after God, without at first knowing that their hearts perhaps yearn to know the Creator.

3. N. T. Wright, *Simply Christian: Why Christianity Makes Sense* (New York: HarperSan-Francisco, 2006).

Whether it is the children of the church or the inquirer, when we speak of what it means to be the church through the lens of the experience of conversion, we come to this discussion with several basic assumptions:

1. Conversion is an extended and complex process, a matter of beginning well. It is the start of a spiritual journey; and indeed, the journey has two parts: first the journey to faith (or as I will suggest below, the journey to baptism), and then the journey as a baptized follower of Christ.

2. The process of coming to faith requires that we learn a language, the language of the Christian theological and spiritual tradition; this language will give meaning and focus to our experience of Christ. But as with all language learning, this will take time, perhaps several years.

3. As often as not, conversion will be a conversion both to the church and to Christ, and the conversion to Christ will be cultivated and nurtured within a church community. Within the church community we learn the language of faith, for indeed the church itself embodies the faith that it proclaims.

4. Therefore the church is a venue in which all, but notably here our children and the inquirers, know the grace of God. The church is a means of grace, the transforming grace of God, when it affirms and lives by Word and Spirit, the critical dynamic and criterion of congregational health. The church is the place of the Spirit, who alone is able to bring about new life. Thus the church is but the midwife of the Spirit's work; the church is both womb and midwife—both the venue of the Spirit's work and the abettor and aide to the Spirit's work, while never assuming the Spirit's role in the life of one who is coming to an adult faith in Christ. The church does not bring about the new birth. This is the work of the risen Christ, who by Word and Spirit enables women and men to come to faith in himself.

5. There is need for intentionality. Any reading of Acts 2:38 and following cannot miss the intentionality of the early Christian community, whose members are described as being "devoted . . . to the apostles' teaching and fellowship, to the breaking of bread and prayers" (2:42). There is the intentionality of being the church; yet there is also the intentionality of the community toward those who are on the way to faith in Christ. Hence, I will be suggesting that we restore the ancient practice that viewed baptism as the pivot point of this intentionality, the focus of the process of coming to faith rather than a personal prayer or confession, however significant these might be along the way. Here then I will speak of the importance of ritual. To borrow Alan Kreider's wonderful phrase in describing the early church's approach to conversion, it needs to be "ritually articulated."[4]

Working with these assumptions, then, I will approach the question in the following sequence. I will speak of the ascended Christ and what his ascen-

4. Alan Kreider, *The Change of Conversion and the Origin of Christendom* (Harrisburg, PA: Trinity, 1999), 7.

sion means for the life of the church. Next I will consider what it means to be the church. Then I will consider the practices or intentionality that should perhaps shape the life of the church as it seeks to be a place where women and men are coming to faith in the ascended Christ.

The Ascended Christ and the People of God

We seek an approach to evangelism that is deeply sensitive to the needs and aspirations of those coming to faith. Yet in the end, evangelism is not a sales exercise seeking customer satisfaction. Further, it is not merely a membership drive for the church as though the church is but a religious club. Rather, it is about being a people, on a journey and in mission, who together are a place and a people in dynamic communion with the ascended Christ. Thus when we speak of conversion and its implications for congregational life, this is where we need to begin: with the central figure in all such discussions, the risen Christ.

The Letter to the Ephesians could not be more explicit on this: the purposes of God begin and end with Christ Jesus. Further, the conversion narratives I have profiled consistently testify to the fact that conversion is not about an encounter with an idea or a principle or "four spiritual laws" or even with the Bible, but rather with Christ crucified, risen, and ascended.

When we speak of the church, we must speak of the faith community in terms of this reality; otherwise we easily fall prey to the default mode of treating the church as nothing more than a religious club. The encounter of conversion is with the one described in Ephesians as the head: Christ. Thus we are in union with the head when we are in union with one another. We are the living church insofar as we are animated by the living head, Christ Jesus. The ascended Christ is in dynamic communion with the church, but more, Christ as the ascended one is overseeing the inbreaking of a new reign, the very reign of Christ by which all things are being made new. And the church is only the church as it too, in response the Spirit, participates in this new reign, typically called the kingdom of God.

The church itself is not Christ, and the church is not to be equated with God's kingdom. The life of the church is derivative from that of Christ; the faith community is not self-sustaining. Its life is oriented not back toward itself but toward the inbreaking of the reign of Christ. So the church is not self-focused and not seeker focused, but Christ focused. Here we must stress that the focus is not on a doctrine or christological principle but indeed on Christ himself and on his work in the world. There is remarkable continuity and discontinuity between Christ and the church: we cannot know Christ and live in dynamic union with Christ if we are in isolation from the church, but we must not then confuse the church with Christ. Further, the church is a sign of and witness to the inbreaking of Christ's reign, but we must not confuse the church with the kingdom.

This is precisely what then allows the church to be a people who know the transforming grace of Christ. Worship is encounter with the living Christ and the means by which the church is empowered to witness to the kingdom in the world. In worship, we are not merely engaged in religious activities; we are rather intentionally in encounter with a living person. If the liturgy is not oriented toward the living Christ, it is a human construction and nothing more; it is hype and nothing more. This is the goal and intent of the Spirit, that we might see Christ and hear Christ and respond to the call of Christ. Thus the liturgy, the worship of the people of God, is oriented on this axis.

All of this is then a reminder that our passion is not merely for religious activities but specifically for the actions and ways of being that enable the church to be a people in encounter with Christ and in mission with Christ in the world. Evangelism is really nothing other than inviting others to meet Christ with the church and to participate with the church in mission in the world. Thus when we speak of intentionality, it will not be about getting people to join the church but rather about being a place where people might meet Christ and join Christ in the work that Christ is about in the world. This has profound implications for the nature of worship, particularly for what we mean by preaching and how we approach the sacramental actions of the church: baptism and the Lord's Supper.

Thus our vision of Christ shapes and informs our understanding of the church. In the preface to his seminal study on the ascension, Douglas Farrow opens with this provocative declaration: "Not since the time of Paul has the question of ecclesial identity been a more pressing one than it is today."[5] Part of what makes this such a compelling question is that all around us is a plethora of responses to what it means to be the church, and the typical response is more pragmatic and methodological than theological. As noted above, we must consider what it means to be church by asking theological rather than purely pragmatic or methodological questions. We will come to questions of practice and method, but we must begin with the fundamental theological questions. If we do not begin here, our pragmatism easily leaves us with no more than marketing or sales gimmicks.

The church is a particular people; they are the called ones, who live out their common life in particular places. Central to their identity is that the faith community gathers for worship, but their energy as a community is simultaneously toward the world. The church then is not an end but a means to the end, to worship Christ and to serve Christ in the world. As a community the church's vision and passion are toward the reign of Christ, both as it

---

5. Douglas Farrow, *Ascension and Ecclesia: On the Significance of the Doctrine of the Ascension for Ecclesiology and Christian Cosmology* (Grand Rapids: Eerdmans, 1999), ix.

has already come and as it will come at the new creation. So their common life, in word and deed, is to witness as a sign to this kingdom—not only as we live now in the light of that kingdom but also as we anticipate the coming consummation of Christ's reign.

Surely the defining challenge in this regard is captured by Robert Webber's phrase "ancient-future." How can the church simultaneously be ancient—intentionally aligned with the historic faith—while also a community that "makes sense" in a postmodern society? For some, this means that the church is defined by the "seeker" and that the presenting needs of the society and of the casual observer become the agenda of the church. Some even argue that the church does not need to look like the church (foreign and overly religious) as it seeks to respond to the felt "spiritual" needs of this generation.

Yet, to the contrary, the church is most effective in its call and mission when it is as churchly as it can possibly be. The church is a witness to the kingdom not when it downplays its identity as the church but precisely when it is very much the church. By being the church, the people of God fulfill their identity and their destiny and accomplish their mission, which includes the worship of the Triune God but also the call to disciple the nations. What ultimately defines our engagement in the world is our very identity as the people of God.

There is another motivation that shapes this conviction that the church needs to be very churchly, especially when it comes to its passion to be a place where people are coming to faith in Christ. Rather than downplaying the churchly character of the faith community in order to connect with non-Christians or make the church seem more palatable, it is all the more crucial that the church be the church—unapologetically so. There are two reasons. First, the ultimate identity of the new Christian is as and within the people of God, and the act of coming to faith needs to actually be consistent with this identity. The experience of coming to faith needs to look and feel like what the experience will be as a Christian. Second, the point of connection with the potential new Christian is precisely their spiritual hunger. They need to know God and know the grace of the Spirit, which can only come through Christ. The church then needs to demonstrate the setting or form in which this is experienced. Coming to faith is not ultimately about coming to the church, but to Christ.

From this, then, we can affirm the following:

- The church is the people of God and needs to live out this identity as thoroughly as possible.
- Worship is a place of encounter and communion with Christ.
- The church is sustained by this encounter, and we need to be deeply conscious of the means of grace, the very means by which Christ sustains his people.

- We can without apology identify with and engage our energies in kingdom practices, which reflect God's purposes in the world.

Thus the focus of the church is not on the potential new Christian. However eager we are for people to come to faith in Christ, they are not our primary passion or concern. They will come, in the timing of God and as the Spirit draws them to himself. As I will note below, there are certainly practices by which we can intentionally be a place where people are coming to faith in Christ. But perhaps what the potential new Christian most needs to appreciate is that she or he is not the focus of our attention; rather, in our worship we are focused on Christ, not on the seeker, and we are about the mission of God in the world. And they are welcome to join us in this vision and mission. In other words, the most evangelistic thing the church can do is just be the church: worshiping, learning, and missionally engaged.

Indeed, when we focus on the seeker, I wonder if the net result is obvious: they naturally think that the church is about responding to *their* agenda, their felt needs. Then if they come to some measure of faith and identify themselves as Christians, they still think the church is there for them. We inadvertently, perhaps, reinforce a consumerist mentality regarding congregational life. The church is not a project. It is not a nonprofit organization that needs a brilliant and charismatic CEO to manage a strategic plan to achieve an organizational mission. It is not an enterprise. The church is not a club, where what defines us is certain religious activities that matter to us and where we are eager to show our vitality by the number of new members we are able to sign up.

Rather, the church is a *people*. This means that what constitutes its common identity and what sustains that identity is something wholly other than that of a project or a nonprofit agency or a religious club. It is a people sustained by Christ, who through Word and Sacrament empowers and sustains them to live in mutual fellowship with each other, to love and be loved. Through Word and Sacrament, Christ equips this people to be agents for truth, justice, and peace in the world. The key to all of this is surely the ministry of the Spirit. There is a powerful interplay between the ascension and Pentecost. Indeed, what defines the church is precisely the reality of ascension-Pentecost. We live in dynamic union with the ascended Christ when we eagerly respond to the grace and initiative of the Spirit. The people of God is the fellowship of the Spirit. This means that the church is not merely a collection of individuals, nor merely a group of people who have a shared experience of a sermon or of singing together—such as those who might attend a football game together. Rather, the church is a fellowship of the Spirit, a mutuality, a participation in the life of Christ and thus in the life of one another. And this is a transforming fellowship: the church is a community that grows in wisdom together, a growth made possible by the members' mutuality.

187

Such a church is a womb in which spiritual conversion and transformation, new life, takes place. The very character of conversion requires this. Though it is theoretically possible that there will no doubt be exceptions—a kind of equivalent to in vitro conceptions—the natural and thus supernatural working of the Spirit is in and through the womb that is the people of God. The church is the very medium through which the Spirit is bringing women and men to faith in Christ. Yet the womb metaphor is tenuous and limited in its use. We also must insist that the church is not the mother of those who are coming to faith in Christ. The church is no more than a midwife, one might say, enabling the work of the Spirit, coaching and encouraging those who are coming to faith. But in the end, it is the work of the Spirit.

In this process, the church thus plays a critical part. It is the setting where the Spirit does the work of the Spirit. By its common identity and character, the church embodies the call to discipleship through its worship, its approaches to learning, and finally through its engagement in the world through missional service. What we must affirm in this regard is that the process of coming to faith in Christ must reflect what it means to live as a community of faith. There is a deep continuity between the experience of coming to faith and the experience of growing in faith. Our practices, by which we seek to intentionally foster the capacity of others to come to faith, need to be deeply congruent with the fundamental character of what it means to be the church.

All of this suggests that "televangelism" is an oxymoron. It cannot be done. By its very nature, evangelism is the act of a faith community living the life of faith and welcoming others who on the way wish to participate in that common life—to worship, learn, and serve. It is real people who worship together, learn and serve together, and together are a pilgrim people. Evangelism is an inherently *communal* practice; the community of faith both speaks and embodies the gospel. In acting out the gospel, they reflect what they say about the gospel—something that cannot be done through the television screen.

More than anything else, what marks this people, what enables this communal practice, is that their identity is marked by the life and witness of Christ Jesus. Also, their life in community is *sustained* by Christ, who is the living head of the church. Thus worship is about Christ—a real-time encounter with the ascended Lord. Learning and penitence are in response to Christ as teacher and Lord, and service arises out of appreciating the way in which the reign of Christ intersects with the world.

Worship is encounter with the ascended Christ. Thus the liturgy is evangelism, not because it is used as an overt way to preach to nonbelievers, but because it is an encounter with Christ. Those who are on the way are welcomed to come along and, as they are able and willing, to also meet the One who hosts this event and who is the center, the dynamic center of the life of this people. This is compelling because in the end people are not argued into faith or convinced by rational argument that Christianity is the "true" way. Rather, they come out of a deep spiritual hunger and walk alongside those who have found the living bread, Christ Jesus, who is Savior and Lord.

This takes us back to the point made earlier about the means of conversion. It is precisely the same as the means by which Christ sustains the life of the church: Word and Spirit. Thus the essence of authentic congregational life is precisely this: that in and through this people, Word and Spirit are happening—the work of Christ in the church and through the church in the world.

When it comes to how the church can most effectively be a sphere where women and men are coming to faith, some distinctive practices can shape the church's capacity to be precisely that. But before I turn to this subject, there are two additional observations that need to be made. If the church is a distinctive people, whose identity is marked by their participation in the life of the Triune God, then we must be attentive to the forms, the symbols, and the means by which we live out this distinctive identity—in our worship, learning, and service. By way of illustration, the church needs to be particularly attentive to its design and use of space and, further, to its design and use of media, notably the widespread use of PowerPoint in Christian worship.

Regarding the location of worship services, we need to consider whether our spaces for worship are congruent with our message or whether they unwittingly undermine that very message. Alain de Botton, in his *The Architecture of Happiness*, observes that religious architecture has its roots in a conviction that who we are is profoundly shaped (determined, even) by what we believe in.[6] Then he observes that "to defenders of religious architecture, however convinced we are at an intellectual level of our commitments to a creed, we will remain reliably devoted to it only when it is continually affirmed by our buildings."[7] He goes on to argue that amid the "commerce and chatter of our societies," which are bent on corrupting our passions, "we require places where the values outside of us encourage and enforce the aspirations within us."[8]

We need buildings, de Botton insists, that help us stay true to our confession. We need buildings, in other words, that are congruent with what we confess. We cannot take a purely pragmatic view of buildings and spaces. If the church is to be an abiding witness—in worship, learning, and service—to the reign of Christ, then the church must press for spaces for worship and learning that are congruent in every way possible with that very confession. The genius of such spatial design, particularly when it comes to worship, is that it will simultaneously sustain both radical hospitality—reflecting the grand welcome of God to one and all—and speak to the transcendent, the reality that there is more to life than bricks and mortar (matter).

6. Alain de Botton, *The Architecture of Happiness* (Toronto: McClelland & Stewart, 2006), 107.
7. Ibid., 107–8.
8. Ibid., 108.

Also, the church needs to reconsider its propensity to depend on PowerPoint as a medium for communication and for enabling worship. In recent years, this medium has come to dominate the practice of both worship and teaching in a variety of theological and denominational communities. It has become an unquestioned medium for projecting Scripture for readings and sermon texts and, most notably, for lyrics of the hymns and songs to be sung. Its use seems to be unquestioned; it is taken for granted as efficient and as appropriate for younger people, who are deemed to be more visually oriented and less inclined to handle printed materials.

But is this medium value-neutral?[9] The problem with PowerPoint is two-fold—at least twofold. First, it is a medium that is inherently fragmenting: all communication is in small, sequential bits that have no meaning in themselves. The grand narrative of Scripture is lost when a few verses are projected on a screen and disconnected from the whole of the biblical text. The lines of a hymn or song are projected in segments, and thus the worshiper cannot get a sense of the whole, but only what the projector gives them, in screen-size doses, sung as they are projected, so that interpretive power rests with the one projecting the segments (or fragments) of the song. The net result is that both the Scripture and the hymn or song are trivialized. Further, increasingly the visual center of worship is not the podium as the center for preaching and teaching, or the communion table as the focus of our worship and representing the presence of Christ, but a screen—often so large and dominant that it overshadows all other potential signs or symbols of our common faith.

The other problem is that with PowerPoint our worship becomes increasingly disembodied and distant from us, projected in digital bits that we do not touch or feel. We no longer feel the weight of the hymnbook; more crucially, we no longer feel the Bible as something of substance that has a beginning, middle, and grand conclusion. We do not see and feel that the Romans text being preached is located toward the end of our Bibles and thus can only be properly appreciated against the backdrop of the Old Testament and the Gospels. Though it is possible to say that this text is being preached in light of the Gospels and the Old Testament, the way we treat the Scriptures (as fragments on a screen) is counterintuitive to the way in which we read the text. We are left with a fragment, with no sense of what comes immediately before and after what is being read and preached, let alone how this text might fit within the grand scheme of biblical history. One wonders if this is but another example of an "architecture" that is inconsistent with the message.

9. My comments here are based in part on an essay by Debra Dean Murphy, "PowerPointless," *Christian Century*, July 25, 2006, 10–11. She references Edward Tufte with her observation that "Power-Point promotes a kind of cognitive style that routinely disrupts, dominates and trivializes content." Then she describes the use of PowerPoint in worship as "the relentless sequentiality that divorces content from context. . . . When the text of a hymn (or, more likely, a 'praise song') is projected on a big screen, it can only be experienced as fragmentary and incoherent" (10).

I am not suggesting that nothing should be projected or that PowerPoint is always inappropriate. Rather, what is at stake is the uncritical use of a technology that now visually dominates the worship of so many Christians. We need to ask, does PowerPoint form and cultivate sensibilities that actually undermine those that are congruent with the gospel? In other words, does the form fit the message—whether the spaces for worship or the media that facilitate that worship?

Intentionality: Toward the Children of the Church and the Inquirer

With this backdrop—the understanding of what it means to be the church—we can now consider practices of the church by which the church is a people where women and men are coming to faith in Christ. Can the church be a community that *lives* the faith, embodying the kingdom vision to which we are called, through practices that enable us to be the church *together*: to learn together, worship together, and work and serve together? If so, how can these practices be engaged in a way that is alert to the journey to faith of those who are on the way, whether they are the children of the church or seekers new to the Christian faith?

Let me begin here by stressing that the church does not need to be a busy place. We are not defined by our level of activity, and we are not more effective if we do more. Indeed, hectic busyness is often counterproductive. I suggest that we think of the church, in this regard, as having four distinctive marks, each of which is "ritually articulated":

1. Radical hospitality (Rom. 15:7): "See how they love one another";[10]
2. Preaching, teaching, and the penitential life;
3. Missional service;
4. Rites of initiation.

In each respect, these practices can be ritually articulated, the first three in the Lord's Supper, the last one in baptism.

1. Radical Hospitality

We need to speak of a *radical* hospitality. Hospitality is not something superficial or incidental to the church's identity but rather one of the fundamental marks of what it means to be the church. First, this is a hospitality first shown toward one another as members of the faith community. The church is marked by the mutual giving and receiving of love. The compelling evidence that Jesus is the Christ is not so much from rational argument as from the

10. Quoting Tertullian, *Apology* 39.7; cf. John 13:34–35.

power of love, within a heterogeneous community; a diverse community is extraordinary because of this very diversity. The world is not surprised when people love their own kind. What catches the attention of the world is where this love is present in a community of racial, gender, age, and socioeconomic diversity. This is surely what the apostle has in mind when in response to the profound differences between Gentiles and Jews in the Roman church (Rom. 14), he urges them to welcome one another in Christ (15:7).

There is no genuine hospitality toward the world that is not first demonstrated within the Christian community. Indeed, it is from the strength of this mutual love that we are able to open our hearts to our children and to those who are on their way to faith in Christ. Hospitality is the vital soil in which conversion occurs: hospitality toward our children and hospitality toward the inquirer or seeker. In so doing, the church is the presence of Christ—toward the child and toward those who are on the way. The hospitality that Abraham offers to the angelic visitors is the abiding example of how we treat those who cross the thresholds of our communities (Gen. 18; Heb. 13:2). We respond to the other with a deep regard for persons—for who they are now, and for who they can and might become.

We receive our children by not demanding that they be anything other than children; they do not need to become miniature "adults" before they are accepted and received, before they are loved and delighted in. As children they know the blessing of the faith community. And that blessing is necessarily intergenerational: the young know the blessing of those a generation older and even two generations older.

For those on their way, hospitality means that we allow them to be seekers, finding their way at their own pace, which is the same as the pace that is moderated and mediated by the Spirit. This is the gift we give the other: hospitality. It begins with attentive listening. We listen to their story, to their joys and sorrows, to their longings and points of disillusionment.

We stress that hospitality is only authentic if we are true to the gospel and to our identity as the church. We do not negate or undermine our own identity when we offer hospitality toward another; Jesus himself was able to offer this hospitality to sinners and to welcome them into his company and to his way, but always on the assumption that they were welcomed into a communion that was oriented toward himself and his kingdom. The child and the seeker are not then the focus. We do not allow children to control the agenda or disrupt worship; we do not orient our worship around the seeker. But along the way we are attentive to their needs. In being true to ourselves, we offer a fundamental generosity toward our children and toward those who are on their way to faith.

Further, we do not need to press for a premature intimacy: we can be genuinely hospitable without feigning or presuming intimacy with the newcomer or seeker. Relationships are built slowly, over time, and true hospitality respects boundaries, both those of the community and those of the person who is a seeker or inquirer.

Two things are critical and essential signs of this hospitality. The first is language: we urgently need a language of faith that is true, authentic, and theologically rich; but our language also needs to consider the understanding of those who are on the way to faith. Further, we urgently need a language that recognizes this very dynamic, that they are *on the way*. Our language needs to be inclusive and generous and nonjudgmental. But, I stress, we never deny that while they are on the way, they are still seekers and not yet baptized followers of the living Christ. Our language must allow both children and seekers to come at their own pace, without pressure or hurry.

Second, our language is complemented by eucharistic hospitality. Few things are so essential to or so powerful an expression of hospitality as meals. If we love one another, we eat together; and if we offer hospitality to another, we offer this through our words, yet also in a meal. Jesus demonstrated his kingdom purposes at meals, banquets, and other festive meals. Through table fellowship, he welcomed those whom he was eager to have come to the grace of life in his kingdom. He preached the gospel, declaring that the kingdom had come. And Jesus demonstrated the central dynamic of this proclamation through meals. He ate with his disciples; he ate with sinners; he ate with his disciples when they were sinners (John 21). We can hardly conceive of Jesus's ministry apart from the meals, and we cannot think of the church's life without meals.

Surely, these are meals that are meals. I am sure that of all the things we did during my first pastorate, the most effective and significant was the regular potluck suppers. Churches have always known that food is an essential part of the church budget!

And yet, of course, when we speak of eucharistic hospitality, we speak of the Lord's Supper. The Lord's Supper is the ordained means by which the love and community of the church is "ritually articulated." It is without doubt an essential means by which the church demonstrates its commitment not only to Christ but also to one another; at this meal we demonstrate our love for one another, and we cultivate or nurture that love.

But what of our children? And what of those who are on the way to faith? Are they to be excluded from this meal? Shall we dismiss the children to their children's church and not have them present for this "adult" event? Shall we advise the non-Christians not to partake unless and until they have made a faith commitment and been baptized? In other words, the widespread assumption in the church is that the Lord's Supper is an act of exclusion rather than inclusion—not hospitality, but a boundary-marking act. But if we are following the example of Christ, for whom meals were an essential counterpart to his preaching, could it be that the Lord's Supper is the way in which our hospitality is "ritually articulated" for both our children and those who are on their way to faith?

Could it be that if you are in our home, we cannot conceive of the possibility that you are not welcome at the Table? One of the dramatic ways in which Christ welcomes people to himself is through the classic combination of word and deed: the gospel preached and then demonstrated at table fellowship. In other words, is there truly any justification for excluding someone from the Table other than that they are confessing Christians who explicitly violate their Christian identity (see 1 Cor. 11:27–32)?

At the very least, some congregations offer children a blessing; this is the least that can and should happen. But why, if they are part of the faith community, the family of God, are they excluded from full participation in a vital and essential rite by which they may experience the hospitality and thus the love of God?

And for the seeker, could the Lord's Supper be a "converting ordinance," to use the language of John Wesley[11] and others? Could it be that they will only feel the force of God when they not only hear the gospel but then also participate in the means by which this Word is demonstrated? In other words, could it be that eucharistic hospitality is one of the essential marks of a faith community where women and men are coming to Christ? The Lord's Supper without the gospel is meaningless, but could it also be that the Word needs to be matched by eucharistic hospitality? Could it be that we need to explore active ways by which, with the full integrity of the Lord's Supper honored, all who wish to come may come—all who long to know Jesus more, even if they cannot as yet call themselves Christians?[12]

2. Teaching-Learning and the Penitential Life

The church is a teaching-learning community, and its commission is to teach the nations to obey. This is how disciples are made (Matt. 28:19–20). Thus there is a deep connection between the educational ministry of the church and its ministry of evangelism. Indeed, evangelism and Christian education are part of a continuum: there is no evangelism without teaching, and through evangelism one is invited to join a teaching-learning community. The genius of this teaching is that it fosters the transformation arising from repentance.

Teaching and preaching are central to congregational life. Without teaching, the church is not the church, and the church does not fulfill its mission in the world. The early church is described in Acts as a community devoted to the "apostles' teaching," or doctrine (Acts 2:42). In this feature, the emerging Christian movement is reflecting its Jewish heritage, with the deep commit-

11. *Works of the Reverend John Wesley,* 7 vols. (New York: J. Emory and B. Waugh, 1831), 3:188, journal entry for Thursday, June 26, 1740.

12. Those who affirm open communion do so on the assumption that the meals Jesus had with "sinners," including the feeding of the five thousand, are one of the sources for the Lord's Supper.

ment to teaching and learning for all, not merely for scholars or teachers or pastors. It follows that teachers play a vital place in the life of the community. The scandal of the evangelical mind lies precisely in downplaying the life of the mind, which is so vital to authentic Christianity.

Hence, the work of nurturing children in the faith and introducing new-comers to the faith will necessarily find expression in teaching-learning. For children, early on they become students eager to grow in understanding, engaging both heart and mind in the exploration of truth. For adolescents, it will mean that youth ministry is not about entertainment, but about teaching and learning. For the newcomer, it will mean that catechesis is integral to evangelism. Evangelism is as much teaching (catechesis) as it is anything else; teaching launches persons on a life of learning, where they appreciate from the beginning that teaching-learning is pivotal to their growth in faith (the beginning of lifelong learning). Thus, evangelism and education are inseparable: education grounds evangelism; evangelism animates Christian education.

The teaching curriculum is surely at least threefold: the Scriptures (viewed through the grand narrative of redemptive history), the ancient faith (introducing young people and seekers to the creedal heritage of the church), and the Christian life—including the life of prayer and spirituality along with ethics and life in the world under Christ's reign.

If this is the content, the goal of teaching is specifically the goal of the Christian life (see chap. 5 above, "To Be a Saint"). Teaching will be oriented toward Christ, understood and experienced as a member of the Holy Trinity; and it will be intentionally oriented toward the specific marks of the Christian life: wisdom, vocational holiness, love for others, and joy.

In all this, it is essential that we always live under Christ's commission: we teach for obedience (Matt. 28:20). Teaching is always oriented toward not merely understanding but especially that we would be wise and live in the light. There is no wisdom without teaching, but similarly, there is no wisdom without lived teaching. This means that by its very nature, teaching leads to repentance: it leads to a change of mind, a change of heart, a change of life. Teaching is always a catalyst for repentance: new understanding leads to new light, new direction, a change of direction and order for the learner's life. If we stop learning, we stop repenting and we stop growing. Both the education of children and evangelism are precisely this: learning, repenting, growing in faith and hope and love, growing *into* faith and hope and love.

Hence, hospitality (number 1 above) is not tolerance; the church is a community deeply committed to knowing and living the truth. You cannot come into the community and not feel and experience the demands of the gospel, the cost and character of authentic discipleship. Thus the church is a *penitential community*: learning and turning, learning and increasingly recognizing the darkness and resolving again to walk in the light. The learning takes the community deeper in its understanding of the nature of the kingdom, and thus repentance naturally follows as the learning opens hearts and minds to the truth. Our hospitality to our children and to those on their way to faith is that they are invited, eagerly so, into a community that has a clear kingdom agenda. The church essentially says: "Join us, as we live under and are formed and re-formed by the Word."

In other words, just as hospitality is etched into the very DNA of the church's identity and way of being, the same could be said of the orientation toward teaching and learning. A church is marked by a learning culture; it is a school of faith. The community is marked by an insatiable pursuit of truth, as reflected in the images of Proverbs 4 and in the longing for truth, wisdom, and life. This teaching and learning call on the capacity of gifted teachers; it also is the fruit of good conversation and interaction, so that the young learn from the seniors, and the seniors are also challenged by those who are young enough to be their grandchildren. Thus the philosopher is learning from the plumber just as the medical doctor is learning from the businessperson.

Both preaching and teaching are vital to this process. They are distinct, but the difference is truly a matter of degrees along a continuum. Preaching takes what is learned and calls the church to live in the light, to live in light of their understanding. Preaching calls for obedience. Teaching, by way of comparison, does not always demand (immediate) action but rather calls for depth, reflection, and growth in understanding, which will often come slowly and incrementally as through teaching we grow in wisdom. But preaching by its very nature requires a response. Teaching fosters critical reflection; preaching calls for submission to the authority of the truth. Yet it is a matter of degrees: all good preaching has an instructive component; the best teachers will often remind their students that the truth calls for obedience. The other difference is that preaching is located within the liturgy and sacramentally re-presents the authoritative teaching of Christ. Preaching more explicitly and clearly opens up the Scriptures as the vehicle for knowing and hearing the ascended Christ. Preaching is not education, though it definitely has a teaching component, and preaching is not public therapy, though there will surely be elements of preaching that foster emotional healing. Rather, preaching is encounter—with Christ, through the Word.

Two other elements of public worship play a critical role in this process of teaching-learning and the penitential dimension. First, the prayers of the people (or pastoral prayer) are essentially the longing of the people of God that "thy will be done on earth, as it is in heaven." Teaching and preaching foster a deepening appreciation of the nature of this will and the inbreaking of Christ's reign. The prayers of the people then ideally reflect this growing appreciation of the nature of God's will. Our prayers are informed by our teaching-learning. Ideally, the prayers of the people reflect that this is a people that is seeking to be aligned with the purposes of Christ (penitence) and that longs for the whole world to know the grace and will of Christ. Thus both the preaching and the prayers reflect a continual call to live in alignment with the inbreaking reign of Christ.

The other essential element is the Lord's Supper as the necessary complement to the ministry of the Word. The teaching-learning of the church is ritually articulated in the Lord's Supper: we have heard the Word, and now we receive the Word, allowing it to dwell richly within us (Col. 3:16). The Word calls for repentance and covenant renewal, and the Table is the ordained means by which the penitential life is ritually articulated in the life of the church.

3. Generous Service to the World in Word and Deed

The church is missionary. Its missional character is as much a part of its DNA as its generous hospitality and its love of learning. The life of the church is deeply oriented toward service in word and deed: locally, in its immediate neighborhood, and globally, as it partners with other churches and agencies to make a difference internationally. The church is a people *together* in service, in active joint participation in the inbreaking of Christ's reign.

Fundamentally, this means that the members of the church are equipped and empowered to make a difference through their respective vocations: nurses are empowered by life in the church to be faithfully engaged in their work, along with their sisters and brothers who are similarly empowered in their vocations, whether they be in business, the arts, education, or religious ministry. This is a reminder that what marks the church as a great church is not its size, not its numbers, but rather its impact through its members in its community. We ask each church, are these people empowered and equipped for the work to which each of them is individually called?

The members of the church are called by Christ to service together—as old and young, long-termer and newcomer, join hands to make a difference, in word and deed, to seek justice, to meet the needs of those in need, and to witness to the person of Christ. As noted, this surely happens locally: together each congregation must ask, how is this church being called to serve this neighborhood, town, or city? Then it naturally follows, how is this church, perhaps in partnership with other congregations or agencies, called to make a difference in the world? No congregation is asked to be all things to all people; instead, each is invited to discern how they are called to witness, in word and deed, to Christ and to be the mouthpiece, the hands, and the feet of Christ in the world. It should be clear to anyone who is even marginally connected to such a community that these people are seekers of peace and justice for all. It is evident in their prayers, in their preaching, and in their response to that preaching.

Our children are invited to join this process early, to appreciate that we are the church together not just as a gathering place in a building but especially as a people in mission, who in the grace of God seeks to make a difference through the exercise of time and talent. The same would apply to those who are seeking Christ: by coming in the door, they are candidates for service! They learn the ways of the kingdom by participating in the way this congregation serves. They learn service by serving, and from the beginning they learn that as they move through baptism, it is etched within their souls that they are entering into a baptized life that is oriented toward generous service.

Both teaching and the engagement of our lives in service are a continual process of learning and exploration and thus of continual conversion. This continual and ongoing conversion is the essential ecclesial way of being if we are to be an authentic people and place where women and men are coming to faith in Christ.

This dimension of congregational life is also ritually articulated by the Lord's Supper. Each celebration of the meal is an act of both calling us out of the world and calling us into Christ's presence while also being the act by which we are once more empowered for the work to which we are called in the world. We urgently need to recover the close interplay between the Holy Meal and the mission of the church: it is an act of hospitality, and it embodies our learning and repentance; yet it also is both our food for the road and the constant sign of our longing that the world would know the grace of the Bread of Life.

Historically, there have been two—at least two—ways in which the close interplay between the Lord's Supper and world engagement has been demonstrated. In my own tradition, it has always been our practice to have a "benevolent offering" collected at the end of the communion service; it is given toward a fund to help those who are in critical need of financial assistance. One might often get the sense that this benevolent offering is only coincidentally collected at the time of the communion service. But there is every reason to appreciate that this action is a sign of our commitment to the poor, to justice, and to the gospel, which is good news to the poor. Indeed, more needs to be made of this, demonstrating that we move from the Table to the world, and that as we do so, we have an action that reminds us of a needy world.

The other classic means of demonstrating the link between the Lord's Supper and world engagement is footwashing. Some view this as a third sacrament; others practice it occasionally as a sign of service to one another within the faith community. Either way, when it is observed, it too is an act by which the church signals that our engagement with the world is marked by the standard and disposition of Christ Jesus himself, who was a servant of all. Like a benevolent offering, it too is a reminder: something not merely for us but also for the world. Thus it is an act by which we are strengthened afresh for generous service to the world in Word and deed.

4. Rites of Initiation

Children grow up in a church community that is marked by three things: radical hospitality, teaching-learning and repentance, and generous service in the world. The same is true of those who are seekers or inquirers: this is how they experience the church as they are welcomed, join a learning community, and early on, even before they are baptized, are welcomed to join Christians in service to the world.

Yet, however powerful it might be to be part of such a community, the church has consistently recognized that women and men who might come to faith in Christ need a process or curriculum by which they make the move to *appropriation*. It is certainly possible that someone may come to faith in Christ and be baptized just by being around Christians and eventually, in a haphazard kind of way, be challenged to be baptized and go through with it. But how many fall through the cracks? How many come to faith without establishing a good foundation for the Christian life that is supposed to follow?

Does the church not need to intentionally shepherd children so that they can genuinely assume adult responsibility for that faith? And does the church not need to give special attention to those who are on their way to faith in Christ so that they do have opportunity to consider the demands of the gospel and do have opportunity to establish a good foundation for the Christian life to which they are called?

This was precisely what happened in the early church; surely the Christian community would be wise to learn and adopt such practices for today. The pattern and approach of the church of Ambrose and Augustine reflects deep wisdom. In his comprehensive study of early Christian baptism, Thomas M. Finn speaks of the process of conversion for the early church, especially in the second century, and then comments:

> The rites distinctive of the journey to Christianity developed quickly into a rich, extended and dramatic liturgical journey. Perhaps more than any other possession of the Church, they account for early Christian survival and spread—such is the power of ritual. In addition, they reveal the fundamental meaning of the Church to early Christians as the place of salvation, more accurately, that community where one finds access to Christ the Saviour.[13]

This ancient wisdom finds contemporary expression in the Rite for the Christian Initiation of Adults (RCIA) of the Roman Catholic Church. My thesis is that evangelical and Protestant churches need a similar means of incorporating new Christians into their fellowship. The genius of the ancient rite and of the RCIA is that this process is, again, "ritually articulated."[14] It is a process that is structured by the life and worship of the church and leads, intentionally, through a process of learning and repentance, to and beyond baptism.

13. Thomas M. Finn, *Early Christian Baptism and the Catechumenate: West and East Syria*, Message of the Fathers of the Church 5 (Collegeville, MN: Liturgical Press, 1992), 3–4.
14. Kreider, *Change of Conversion*, 7.

The RCIA process is quite simple and rests on an ancient understanding of how people come to faith in Christ.[15] It is structured around three turning points. The first is the catechumenate: a person is accepted into a cohort of fellow seekers, who will walk together and discuss together their questions about the faith. Typically the group, the catechumens, will meet weekly and accept guidance from a mature Christian, though the focus will be not so much on teaching as on responding with good instruction to the questions raised. In some cases, the catechumenate is ongoing throughout the year; in other cases it begins in the fall and lasts through the first part of the next year.

The second phase is the season of Lent. A catechumen who confirms the intent to be baptized and become a Christian then enters into a more intense time of focused study, reflection, self-examination, repentance, and heart preparation for what is yet to come. For the rest of the church, Lent then becomes a season in which they reaffirm their baptismal vows and deepen their walk with Christ.

The third phase is the actual rites of initiation, followed by a period of postbaptismal teaching. This really is the nodal point of the conversion journey, as in the description of the early church's practices (see under Ambrose, Augustine, and the early church in chap. 3 above). Holy Week becomes the focus of the journey; through the celebrations of the week, the candidates for baptism join the community for the celebration of the Paschal Feast anticipating the Easter vigil, the Saturday night of this special week, when they will be the focus of attention. The rites of initiation are threefold: baptism, chrismation, and Eucharist.

Then this is followed by a season typically called "mystagogy," where the newly baptized continue to be instructed and grounded in their new faith. "Mystagogy" means that they are introduced more deeply to the mysteries of the Christian faith and are integrated fully into the life of the church. In some cases, this lasts one week; in other cases, it is a period of forty days up until Pentecost Sunday.

For the Roman Catholic tradition, each of these steps requires a formal liturgical rite: they are welcomed into the order of catechumens so that all know who is making this initial inquiry into the faith. Then they are granted a special blessing on the first Sunday of Lent as they publicly declare their intention to be baptized. Baptism, at the Easter vigil, is the climactic event when the whole faith community, which has walked with them and alongside them through the process, now surrounds them and affirms with them their new faith and their membership in the church. The first Sunday of Lent is es-

15. See the following resources: *Rite for the Christian Initiation of Adults*, Canadian ed. (Ottawa: Publications Service of the Canadian Conference of Catholic Bishops, 1987); *Rite for the Christian Initiation of Adults*, United States ed. (Washington, DC: United States Catholic Conference, 1988). As a helpful secondary source, see Thomas H. Morris, *The RCIA: Transforming the Church; A Resource for Pastoral Implementation* (New York: Paulist Press, 1997).

sential to the process; it is the public call but also the public acceptance that one is called to accept one's election and thus the call to baptism. They begin to prepare for baptism. Part of the value of this process is that those to be baptized are part of a cohort of fellow catechumens.

The language and even much of the undergirding theology will no doubt be different for an evangelical or Protestant church community. But the ancient wisdom still applies and merits consideration: the value of an intentional process by which those who are on the way are gently encouraged and given a way, a track or curriculum, that will lead to baptism, a process structured by the liturgical life of the church.

For many evangelical congregations, baptism once a year, at the Easter vigil, will not be sufficient; they will want to have more opportunities for adult converts to be baptized. So perhaps Easter would be one opportunity, along with Pentecost Sunday and the first Sunday of Advent. In each case the forty days before these Sundays would be times in which those who intend to be baptized announce their intentions and move into a season of intentional study, meditation, reflection, and repentance—preparation for their baptism. But the process by which seekers can join with fellow seekers in guided conversation with mature Christians who can walk with them and help them make sense of the faith and of their own experience to date would be ongoing.

I need to add: What we have to say about the church and those who are coming to faith has equal applicability for our children, for the children of the church. The community of faith has a dual calling and responsibility: to those who are seeking and to those who grow up "in the faith." It would appear that the way in which we respond to both may well be remarkably similar. Some congregations may want to have a separate track for their young people; others may invite them to join in with the conversations of those who are entirely new to Christian faith. Either way, here too we need a process, a way in which the young can raise their questions, reflect on their experience, and come to clarity about their own commitments and their readiness to move into adult faith.

The process requires and indeed demands two essential features: good teaching and effective sponsorship, companions on the way. The catechumen is being converted to Christ and to the church, as the community gradually welcomes the new believer into their company, step by step. A sponsor, one member of the community, walks alongside the catechumen in this journey to baptism.

However it is formulated, the ancient wisdom then suggests four stages, marked by three rites of passage or transition:

1. *A period of exploration, the pre-catechumenate.* This is a season in which the questions and interests and concerns of the inquirer take center stage; the church through its processes would be more inclined to respond to questions

rather than raise them; the process would emphasize what is of concern to the person who is interested in the Christian faith and has questions about it.

Rite of hospitality. If the inquirer would like to move to the next phase in the pilgrimage, then through a formal rite of hospitality they would be formally welcomed into the catechumenate. Now the whole community would recognize that they have responded to the invitation to make the journey toward Christian faith.

2. *The catechumenate*. Now the focus would shift slowly but surely away from the agenda set by the inquirer to the calling of the church: this would be a formal introduction to the teachings of the faith, the calling to holiness and what it means to be a Christian. But it is merely a matter of degrees: even during the period of exploration, the inquirer would be learning about the faith, and during the catechumenate those who are facilitating the process would certainly be responsive to the particular points of concern or interest of the one who is coming to faith. During the catechumenate we begin to adopt the posture and disposition of a learner, as we move toward incorporation into a teaching-learning community. We learn what it means to live under the authority of Scripture and remain faithful to the ancient creeds of the Christian church.

Rite of election. If a catechumen is ready to move ahead and accept the call of Christ, then through a formal rite of election both the church and the individual indicate this, publicly and clearly. They are not merely on the road to faith; they have now also accepted the call to formalize this through baptism. If baptism comes with the Easter vigil or Easter, then the rite of election would naturally fall on the first Sunday of Lent, thus following the ancient practice of taking forty days to prepare heart, soul, and body for baptism.

3. *Period of purification*. Then, for a period of forty days, either Lent or the forty days before the scheduled baptism, the inquirer who then became a catechumen is now a candidate for baptism. This period is not so much a learning time, though there is always more learning as we grow into the faith. The primary focus, rather, is on the intensity of Christ's call on our lives and on our examination of heart and soul to confirm this call and to enter into Christian discipleship.

The church has always recognized the sacramental quality of a period of forty days, reflecting the experience of Christ in the desert as he prepared his heart and soul and body for the life and ministry to which he was called.

Rite of baptism and chrismation. Then, either at Easter or, as suggested above, at another significant point in the church calendar, the candidate is baptized, anointed with the oil of the Spirit, and formally welcomed into the faith community. While certainly active in the community as an inquirer, as a catechumen, and then as a candidate, now through baptism the candidate is marked as a sister or brother in the faith.

4. *Mystagogy*. Mystagogy means being led into the mysteries of the faith. However this last phase is described, there is much value in allotting six or seven weeks immediately after baptism—perhaps up until Pentecost Sunday, if the baptism came at Easter—for teaching that fosters a healthy transition into full discipleship, congregational life, and ministry. For many it will be a time to reflect on the meaning of their personal vocation, how Christian discipleship marks the whole of their lives, including their work in the marketplace. For others it will be a time of reflection on their particular avenue of Christian service within the faith community as they discover how God has gifted them to contribute to the church's life. For all, it can be an introduction to the life of prayer and perhaps to disciplines of the spiritual life by which they will appropriate the grace of God and grow in faith, hope, and love. Whatever the focus, the critical point of this season is for us to signal that conversion is only a beginning of the pilgrimage, only the foundation on which one will now build, in response to Christ's call and the Spirit's enabling.

Both in the ancient church and in contemporary adaptations of this approach to fostering the journey to faith, a spiritual companion is often assigned to each catechumen, not as an evangelist—for the whole Christian community plays this role—but as a friend who listens, encourages, and supports the new Christian on their journey to baptism and through at least the initial weeks of their Christian pilgrimage. This is the genius of the ancient approach: when we speak of conversion, we speak of a journey, a pilgrimage of faith, or better, of an emerging faith. It is a journey to Jesus: the Father calls us to Christ, and the Spirit superintends the journey into the arms of Christ.[16]

The Ascended Christ

In all of this, two complementary points must be made. First, conversion must include the two fundamental elements that were so important in the experience of Augustine: a reordered understanding and a reordered life. These are the two pivotal and essential tracks on which the train of conversion will run. To come to Christ means that we come to a new vision of reality, a new understanding. And this requires teaching. There is no conversion without teaching. But then the other track is reformation of life and behavior, a moral alignment with the inbreaking reign of Christ. Here too, there is no conversion until and unless we learn obedience.

Second, we also must insist that while the process of conversion requires both, we cannot reduce conversion to new understanding and moral reform. A person could have new understanding, even a deeply biblical and theologi-

---

16. "Journey to Jesus" is the title of the approach suggested by Robert E. Webber in his *Journey to Jesus: The Worship, Evangelism, and Nurture Mission of the Church* (Nashville: Abingdon, 2001), which is another approach based on the ancient wisdom of the early church.

cally sound understanding, and a person could be moral; but this does not make them a Christian. What makes one a Christian is an encounter with the living Christ.

Thus the work of the church is first and foremost worship, the liturgy, as typically offered on a Sunday morning. The liturgy of the church is, as the word *liturgy* itself suggests, the *work* of the people of God. Every other action of the church flows from it and leads back to worship. As the primary work of the people of God, nothing can or need diminish this commitment. Then, as a people who know, love, and serve Christ, we offer radical hospitality to our children and to the inquirer. We are a teaching-learning community, seeking to know and live the truth. And together we engage in generous service, to our community and to our world. Then, together, we welcome into the faith those whom Christ, by the Spirit, is bringing to himself.

Index

✣